INTELLECTUAL ADVANCEMENT THROUGH DISCIPLINARITY

TRANSGRESSIONS: CULTURAL STUDIES AND EDUCATION
Volume 19

Scope
Cultural studies provides an analytical toolbox for both making sense of educational practice and extending the insights of educational professionals into their labors. In this context *Transgressions: Cultural Studies and Education* provides a collection of books in the domain that specify this assertion. Crafted for an audience of teachers, teacher educators, scholars and students of cultural studies and others interested in cultural studies and pedagogy, the series documents both the possibilities of and the controversies surrounding the intersection of cultural studies and education. The editors and the authors of this series do not assume that the interaction of cultural studies and education devalues other types of knowledge and analytical forms. Rather the intersection of these knowledge disciplines offers a rejuvenating, optimistic, and positive perspective on education and educational institutions. Some might describe its contribution as democratic, emancipatory, and transformative. The editors and authors maintain that cultural studies helps free educators from sterile, monolithic analyses that have for too long undermined efforts to think of educational practices by providing other words, new languages, and fresh metaphors. Operating in an interdisciplinary cosmos, Transgressions: Cultural Studies and Education is dedicated to exploring the ways cultural studies enhances the study and practice of education. With this in mind the series focuses in a non-exclusive way on popular culture as well as other dimensions of cultural studies including social theory, social justice and positionality, cultural dimensions of technological innovation, new media and media literacy, new forms of oppression emerging in an electronic hyperreality, and postcolonial global concerns. With these concerns in mind cultural studies scholars often argue that the realm of popular culture is the most powerful educational force in contemporary culture. Indeed, in the twenty-first century this pedagogical dynamic is sweeping through the entire world. Educators, they believe, must understand these emerging realities in order to gain an important voice in the pedagogical conversation.

Without an understanding of cultural pedagogy's (education that takes place outside of formal schooling) role in the shaping of individual identity--youth identity in particular--the role educators play in the lives of their students will continue to fade. Why do so many of our students feel that life is incomprehensible and devoid of meaning? What does it mean, teachers wonder, when young people are unable to describe their moods, their affective affiliation to the society around them. Meanings provided young people by mainstream institutions often do little to help them deal with their affective complexity, their difficulty negotiating the rift between meaning and affect. School knowledge and educational expectations seem as anachronistic as a ditto machine, not that learning ways of rational thought and making sense of the world are unimportant.

But school knowledge and educational expectations often have little to offer students about making sense of the way they feel, the way their affective lives are shaped. In no way do we argue that analysis of the production of youth in an electronic mediated world demands some "touchy-feely" educational superficiality. What is needed in this context is a rigorous analysis of the interrelationship between pedagogy, popular culture, meaning making, and youth subjectivity. In an era marked by youth depression, violence, and suicide such insights become extremely important, even life saving. Pessimism about the future is the common sense of many contemporary youth with its concomitant feeling that no one can make a difference.

If affective production can be shaped to reflect these perspectives, then it can be reshaped to lay the groundwork for optimism, passionate commitment, and transformative educational and political activity. In these ways cultural studies adds a dimension to the work of education unfilled by any other sub-discipline. This is what Transgressions: Cultural Studies and Education seeks to produce— literature on these issues that makes a difference. It seeks to publish studies that help those who work with young people, those individuals involved in the disciplines that study children and youth, and young people themselves improve their lives in these bizarre times.

Intellectual Advancement through Disciplinarity

Verticality and Horizontality in Curriculum Studies

By

William F. Pinar
University of British Columbia

SENSE PUBLISHERS
ROTTERDAM / TAIPEI

A C.I.P. record for this book is available from the Library of Congress.

ISBN 978-90-8790-236-0 (paperback)
ISBN 978-90-8790-237-7 (hardback)
ISBN 978-90-8790-238-4 (e-book)

Published by: Sense Publishers,
P.O. Box 21858, 3001 AW Rotterdam, The Netherlands
http://www.sensepublishers.com

Printed on acid-free paper

TABLE OF CONTENTS

TABLE OF CONTENTS

PERMISSIONS

I gratefully acknowledge the following publishers for their permission to reprint: Peter Lang Publishing, Lawrence Erlbaum, Routledge, Falmer, Pacific Educational Press, and Teachers College Press.

INTRODUCTION

Disciplines are now experiencing a legitimation crisis.

Mitsuhiro Yoshimoto (2002, 369)

Skepticism toward disciplinarity[1] is deeply entrenched in our field, intensified, perhaps, in progressive education's efforts to reconfigure the school curriculum as child-centered or focused on social reconstruction.[2] Skepticism toward disciplinarity had also been affirmed by Franklin Bobbitt and W. W. Charters' ascription to adult activity the organizer of the school curriculum (Pinar et al. 1995, p. 96ff.). In later synopses of possible designs of the school curriculum, the academic disciplines represented only one of five possibilities[3] (see Pinar et al. 1995, p. 686). Add to these historical dispositions the contemporary legitimation crisis to which Yoshimoto refers, and the rage for interdisciplinary, trans-disciplinary, post-disciplinary – anything *but* disciplinary – research and curriculum becomes intelligible.

Acknowledging the discipline-specific historical context in which one's topic becomes intelligible is one marker of disciplinarity. To know a discipline obligates one to acknowledge the already-existing conversation in which one is presuming to participate. In certain North American cultural traditions – certain indigenous peoples (see Grant 1995, p. 212; Hampton 1995, p. 29) and among certain African Americans (Christian 1997, p. 367) for instance – the significance of ancestors can be spiritual as well as intellectual. In cultures characterized by presentism, the aged are often warehoused in assisted-living or "nursing" homes; the dead are often forgotten.

Within the culture of the academic field of education, those who have gone before are regularly relegated to the "lit. review section" graduate students are forced to complete before they focus on the "real" research at hand. Even for established scholars, those who have gone before become relegated to "shoulders on which we are standing," prosthetic props to our own narcissistic achievement. Just because someone is old (or young) or dead does not qualify him or her for respect, but neither should it reduce that person to body parts.[4]

We treat our contemporaries not much better, unless – again, thinking of the graduate student example – they are on one's Ph.D. committee, in which case copious referencing may be advised. As I have complained before (see Pinar 2004a, p. 171), in the academic field of education publications are too often relegated to c.v. items, commodities to be counted, their value assessed on the basis of the reputation of the publisher or the number of times they are cited by others (see Miyoshi 2002, p. 27). Self-referencing is common; while that practice can represent a form of pedagogy, it risks reducing a complicated conversation to a monologue.

The intellectual content of the article or book may be acknowledged – and then too often reduced to a phrase – but infrequently seriously addressed, not even, I suspect, in many graduate classes, where more than a few of our teacher-students press us to listen to their "classroom" issues.[5] There are those who justify such

xi

hijacking of college or university curriculum by claiming that the academic field of education is "applied," but I suspect their "hospitality" to these monologues may also be in the service of propping up enrollments and soliciting favorable student evaluations of one's teaching.

In many graduate classes I have taught over the past thirty-five years, tired teachers have willingly engaged in complex contemplation of the multiple readings I have assigned. Hardly have I been the only education professor to link teachers' daily frustrations to assigned readings, enabling teachers to rearticulate what may have at first seemed to be unique dilemmas as shared, and sometimes solvable, professional problems. There is, of course, an experiential foundation to one's professional expertise that follows from study, teaching, and other forms of professional labor in schools and other educational agencies.

Linking lived experience to scholarship is exactly the academic enterprise, as I understand it. At least in the humanities and the arts, the academic curriculum can provide intellectual passages between subjectivity and society, from the past to the future through the present (see Pinar 2004a). Without intellectual labor, the subjective can subsume the world; without intellectual labor, the social can subsume the subjective. While it cannot provide protection against narcissism or totalitarianism, intellectual labor enables understanding of what we experience in the world (Jay 2005).

Add to these complexities of our profession the parasitic relation between many faculty and their employers. Run like businesses, corporatized colleges and universities expropriate faculty time – sometimes rationalized by invocations of "faculty governance" – for redeployment in the administration of the organization. More than a few faculty – preoccupied with meetings (both in-house and with public and private schools and with other educational agencies), grant-writing, the teaching of classes, the supervision of graduate students, and the detailed documentation of these activities – report insufficient time to study the intellectual production of their field.[6]

Given the crisis of U.S. colleges and schools of education – due, in large part, to the Bush Administration's assault upon them (see Pinar 2004a, p. 216ff.) – and the de facto nationalization of especially mathematics and science curriculum, Departments of Curriculum and Instruction disappear, replaced by departments of Teaching and Learning, or, at Louisiana State University for example, by a Department of Educational Theory, Policy and Practice. Bernard Silberman (see 2002, p. 304) worries that "when money is short, those areas of university life that are not firmly anchored in a departmental structure are the first to be accused of intellectual shallowness." The disappearance of Departments of Curriculum and Instruction not only testifies to administrative and faculty capitulation to curricular control by others (and a self-degrading compulsion to market ourselves); it threatens the survival of curriculum studies as an academic discipline.

The intellectual labor of understanding – the labor of comprehension, critique, and reconceptualization – constitutes the discipline of disciplinarity. Through such self-reflexive and dialogic labor one can contribute to the field's intellectual advancement and to one's own. Appreciating the simultaneity of these contributions requires us to replace Schwab's syntactical and substantive structures of the disciplines (see Pinar et al. 1995, p. 161). Focused on methodology and the concepts research methods generate, Schwab's schema seems more appropriate to the natural and social and behavioral sciences than it is to the humanities and the arts.[7]

Replacing these structures are, I suggest, two more appropriate structures for a discipline associated with the humanities and the arts and focused on the education of the public. These structures are more intellectual dispositions than inviolate orderings. While they may not be "unpredictable," as Brent Davis (2005, p. 128) suggests, they would, no doubt, be characterized by a "complex emergence." My initial and provisional statement of them here is intended to start, not to end, a disciplinary conversation.

VERTICALITY AND HORIZONTALITY

The first of the disciplinary structures I propose we cultivate is verticality, by which I mean the intellectual history of the discipline. What ideas formulated in earlier eras inform those in ours? My acknowledgement of our long-standing skepticism toward disciplinarity in the opening paragraph is a superficial example of this necessary disciplinary practice. Concepts have histories (see, for example, Tanaka 2002, p. 87), histories that require elaboration if present usage is to have disciplinary resonance. If they are to have subjective resonance, they must have meaning within our individual life histories as well.

For example, "learning" is a concept discredited by Dwayne Huebner, the brilliant curriculum theorist whose seminal work was conducted during the 1960s (see Chapter 14). Huebner showed that educational psychology was over-identified with academic psychology (and, during his period, with behaviorism), thereby effacing questions of politics and culture, not to mention those associated with student interest and teachers' academic freedom. In a series of essays I collected and introduced thirty years later, Huebner (1999) argued convincingly that we must employ intellectual traditions other than those associated with academic psychology in order to advance our understanding of curriculum.

Appreciating Huebner's work on the topic as definitive, in *Understanding Curriculum* we tried to stuff the learning genie – and its complementary concept, instruction - back in the bottle by subsuming these within various discursive efforts to understand curriculum (rather than giving the concepts their own chapters). Forty years after Huebner's crucial contribution, and inspired by another scholar of that generation – Robert McClintock – I argued that "study" is a more appropriate term for understanding educational experience, as it incorporates issues of agency and volition, interest and curiosity as well as interpellation and knowledge acquisition (2006b, pp. 109-120). In fact, I have argued that "study" – not "instruction" or "learning" – constitutes the site of education.

To study the discipline's verticality, historical studies are primary, as history is the first casualty in the futurism of the present (see Pinar 2004a, p. 133). Despite the existence of a robust specialty of curriculum history (Kridel and Newman

2003), its intellectual centrality to the field is inadequately acknowledged institutionally. No department or college or school of education should be without at least one curriculum historian; a center or institute of curriculum history could provide a significant disciplinary signature for any institution aspiring to contribute to the field's intellectual advancement.

Like the discipline of intellectual history (see Pinar 2006b, pp. 1-14), verticality documents the ideas that constitute curriculum studies.[8] There is, of course, no one disciplinary conversation, no one collective history. Moreover, disciplinary conversation is hardly held in a sound-proof room. The sounds of events outside the field – cultural shifts, political events, even institutional reorganizations – influence what we say to each other and to schoolteachers. So while I define verticality as the intellectual history of the field, such history requires sustained attention to the external circumstances in which those ideas take form.[9]

From abstraction, verticality becomes concrete and embodied through biographical studies of individuals and their contributions to the field. Philip Jackson's (1992) intellectual history of the field – focused on three individuals (Bobbitt, Tyler, Schwab) – documents the significance of this form of verticality to curriculum studies (see, too, Pinar et al. 1995, p. 33). Perhaps due partly to residues of the anti-narrative, structural, *Annales*-style history (see Gallagher and Greenblatt 2000, p. 53) and to post-structuralism's (see Pinar et al. pp. 450-514) rejection of phenomenology's preoccupation with lived experience, disciplinary emphasis upon individuals has been eclipsed by attention to social forces and *mentalités* (see Tröhler 2006, p. 91 n. 10). Biographical studies and volumes of collected works (see, for instance, Macdonald 1995; Huebner 1999; Pinar and Irwin 2005) provide us personifications of social forces and *mentalities* as they are articulated through disciplinary forms.[9]

The second disciplinary structure is horizontality: analyses of present circumstances. Horizontality refers not only to the field's present set of intellectual circumstances – as, for instance, I attempted to portray in my 1978 the state-of-the-field address (Pinar 1994, pp. 77-99) – but as well to the social and political milieus which influence and, all too often, structure this set.[10] Study of the "external" circumstances of the field must be accompanied by ongoing attention to the field's intellectual history, as its history will configure scholars' responses to their present political and social circumstances. Horizontality and verticality are intertwined disciplinary structures, as I trust I demonstrated in *What Is Curriculum Theory?* There I showed how political conservatives exploited gendered and racial associations with public schooling to distract the public from conservatives' impoverishment (and incarceration: see Pinar 2001, p. 1003ff.) of the middle and lower classes.

It almost goes without saying that no totalistic grasp of the field's structures is possible. We are participating in a conversation larger, more complex, and finally elusive than any single individual or school of thought can grasp. We are all partisans, if citizens, of a larger intellectual body politic (see Pinar 2006b, p. 154). Despite our disagreements, however, a fundamental loyalty to the that larger intellectual body politic – curriculum studies - and to its advancement would seem to be a precondition for "citizenship."

I am, then, proposing that verticality and horizontality structure the disciplinarity of curriculum studies, and that the cultivation of these enables – but does not guarantee - the field's intellectual advancement. Without knowledge of the intellectual history of curriculum studies, without understanding of its past and present circumstances (both internal and external to the field), one cannot contribute to the field. One cannot advance its conversation and thereby complicate our understanding. Nor without such knowledge can one claim expertise.

PRESENT CIRCUMSTANCES

Surely I am restating the obvious. But if it is obvious that knowledge of the field's past and present circumstances is the prerequisite to expertise and participation, then why do courses in curriculum history and theory not constitute the core of every graduate program in curriculum studies? To understand why such courses are often missing in graduate programs, we can look to the internal culture of the larger academic field of education in which curriculum studies is embedded. That culture is characterized by

1) presentism (Pinar 2004a, p. 3),
2) an obsession with social engineering (Pinar 2006b, p. 109), and
3) defensiveness over its academic status (see Pinar 2006b, pp. 121-152).

These converge in research projects devisable as interventions in school policy or practice and that sometimes disparage the "merely" academic curriculum.

The reign of ethnography in educational research heightens the culture of presentism, as it reports "what is," too often with a minimum of theory. Ethnography originates in social science, specifically anthropology; it surfaces in a number of fields, including area studies (such as Japanese studies), wherein "fieldwork" has been considered *de rigueur*. Discussing Japanese Studies, Silberman (2002, p. 309) observed that "training in any kind of social science (with the exception of economics in the last several decades) concerning another society requires presence and research in the field." The exoticism of so-called primitive cultures helped rationalize early anthropological research; in schools ethnography aspires to make the all-too-familiar somewhat strange. Without theory, ethnography always disappoints. Given the Bush Administration's insistence on funding only quantitative research, one is hesitant to criticize any form of qualitative research, but the truth is that too often educational ethnography only restates the obvious. Why knowledge of what five teachers in rural Pennsylvania think of *No Child Left Behind* is necessarily superior to knowledge of what Jane Addams thought about associated living is not obvious to me. If what five teachers think of NCLB were linked to Jane Addams' conception of social ethics: well, that might be interesting, that might contribute to disciplinary knowledge and thereby to the intellectual advancement of the field.

Because – thanks to politicians' scapegoating of teachers – the U.S. public school is always perceived to be in some sort of "crisis," because the "discovery" of "what works" waits for us in the future, because no one – either in the academy or in Washington – believes us education professors (whatever we say), we scramble for solutions to present problems created by others. These are problems – low test scores, most prominent among them, but also what used to be termed delinquency (see Lasch 1995, p. 160), now construed as matters of disciplinarity in Foucault's sense - we cannot, in principle, solve (see Pinar 2006b, 145). (If we dispense with the curriculum and become test coaches rather than teachers, probably we can increase test scores.) Like abused housewives, we scramble to cover-up the patriarchs' philandering, dutifully focused on the household tasks they assigned us (Pinar 2007b).

If university-based scholars were able to engage in conversation not already overdetermined by politicians' school "deform" legislation, what would we say to our colleagues in the schools? What would inform our replies to our school colleagues' questions (should our school colleagues have questions)? What disciplinary knowledge informs our professional "insight"? Without knowledge of curriculum theory and history, upon what do we rely? In what are we knowledgeable if we do not know the field in which the academic degrees we hold are conferred?

In order to speak freely and frankly with schoolteachers – should the opportunity ever occur – we cannot only be complaining about the state of things, quarreling among ourselves over who is to blame, and forever writing the introductory textbook we hope will be adopted in large and multiple undergraduate classes (from which we can profit sufficiently to take early retirement). Through this last imperative - the quintessential instance of a market-driven discipline (see Spivak 2003, p. xii) – ideas are reduced to their lowest common denominator. Without an intellectually vibrant field – and the prerequisite for vibrancy is the ongoing, rigorous, ever more sophisticated attention to the intellectual production of the academic field – upon what are graduate students and colleagues drawing to speak to school-based colleagues?

Our primary professional obligation is, then, to the academic discipline to which we claim affiliation and expertise and to which we dedicate our working lives. Our primary scholarly commitment is to that field's intellectual advancement, not to its exploitation for profit or power, not to its silencing in fear of offending politicians. We can contribute to that intellectual advancement by attending to the disciplinary structures of the field: its verticality and horizontality. In an effort to organize such attention, I proposed the establishment of a "canon project" at the 2007 annual meeting of the American Association for the Advancement of Curriculum Studies (AAACS), held April 6-9 on the campus of the University of Illinois in Chicago.

THE CANON PROJECT

Quite aside from the U.S. field's historic skepticism toward disciplinarity, the very concept of "canon" produces consternation, associated as it is with the "canon wars" of the 1980s, struggles to critique Eurocentrism and to incorporate women's and African American as well as other so-called minority literatures into the curriculum. The concept of "canon" was affiliated with conservative curricular control. Worse, the concept is now also associated with E. D. Hirsch's profiteering attempts (see, for example, 1999) to turn back the educational clock one hundred years, substituting the memorization of facts for understanding. At the outset, canon as a concept in curriculum studies is almost a slur. A proposal to install one must seem, upon first reading, an eccentric suggestion at best.

In the context of U.S. curriculum studies, however, my proposal to construct a canon is, I insist, a *progressive* move. In a presentistic field dispersed along multiple and often apparently unconnected specialties, torn by conflicting characterizations of its history and mission, a bibliographic statement of the core knowledge of the field would provide disciplinary infrastructure in a turbulent period wherein stabilization might set the stage for intellectual advancement.

Speaking of their own field – area studies generally, Japanese studies specifically – Masao Miyoshi and D. H. Harootunian (2002, p. 8) acknowledge that disciplinary mappings, depicting the chronologies of discourses, are especially "difficult to compile at a moment like ours where the central authority for evaluation has largely vanished from the arena of scholarship." No doubt there are those who welcome this absence, imagining that it leaves the field unhampered, able to develop freely and creatively. "And yet," Miyoshi and Harootunian (2002, 9) point out, "a total absence of attempts to sort out, interrelate, and map out ideas and analyses could result in a loss of critical scholarship, coherent reference, and articulate knowledge." To put the matter more bluntly than do they, without disciplinary structure there is no discipline.

Efforts to provide bibliographic mappings of curriculum studies are hardly unprecedented. William H. Schubert and his colleagues (et al. 2002; 1988) have provided bibliographies and genealogies that ought to be studied by every doctoral student. One of Schubert's colleagues on the genealogical project, Craig Kridel (1999-2000; 1999), has listed what he suggests are the most important books published during the twentieth century; as well he has documented Bergamo Conference presentations. Complementing these contributions are the bibliography prepared by Professor Edmund C. Short[11] and the references to *Understanding Curriculum* (Pinar et al. 1995, pp. 869-1034).

Incorporating these contributions, and adding the organizational force sponsorship by the American Association for the Advancement of Curriculum Studies (AAACS) would provide, the Canon Project would make available on the AAACS website a bibliographic mapping of key texts in the intellectual history of curriculum studies. Who among us would disagree that the work of Bobbitt, Tyler, and Schwab constitutes the "basics" – the first level - of curriculum studies knowledge? (To the put matter conversely: who can claim expertise in curriculum studies without knowing about these figures and their work?) There are debates regarding the significance of their contributions, and these scholarly debates and commentaries could be linked hypertextually.

To illustrate: Philip Jackson's 1992 essay on the history of the field – acknowledged earlier – could be linked to Peter Hlebowitsh's (2005a) revisionist analysis of it, Hlebowitsh's entry then linked to Ian Westbury's (2005) and Handel Wright's (2005) commentary on his revision, themselves linked to Hlebowitsh's (2005b) rejoinder to them. Also accessible would be links to bibliographies concerning each of the three: Bobbitt, Tyler, and Schwab. We can think of this disciplinary architecture as a form of curriculum design (Pinar 2004a, p. 155), a disciplinary complement to John Willinsky's Public Knowledge Project.[12] Bibliography mappings concerning the work of those following Schwab could be built, as Nicholas Ng-A-Fook (2007) has suggested, collectively, perhaps after the model of Wikipedia.

Even if there is consensus that knowledge about Bobbitt, Tyler, and Schwab constitutes a base-line of curriculum studies expertise, probably there will be little agreement concerning their contemporaries and the significance of their contribution. For instance, how important is William Bagley's work? Perhaps he would be listed on a second page (after the first page listing Bobbitt, Tyler, and Schwab), with a link to contemporary debates concerning his importance: see, for instance, Ravitch 2000, p. 121). The elephant in the room is Dewey (and, I think, Addams and Du Bois), and Dewey's work – given that it is larger than curriculum studies but with enormous significance for the field - merits a separate page(s), with links to contemporary treatments of his (their) continuing influence. On another page one might list the scholarship of Maxine Greene, Dwayne Huebner, and James B. Macdonald, as it provided the passage to the Reconceptualization of the 1970s.[13] Scholarship after theirs is too close-at-hand for us to judge, but it could be listed according to mapping schemes (including the Wikipedia model mentioned earlier) those participating in the Canon Project construct.

Given the contentious character of canon formation, a widely respected scholarly figure, one disaffiliated with any particular "camp" or "cause," must be chosen to undertake leadership of The Canon Project. There could be three to five other members, with as many consultants as the Canon Committee deems appropriate.[14] Before installation on the AAACS website, there could be a consultation with the general membership as well. Depending on swiftly the Committee is able to move, their report could be issued in the next three to five years. My suggestion is that updating and possible revision of the Canon website be undertaken every ten years.

Despite our field's long-standing skepticism toward disciplinarity, despite the concept's conservative connotations, the cultivation of curriculum studies' disciplinarity – its structures of verticality and horizontality – is progressive labor compelled by present reactionary circumstances. It is labor each of us – as individual disciplinary specialists – is obligated to undertake. Such individual labor will be given focus and intensity by a collective canon formation, a project appropriately undertaken by an organization dedicated, as its name declares, to the advancement of curriculum studies.

The Canon Project will not be without controversy, nor should it be. The key curriculum question in the United States – what knowledge is of most worth – is

a
not quiet question. It is a call to arms as well as a call to contemplation; it is a call
to complicated conversation. It is our uniquely vocational call. Despite the
potential political significance of curriculum studies, there will be those who split
its disciplinarity from the possibility of political action. They will ask: Do not
disciplinary obligations take us out of the public "arena" (Pinar 2004a, p. 205),
preoccupying us while school "deform" destroys the progressive project of
educating the public? What politically vibrant roles can scholars play from their
disciplinary locations? Can these locations provide levers by means of which we
might negotiate a "new deal" for U.S. schoolteachers and for ourselves? How can
we strengthen our discipline intellectually so that it becomes eligible for political
significance?

It is through the discipline that we work to understand – and thereby change –
the world. It is through study and teaching of the discipline that we work to educate
the American public. If educated, the public will insist on shifts in opportunistic
political policies that exploit schoolteachers, demean schoolchildren, and threaten
to destroy any educational process within schools. Through our remembrance of
things past we witness to a future foreclosed by predatory politicians distracting
Americans from politicians' plundering of the public sphere. The discipline is the
site from which we attempt to intervene in that larger public sphere.

In his discussion of the scholarly journal *Critical Inquiry*, James Chandler
recalls Foucault's notion of the specific intellectual, the contemporary figure that
has replaced the so-called universal intellectual. This latter figure was, Chandler
suggests, a product of the Enlightenment; Foucault named Voltaire as the first of
this category and Sartre as the last. No longer positioned to speak as the collective
conscience of society, the specific intellectual speaks from particular disciplinary
locations within society, most often through the university, structured as it is by the
academic disciplines. *Critical Inquiry's* "distinctive contribution," Chandler (n.d.)
suggests, stems from the initial framing of its project through the notion of
discipline rather than theory and, concomitantly, from its insistence on a kind of
writing that, while resolutely academic, is nonetheless intended to be intelligible,
even useful, to academics in other fields.

While curriculum development after the Reconceptualization aspires to be
"intelligible, even useful" to our colleagues not only in other fields but in the
schools (see, for instance, Pinar 2006a, b), this present argument for cultivating the
disciplinarity of curriculum studies derives from my judgment that writing in our
field is often not "resolutely academic" enough.

For Chandler, disciplinarity is in the service of "interdisciplinary connection and
exploration." This apparently paradoxical point can be bypassed in the enthusiastic
pursuit of interdisciplinary or trans-disciplinary scholarship. Neither of these latter
orders of scholarship is possible without disciplinary expertise. Neither, I am
suggesting, is political action likely without disciplinary expertise. And for both
historical and contemporary reasons outlined at the outset, the disciplinarity of U.S.
curriculum studies remains insufficiently founded. "Founded" means "to set or
ground on something solid," in our case knowledge of the field's history. It means
also, the dictionary tells us, "to establish (as an institution) often with provision for

future maintenance."[15] Specifying the past in the present can provide passages to the future. While the entrance to the future is located somewhere in the present, entry will occur through study of the past.

"A DEFINITIVE FUTURE ANTERIORITY"

Verticality and horizontality are hardly self-enclosed structures, then: they are turned outside themselves, attuned to history, society, and subjectivity. In an essay on the field of comparative literature, Spivak (2003, p. 5) worries that "diagnostic cartography does not keep the door open to the 'to come'." To create passages to futures foreclosed by present circumstances, Spivak (2003, p. 5) implies we must act calmly and courageously, in defiance of the present for a future only we (as disciplinary specialists) can imagine: "For the *discipline*, the way out seems to be to acknowledge a definitive future anteriority, a 'to come' –ness, a 'will have happened' quality." Rather than becoming demoralized over present circumstances (or, after Dollard [1939], directing our frustrated aggression toward each other and toward teachers), Spivak is implying, I think, that we can find the future by virtue of our conduct in the present. Rather than being defeated by the present, we can act as if the future lay open before us, unobstructed, waiting for us to move into it. In practical terms, for example, we can teach our students a series of scholarly moves that support the disciplinary structures of verticality and horizontality. These include, I suggest, synopses, analyses, critiques, extensions, and even the replacement of extant concepts. In order, these intellectual maneuvers and tactics of study can enable us

1) to grasp, on its own terms, what is written in curriculum studies,
2) to situate these concepts(s) within pertinent historical disciplinary traditions and present disciplinary circumstances,
3) to critique the concepts(s) on their own terms and from perspectives and proposals already extant within the intellectual history and evident in the present circumstances of the field,
4) to extend the idea(s) by adding to or revising these concepts (and perhaps drawing upon scholarship outside the field), and
5) to replace the concept(s) with "new" ones that perform their specific labors of understanding in a more satisfactory fashion (with more explanatory force, for instance) that the initial conceptualization.

None of these constitutes a categorical imperative. Certainly there are concepts to be praised, not critiqued, not replaced.[16]

Whatever maneuvers are to be made, careful study of the intellectual production of the field is the first and persisting step in the cultivation of disciplinarity in curriculum studies. The above conceptualization of scholarship as "steps" in a "sequence" is atomized and thereby misleading, as it implies that conceptualization is strictly sequential. And it assumes the subjective integration of intellectual work in society in a particular historical moment (Pinar 1994).

As a trace of the past, the present foreshadows the future unfolding. As Sekyi-Otu (1996, p. 184) writes in a different but pertinent context: "Necessary for the radical transvaluation of the ends and instruments of modernity is the critical dialogue of inherited and nascent life-worlds." The disputational scholastic tradition in which academic work in the West resides (see Doll 2005, p. 23) intensifies the competitive, indeed adversarial, disciplinary positioning "complicated conversation" toward intellectual advancement probably provokes. Intensified, dispute can silence, not advance, conversation, except, perhaps, in a Talmudic tradition (see Block 2004).

In its Western vernacular sense, conversation can press against formalistic structures. "[W]hen I think of conversation," Donna Trueit (2005, p. 78) writes,

> it is not as a disciplinary form, but quite the opposite; conversation runs and spills, in the present recalling the past and, simultaneously, anticipating the future. The action of conversation is that it plays with meaning and relations, transgresses, narrates and questions, and in so doing begins to recognize and then challenge the bounds of certainty.

In this definition, stressing its spontaneous and improvisational character, conversation – like jazz (see Aoki 2005 [1990]) – proceeds within specific histories, structural forms, and social relations, recalling the past as it invites the future into the present.

Modernist senses of progress – structured by consumer capitalism and technological development – can create the illusion that what is "new" is "better." Critiques, extensions, even replacement of existing concepts do not necessarily represent intellectual advancement. Judgments of intellectual advancement or breakthrough (Axelrod 1979) are never neutral; judicious judgments are by definition delayed. They must be formulated carefully, which is to say respectfully, so that disciplinary participants can make their judgments based on ample and explicit evidence and self-disinterested explanation, not prejudice or ideology. Intellectual advancement is a retrospective judgment that what is formulated as "new" does, in fact, represent a qualitative advancement over what now we understand to be the case. Ornamental refashioning of past concepts – novelty - represents a field's intellectual devolution, not its advancement.[17]

"PLANETARITY"

As an academic discipline, curriculum studies is always already structured by the worldliness of schools, teachers, and the children they teach. Such worldliness is comprised of the lived experience of those who work in schools. In the present historical moment, worldliness is also informed by planetary time, by the impending apocalypse capitalism and copulation threaten (see Pinar 2007a). Constructing ourselves as "human" – in contrast to the "planet" – is no longer a strategic essentialism, but a deeply dysfunctional one. Appreciating that the biosphere subtends the species on whose behalf we must now conduct our educational labor constructs us simultaneously as a "we" and a "them," a paradoxical subjectivity expansive enough to welcome what is foreign, including the non-human.

In imagining the internationalization of curriculum studies, I have been inspired by the early twentieth-century communist idea of workers worldwide united.[18] In that fantasy, however, what bonds curriculum workers is not political ideology or even anti-capitalism but anti-neo-liberal school "deform." What might bond us as well, I have fantasized, is a shared sense of the profession we might articulate through scholarly conversation, supported by intellectual and organizational infrastructure. The international handbook (Pinar 2003) supports the formation of the former, while the international association (IAACS), its affiliated national and regional associations (such as AAACS), and academic units such as the University of British Columbia's Centre for the Study of the Internationalization of Curriculum Studies support the latter.

Even more than neo-liberal school "deform," however, the degradation of the biosphere constitutes everyone's emergency, the catastrophe already underway, the compelling "common democratic project" (see Carlson 1998, p. 218). The ecological crisis requires of us to cultivate what Spivak (2003, p. 71) terms "planetarity," in which, she suggests, we human beings constitute a "species of alterity" (2003, p. 72). If a species of alterity, we ourselves are the "they" who threaten Life itself. "If we imagine ourselves as planetary subjects rather than global agents, planetary creatures rather than global entities," Spivak explains (2003, p. 74), "alterity remains un-derived from us; it is not our dialectical negation, it contains us as much as it flings us away." *We* are the "other," then, not only to ourselves, but, it turns out, to Life itself.

Rendered a "we" by a common enemy – ourselves – might we unite in a common curricular cause? "Internationalism," Spivak (2003, p. 92) asserts, "can, today, shelter planetarity," providing a "displaced site for the imagination of planetarity" (2003, p. 95). Spivak does not specify how; perhaps she imagines that in trans-national solidarity we can structure the species-wide allegiance it will take to protect the biosphere from extinction. Perhaps she imagines internationalism as providing protection for diasporic social formations (see Savran 1998, p. 285), wherein migratory flows (forced and voluntary) redistribute populations and thereby provide opportunities for hybrid forms of culture. Cosmopolitanism (see Anderson 2006) may prove to be the complement of internationalism, a dispositional passage to planetarity.

Within curriculum studies, internationalism calls curriculum workers worldwide to unite, and not only against neo-liberal school "deform." In this mobilization, it is incumbent upon us to honor – by studying – the specificity of the local. Internationalization is an opportunity to become engaged with each other in the study of localities in the name of solidarity for sustainability. Rather than recode the specificity of the local into a standardized (that means usually European and North American) language that effaces the local, those of us engaged in the internationalization of curriculum studies seek to incorporate local languages into common curricular knowledge.

It is the irreducibility of the local in the internationalization of curriculum studies that prompted me to invite contributors to the *International Handbook of Curriculum Research* (Pinar 2003) to focus on the intellectual histories and present circumstances of nationally-distinctive curriculum studies fields. For those persuaded that the nation is disappearing as structure of influence and source of meaning, this organization seemed quaint (see Benavot and Truong 2006, p. 3). Just as early twentieth-century communists appreciated, the nation can be a focal point of resistance to global capitalism. For us, the nation – and region and other categories of the local, including the indigenous – is a local instance of planetary species. As does Elaine Riley-Taylor (see 2006, p. 65), we can link "the loss of biodiversity and the homogenization of cultural pluralism within the planetary context." As a unit of military, economic, and cultural aggression, the nation remains a profound problem; but as a symbol for the local, as a passage through which the local is symbolized and articulated, especially in political terms, it remains a concept, and a reality, we cannot as yet regard as past.

It is in this political sense Spivak may be construing "internationalism" as a "displaced site" for planetarity. Internationalism becomes a "parallel universe" to, or to change metaphors, a micro-structure of, planetarity in which we restructure daily practice toward sustainability, a concept, for Spivak, that cannot be rendered uncritical, or isolated from the sphere of the political (see Spivak 2003, p. 72) and, I would add, subjective. In fact, she suggests, "to talk planet-talk by way of an unexamined environmentalism, referring to an undivided 'natural' space rather than a differentiated political space, can work in the interest of this globalization" (Spivak 2003, p. 72). The complexity of internationalization – a complexity layered in genealogical formations that renders history the key discipline of our time – not only prepares us to live "ecologically," it constitutes the maize through which we must walk alone and together if we are to survive.

If we can imagine ourselves as "we" and also as "other" in understanding the present through study of the past, can we educate ourselves toward sustainability? Such "planetarity" requires, I suggest, "internationalism" configured as self-skeptical solidarity committed to the subjective and social reconstruction of the public sphere. This public sphere is a biosphere in which the social is but an element. It is a "public" we can labor – as specific intellectuals, as disciplinary specialists - to reconstruct through the curriculum.

The questions are large – the fate of not only our species is at hand – and our locations small and specific. Even in gracious submission (see Pinar 2004a, 65), we can work as individuals toward our common causes: the intellectual advancement of curriculum studies, on behalf of the education of the public, toward sustainability. Is it too curricular a view to suggest that, for us, each is prerequisite to the other? Unless we can find ways to influence the curriculum, ecological events will. Perhaps the impending catastrophe will provide us the leverage we require to change the debate from test scores to what knowledge is of most worth.

First posed by Herbert Spencer in the nineteenth century, that question reverberates today as the key question of U.S. curriculum studies. "What knowledge is of most worth" is a question that requires its reiteration, perhaps, even, in every class: it is a provocation to complicated conversation. Asking "what knowledge of most worth" invites everyone's reply, even when individual voices are blended in a chorus, demanding sustainability. As my Brazilian colleague Elizabeth Macedo (2007) points out, asking "what knowledge is of most worth" is not an invitation to the Ministry (certainly not the Bush Administration's Department of Miseducation) to provide a curricular answer in the form of official knowledge. Asking the question installs, in Macedo's phrase, a "space of enunciation"; it provides the ongoing political and intellectual opportunity for us subjectivity-existing individuals to testify through the discursive means the academic disciplines supply to our lived experience of public events. In asking the question as disciplinarity specialists, we are testifying to our jurisdiction over the school curriculum. Informed by disciplinary expertise, in consultation with university and school colleagues, with parents, and responsive to the students in our charge, we can provide provisional, revisable, answers to the question. For curriculum studies scholars, it is a moral as well as political and, finally, planetary question we pose.

NOTES ON THE STATE OF THE FIELD

What knowledge is of most worth within U.S. curriculum studies? As of this writing, there are several efforts underway to answer that question. In addition to the American Association for Advancement of Curriculum Studies' Commission on the Status of Curriculum Studies in the United States and the Association's Canon Project, there was a state-of-the-field conference held in February 2006 at Purdue University. Focused on "the next moment" in the field, the conference was chaired by Professor Erik Malewski. An expanded version of the proceedings is forthcoming (Malewski in press). There is the *Sage Handbook of Curriculum and Instruction* (Connelly, He, and Phillion in press), revised editions of Patrick Slattery's (2006) *Curriculum Development in the Post-Modern Era*, William H. Schubert's (et al. 2002) indispensable bibliographic history of the field, Dan Marshall's (et al. 2006 [1999]) *Turning Points in Curriculum*, and Janet Miller's (2005) retrospective (see Chapter 2). There is a special issue of *JCT* devoted to the issue.

In that special issue (volume 22, issue number 1), Ted Kafala and Lisa Carey (2006, p. 25) forefront political struggle and the "juxtaposition" of discourses (Pinar 2006b, p. 9) as presaging the "next generation" of curriculum theory. Kafala and Carey (2006, p. 25) acknowledge the significance of cultural study and criticism, a calling derived not only from the Birmingham School (see Edgerton 1996, pp. 18-22) and its African resonances (see Wright 2004), but, within the U.S., the "New York School" of the 1950s and 1960s, personified by Susan Sontag and, I suggest in Chapter 15, by Maxine Greene. "With this in mind," Kafala and Carey (2006, p. 25) continue, "we must also view the possibility of a 'next generation' with some sense of irony, as "the methods and practices of curriculum theorizing are not essentially 'new,' but are the restructuring and appropriation of valuable past practices." Those acts of restructuring and appropriation summarize the steps toward intellectual advancement that I outlined earlier.

Not only the "methods" and "practices" of the "next generation" recall those of the previous generation, the sense of "turning point" (see Marshall 2006, et al.) also recalls a previous moment. Like the early 1970s (see Pinar et al. 1995, pp. 186-239), we are, it seems, at a pivotal point in the history of the field. Unlike the early 1970s, the field is not moribund. It is intellectually very lively, complex, variegated. The field is threatened less by its internal complexity than by external political conditions, both in Washington and in many departments, schools, and colleges of education, too often administered by bureaucrats forced and opportunists eager to submit to Washington's (and their local Provost's) commands. While we cannot control these external circumstances, we can attend to internal conditions, namely how we conduct ourselves in the midst of these often hostile circumstances. In that micro-version of sustainability that is, I am suggesting, disciplinarity, we testify to the future by protecting the past. By undertaking the construction of a curriculum studies canon, we can install verticality and horizontality as intersecting structures of scholarly endeavor. No longer warm-ups to the main attraction, "lit. reviews" become the focus of the doctoral dissertation research, even when this research is in service of developing curriculum for our colleagues in the schools (Pinar 2006a, b). The format of research essays invited by the *Journal of the American Association for the Advancement of Curriculum Studies* (JAAACS) becomes the format of the field's scholarship for foreseeable future.[19]

In the triumph of postmodernism over Marxism (see Pinar et al. 1995, pp. 304-314), and not only in curriculum studies, the field has fragmented into multiple specializations. Among the categories of post-1995[20] scholarly production are: 1) curriculum history, 2) curriculum politics, 3) cultural studies, 4) race theory, 5) women's and gender studies, including queer theory, 6) post-colonial studies, 7) Jewish curriculum studies, 8) disability studies, 9) narrative (including autobiographical, autoethnographic, and biographic) inquiry, 10) complexity theory, 11) environmental studies, 12) psychoanalytic studies, 13) technology (especially computers), 14) arts-based research, and 15) internationalization.

History is central to the contemporary field. Certainly it is the site of ideological struggles: I think (as noted earlier) of Diane Ravitch's *Left Back*, in which, among other revisionist moves, she makes a whipping boy of Kilpatrick (see Ravitch 2000, 181-182) and installs Bagley as something of an unsung hero (see Ravitch 2000, 245). As well, I think of the challenges to the contemporary field posed by Peter Hlebowitsh (2005) and William Wraga (1999), challenges centered on questions of history. Herbert Kliebard's successor at Wisconsin, Bernadette Baker, has written a (2001) monumental history that requires serious attention, as does Kliebard's post- *Struggle for the American Curriculum* publications (1999, 2002). Eugenics continues to be an important topic of historical research (see Winfield 2007) and the Kridel-Bullough (2007) narrative study of the Eight-Year Study poses several challenges to the contemporary field.

In the last ten years we have seen the book collections of life-times of essays composed by prominent scholars now retired or deceased: among them James B. Macdonald, Dwayne Huebner, and Ted Aoki. There have been collections dedicated to retired scholars – I think of two: one dedicated to Maxine Greene, one to Herbert Kliebard – as well as collections extolling the virtues of those still working (Peter McLaren, for example) and collections critical of influential theorists (for instance, Bowers' collection critical of Paolo Freire). The centrality of history to contemporary studies (in itself and as a site of ideological struggle and intellectual debate) is also indicated by the fact that one of the two chapters focused on U.S. scholarship in the *International Handbook of Curriculum Research* is devoted to curriculum history (Kridel and Newman 2003).

Other events point to the history as the central specialty in contemporary U.S. curriculum studies. Distinguished twentieth-century scholars have been remembered (Kridel 2002, 206). Essays important to the Reconceptualization have been collected (Goodson 2005; Miller 2005; Pinar 1994), an indispensable bibliographical record (Schubert et al. 2002; see also Schubert et al. 1988) has been revised and reissued; a collection of key curriculum documents issued (Willis et al. 1994), essays appearing in the *JCT* – the key journal of the 1970s Reconceptualization – have been collected (Pinar 1999); and revised synoptic texts have appeared or are forthcoming (among them, as noted, Patrick Slattery's (2006 [1995]) *Curriculum Development in the Postmodern Era*, and a revised edition of *Turning Points* (Marshall 2006 [1999], as well as the Marsh and Willis textbook 2004). Readers are organized, at least in part, historically (see Flinders and Thornton 2004; Cuban and Shipps 2000). Even post-1995 discourses – such as complexity theory – sometimes situate themselves within the history of the field (see Doll et al., 2005). Curriculum theory worldwide is now reported historically (see, for instance, Green 2003; Lopes and Macedo 2003; Moreira 2003; Sabar and Mathias 2003; Zhang and Zhong 2003). This centrality, I am arguing here, is to be embraced by installing it as a fundamental structure of the discipline, i.e. as verticality.

By curriculum politics I mean not only political curriculum theory (as depicted in chapter 5 of *Understanding Curriculum*), but, as well, scholarly responses to what I have characterized as the "nightmare" that is the present (Pinar 2004a). Prominent in this category of scholarship are the 1995 Tyack and Cuban history of school reform and the Berliner and Biddle refutation of the "manufactured" crisis. Additionally, there is historical work on curriculum politics: I think of Zimmerman's (2002) review of racial and scientific controversies in the twentieth-century U.S. school curriculum. Kevin Kumashiro's (2001, 2004, 2007) anti-oppressive education initiatives belong in this category, as do efforts to redefine curriculum studies as curriculum work (Gastambide-Fernandez and Sears, 2004) and curriculum wisdom (Henderson and Kesson 2003), although this latter text also extends previous mythopoetic scholarship associated with James B. Macdonald and Mary Aswell Doll.

Cultural studies is itself a vast area as well, often separated from curriculum studies (something I argue against: see Pinar 2006b, chapter 5), in some instances a continuation of the political emphasis of 1970s Marxists, although now rarely Marxist and often focused on popular culture (Edgerton 1996). The most expansive conceptions of this area subsume within it the identity-politics specialties (such as black studies, queer theory), but I resist that, even while I am critical of the more "essentialist" identity politics positions, wherein one's individuality disappears into a collective identity (see Pinar in press).

Race continues to be center stage in the field, even if the debates on multiculturalism are by no means limited to African American issues. As with the other areas mentioned here, the scholarly sources I list are illustrative only, but among the most prominent must be James Banks, Geneva Gay, Gloria Ladson-Billings, Joyce King, Cameron McCarthy, William Watkins. With Watkins' historical scholarship, again we see that what were distinct discourses a decade ago are now mixed. Some multicultural scholarship has been influenced by "critical race theory" (see Ladson-Billings and Tate 1995), scholarship not always originating in but significant for curriculum studies (Delgado and Stefancic 2001). In addition to scholarship on Native American, Latino/Latina, Chicano/Chicana, and Asian-American curriculum issues, there is continuing work on the problem of whiteness (Stokes 2001; Kincheloe et al. 1998; Roediger 1999; Frankeburg 1997; Cooper 1995; Pinar 2006a).

Women's studies have been conducted historically. The collection *Founding Mothers* (Sadovnik and Semel 2002) is suggestive: in it$ are essays on, among others, Marietta Johnson, Margaret Naumburg, Helen Parkhurst, Ella Flagg Young, Laura Bragg (also the subject a book-length study by Louise Anderson Allen), Margaret Willis, Susan Isaacs, Lillian Weber, and Deborah Meier. The Crocco-Munro-Weiler (1999) collection is also illustrative of historically-focused women's studies; in it Jane Addams, Ida B. Wells, Helen Heffernan, Corinne Seeds, Elizabeth Almira Allen and Marion Thompson Wright receive attention.

Gender studies – and, specifically, queer theory in education (Pinar 1998c) – have become even more prominent in the post-1995 period. James Sears continues to be the primary male figure here, publishing important historical studies (1998a, 2006) as well as "queering" education (Sears 2005; Letts and Sears 1999; Sears 1998b). There is a collection on "thinking queer" (Talburt and Steinberg), as well queer theory of race (Pinar 2001; Stokes 2001; Somerville 2001). Again, one notes that post-1995 scholarship is characterized by mixed versions of what were depicted in *Understanding Curriculum* as distinct discourses.

Inspired by the work of Frantz Fanon, Edward Said, Gayatri Chakravorty Spivak, and Homi K. Bhabha, postcolonial studies has achieved prominence in contemporary scholarship (Willinsky 1992), including work on decolonization (Pandey and Moorad 2003). Cameron McCarthy (Dimitriadis and McCarthy 2001; McCarthy 1998; Matus and McCarthy 2003) continues to play a major role, as he did in the establishment of "race" as a central strand in the reconceptualized field (see Pinar et al. 1995, chapter six). Nina Asher and Gaile Canella have made also notable contributions to post-colonial studies.

As Alan Block's study makes clear, none other than Joseph Schwab pioneered Jewish curriculum studies. Such a phrase may suggest to many work done in Israel (think of the Seymour Fox collection, for instance) and in the Diaspora focused on introducing Jewish students to their religious and cultural traditions, and that work is to be included in this category. Block (2006) insists he is not creating a new specifically Jewish discourse; rather, he explains, he is contesting what seems to him to be Christian conceptions of education. Important too is the work of Marla Morris (2006), whose work on the Holocaust is, to my mind, an exemplary example of contemporary scholarship in any category (see Morris 2001).

Disability studies – focused on images of physically disfigured bodies in American culture and, specifically, literature (see Thomson 1997) and including challenges to bureaucratic categories of disability and, specifically, special education (see Brantlinger 2005; Bernadette Baker 2002a, b) – have become prominent. Critiques of gifted education (Sapon-Shevin 1994) have also challenged bureaucratized conceptions of ability.

Like other post-Reconceptualization curriculum discourses, autobiographical curriculum theory has dispersed into other scholarly spheres, among them cross-cultural theory (Wang 2004; Li 2002), psychoanalytic theory (Pitt 2003), women's studies (Neumann and Peterson 1997), studies of place (Casemore in press; Whitlock 2007), innovative pedagogical practices (Oberg 2004; Salvio 1998), social theory (Goodson 1998); and ecological studies (Krall 1994; Doerr 2004). At least one sector of autobiographical studies has been renamed narrative inquiry (not only the genre associated with F. Michael Connelly and D. Jean Clandinin, but the more phenomenologically focused scholarship of Leah Fowler). Biographical studies continue (see, for instance, Salvio 2007); Craig Kridel's (1998) collection is key here.

Complexity theory in education has become something of a movement, with a conference and a journal. William E. Doll, Jr. introduced complexity theory to the field in his 1993 postmodern view of curriculum, and he has continued to play a major role in it, publishing (with Jayne Fleener, herself the author of a complexity theory-inspired book entitled *Curriculum Dynamics*, and Donna Trueit and John St. Julien), a collection of essays on the subject entitled *Chaos, Complexity, Curriculum and Culture*. Brent Davis has emerged as a prominent player in this domain, publishing a genealogical study of the idea (2004) as well as, with Dennis Sumara and Rebecca Luce-Kappeler (2000), an introductory textbook for prospective teachers.

Environmental, sustainability, and other ecological studies have exploded since the early 1990s. C. A. Bowers is the most prominent scholar, but Noel Gough's scholarship has also been influential. Important, too, is the eco-feminist work of Elaine Riley-Taylor and the environmental-autobiographical work of Marilyn Doerr. I, too, have acknowledged the primacy of sustainability in curriculum work (Pinar 2007a).

There is continued scholarly interest in psychoanalysis in education, led by Deborah Britzman (1998, 2003, 2006), Appel (1999), D. Aoki (2002), Atwell-Vasey (1998), jagodzinski (2002), Taubman (1990), Pitt (2003), Todd (2003) and Gilbert (2004). It is also evident in a number of important theoretical studies not primarily psychoanalytic in orientation, among them Grumet's (2005 [1976]; 1988) autobiographical and feminist studies, Block's (1997) critique of the school's psychological violence against the child, Ellsworth's (1997) theorization of teaching as a mode of address, Morris' (2001) investigation of curriculum and the Holocaust, Todd's (2003) elaboration of an ethics of education, and in Webber's (2003) study of spectacular school violence. I employed psychoanalytic theory in my effort to understand what I took to be the "queer" dimensions of racial subjugation (Pinar 2001).

The prominence of technological studies surprises no one. Chet Bowers is prominent here as well, as is John Willinsky, Larry Cuban, Karen Ferneding and others. While Bowers, Cuban, and Ferneding are all critics (in different ways), Willinsky demonstrates the enormous potential of what he terms the "access principle" in making academic knowledge public and usable, a sophisticated form of curriculum design.

In understanding curriculum aesthetically, Eisner's work continues to be prominent, as is work by Philip Jackson (with his 1999 book on Dewey's aesthetic theory), Tom Barone, Donald Blumenfeld-Jones, and Rita Irwin. Irwin has stressed the generative interrelations among the roles of artist, teacher, and researcher in what she terms A/R/Tography (Irwin and de Cosson 2004). The study of visual culture has become important as well (Mirzoeff 1998; Jay 1993).

Scholarly interest in the study of curriculum internationally is not a new phenomenon. In the early decades of the twentieth century, internationalism – associated with political movements on the Left – was advocated by U.S. progressives like Counts and Brameld. Until recently, however, much of the North American scholarship devoted to understanding curriculum internationally was conducted in Canada (see, for instance, Goodson 1988; Carson 1988; Willinsky 1992; Smith 2003; Aoki 2005 [1981]). Despite calls (see Rogan and Luckowski, 1990; Rogan 1991) for U.S. scholars to attend to international developments, not until the last decade did a synoptic textbook devote a chapter on the subject (see Pinar et al., 1995, chapter 14). Since then, developments have been rapid, supported by the establishment of new organizations, among them the International Association for the Advancement of Curriculum Studies (IAACS) and its U.S. affiliate, the American Association for the Advancement of Curriculum Studies (AAACS).

ORGANIZATION OF THIS BOOK

I open with a statement of "abundance," that of David W. Jardine, Sharon Friesen, and Patricia Clifford. In this season of great untruth (Smith 2006), we can take heart from their phenomenologically-informed wisdom (see Garrison 1997; Henderson and Kesson 2003). No longer constrained by its philosophical antecedents, phenomenology during this "next [i.e., present] moment" in North American curriculum studies is also political and, specifically, ecological. Jardine and his colleagues challenge the political character of school "deform" by focusing on the abundance amidst the scarcity of "standards" and "accountability."

Referring to Deborah Britzman's (2003) revision of *Practice Makes Practice*, I point to the unwritten political chapter in *Curriculum in Abundance*. (Perhaps that is the political strategy of "post-critical" scholarship [Pinar 2000 (1975), xv]: critique the extant order by attending to what is everywhere but "not yet," in Maxine Greene's [see Pinar 1998a, 1; this volume, Chapter 15] memorable phrase, and in doing so, attempt to midwife the "next moment.") Jardine and his colleagues dwell in this "next moment," one in which "abundance" is everywhere, in spite of global warming and the overheating of classrooms focused on "outcomes." We are steadied, and maybe mobilized politically, by discerning the fullness around us.

From (waking up from) the nightmare that is the present, in Chapter 2 we return to the past, a past very much present. In the collected essays of Janet L. Miller (2005), we glimpse the last thirty years of U.S. curriculum studies, from its Reconceptualization (1970-1979) to its Internationalization (2001-). It is a portrait at once personal and public, one that testifies to the political potential of autobiography and to the autobiographical animus of politics. Because we have been friends for thirty years, my preface is also personal, and readily I refer to "Janet." As personal, as focused on scholarship I admire, I fail in my critical capacity, but it is a "failure" I defend: what is there to critique in this work, I wonder? Janet has complicated the curriculum theory of autobiography by incorporating concepts of difference and grounding always this theory in the daily practices of teaching and study. The central image of these essays – Picasso's *Guernica* – not only underscores the centrality of aesthetic experience in Janet's educational experience (certainly it is central in her theorizing, as the lyricism of her prose testifies), but the painting's thematics (assault, injustice, struggle, survival) restate, in its global-historical terms, our generation's "local" experience working the tensions (as Janet would say) in our small corner of the world: U.S. curriculum studies. Despite the catastrophe that is the right-wing ascendancy in U.S. national politics and despite the turmoil and bitterness circulating within the field, Janet Miller has remained focused on "what should be and what might be."

Chapter 3 is a speech, first given at the University of British Columbia at the first Provoking Curriculum Conference. Ted Aoki was present that day, as was my co-editor of Aoki's collected works: Rita L. Irwin. In the speech I focus on Aoki's pedagogical genius. Most of the essays Irwin and I collected were speeches Aoki had given to various conferences. Ted's attunement to each conference theme and its participants conveys both his phenomenological wisdom and poststructuralist playfulness. In one sense, his essays constitute classroom lessons, or, in another sense, conceptual jazz performances in which those in attendance were (recalling Alexander Pope's well-worn but still useful formulation) both entertained and instructed. Phenomenology's skepticism toward ocularcentrism and poststructuralism's preference for performativity are audible in Aoki's accomplishment.

What had been discernibly distinct discourses in the 1980s – understanding curriculum as autobiographical, aesthetic, and historical text – merge in A/R/Tography, the study of the confluence of artistry, research, and teaching. Resonant with Aoki's contribution (upon which several contributors draw), Rita L.

Irwin's conception of A/R/Tography enables artists who teach and conduct research to study subjectivity and sociality through text and image. In the collection to which I wrote an afterward (see Chapter 4), A/R/Tography is illustrated through quilt making, painting, sewing, collage, journaling (visual and textual), graffiti, sculpture, and studies in the history of art education.

Kevin Kumashiro responds to debates in the 1980s (see, for instance, Pinar et al. 1995, p. 255) regarding the accessibility and translatability of so-called critical curriculum scholarship to classroom teachers. Reflecting post-1980s curriculum scholarship, Kumashiro draws upon multiple discursive traditions within the field - the political, feminist, multicultural, queer, and postcolonial most prominently – in his focus upon oppression. Sharing Dwayne Huebner's criticism of educational psychology, Kevin underscores the limitations of that disciplinary tradition in enabling students to understand, and take action against, oppression. For Kumashiro, "resistance" is not only a concept in political curriculum theory (Pinar et al. 1995, p. 252ff.), it is a subject prospective and practicing teachers ought to study (2004, p. 24). The "standard" to which Kevin would hold teacher education programs is activism (2004, p. 43), but not the macho Marxist kind (2004, p. 47). In Kumashiro's work, the well-worn tension (see Pinar 2004a, pp. 230-231) between theory and practice dissolves (see Chapter 5).

As we see in Chapter 6, the work of William Reynolds also testifies to the power of a theoretically sophisticated practice. Bill labored to create a common language, the expression of which enables students and colleagues to articulate their experience of school "deform." Inspired by the great curriculum theorist James B. Macdonald, Reynolds works hermeneutically, with a historical consciousness (Seixas 2004), toward democratic community, through a curriculum of compassion. Grounded politically, Bill critiques each phase of politicians' manufacture of the ongoing school "crisis." Informed by critical theory, autobiography, phenomenology, and post-structuralism, Reynolds' scholarship not only chronicles and critiques the major political calamities of the last twenty-five years, it provides "lines of flight" for those who can glimpse the moment after the nightmare ends.

The nightmare that is the present is not only political and public, it is personal. In Chapter 7, I marvel at Alice Pitt's theorization of "the play of personal." For Pitt, hermeneutics is a psychic activity. Working from Winnicott (and Felman, Freud, and Kaja Silverman) and recalling Grumet's *Bitter Milk*, Pitt situates the teacher/student relationship in a series of significant relationships, including that of mother/child and analyst/analysand. The individuation of the "self" requires self-protection as well as self-assertion. In Pitt's work "resistance" – first theorized by Marxist scholars in the 1980s as a clarion call to struggle, later gendered (Pinar 1998 [1983]; Munro 1998a, 28; 1998b) as provocation to self-reflective activism – assumes its psychoanalytic sense as psychic problem to be worked through. Pitt is sober about the potential here: she cautions us against demanding too much of the personal. Its temporality is implied by Freud's neologism (*Nachtraglichkeit*), a term he devised to explain how the experience of trauma is deferred – and, I would add, displaced - into other subjective and social spheres, where it is often no longer readily recognizable. Pitt's use of the term inspired me to employ it in *What is Curriculum Theory?*

The gap between the subjective and social provides opportunities for pedagogy, for autobiography, and especially for women traumatized by living in patriarchal, misogynistic cultures. As opportunity, the personal is constructed – as it was, evidently, for the poet Anne Sexton (Salvio 2007) – and performed in specific contexts, with specific audiences in mind, toward specific ends. The personal is, Pitt adds, an effect of the subject's libidinal ties to specific others. Self-structuring attachments engage not only other persons, but subjective processes (among them study) and possessions (among these, knowledge) as well. The resistance of the patient (or the student) engenders the destitution of mastery, as more than a few therapists (and teachers) keenly know. At the center of education is a "knot" not easily – indeed, fit to be – (un)tied.

In Chapter 8, the "knot" of educational experience and its representation is untied in a collection of pieces that must surely be seen as the summit of poststructuralism. To the sober, it must seem these contributors tied one on, but in my view they were stating their solemn vows, intertexually tying the knot that weds educational experience to its representation. Aoki is the master teacher here ("scholar and sensei" Marylin Low acknowledges), but his students are not disciples. Rather, they are poets and teachers articulating "living pedagogy" from their own displaced spaces. A collage comprised of self, place (see Chambers 2003a, 234), and curriculum becomes visible, or should I say audible, as each writes from the spaces in-between each location, ecstatic moments of *"sublime openness,"* as Pat Palulis (2003, 259, emphasis in original) puts it.

From the sublime to the horrific in Chapter 9, as we face the aftermath of the Holocaust. This scholarship depicts what is at stake in a curriculum of memory and commemoration. Like post-Reconceptualization genres, this collection I am introducing – edited by Marla Morris and John Weaver - is informed by what had been before distinct discourses, among them efforts to understand curriculum as autobiographical, theological, gendered and political text. Given the attention given to Martin Heidegger, phenomenology is at issue here as well. We are confronted, as the title of the collection asserts, with "difficult memories."

The annihilation of German gays and lesbians during the Holocaust situates contemporary controversies concerning sexual minorities in the United States. Right-wing extremists have indeed called for their – our – annihilation. As Kate Evans (whose book I am introducing in Chapter 10) points out, questions of identity are simultaneously local and global. They are, I would add, historical. Emotion is a major category of analysis in Evans' study of four preservice teachers. (Emotion is a subject also taken up by several major contemporary scholars, among them Megan Boler, Deborah Britzman, and Alice Pitt.) Evans shows how, in heteronormative settings, gays and lesbians are required to perform emotional labor, simply in order to function. Now we understand that what we feel is also a social and political matter.

The fantasy of queer-as-child-predator haunts gay and lesbian teachers, as Evans' discussion of anti-gay incidents in schools underscores. In calling for teacher education to challenge the ignorance and prejudice that makes such incidents possible, Evans makes plain the fascism of conservative calls for curriculum "alignment," including the Bush Administration's insistence upon "evidence-based" research on "what works." In such misnamed research, the heterosexist homophobic status quo is institutionalized as "reality," and the psychological annihilation of gays and lesbians is enacted. Thanks to Evans' theoretical and ethnographic savvy, our understanding of curriculum as gender text is advanced as it is rendered vivid and concrete. The installation of emotion as political labor is an important theoretical contribution, advancing our understanding of curriculum as autobiographical, as political, and as gendered.

In Chapter 11 I introduce Tom Barone's essays. At once aesthetic, autobiographical, and political, they illustrate how once distinctive curriculum discourses have blended during the "next moment." Barone's scholarship is a socially committed literature, thoughtfully theoretical and in service to practitioners in the schools. In order to testify to the truth of the present moment, Tom moves away from social science toward the humanities (specifically the literary), privileging metaphor over literalism, fiction over fact. Victims of a callow culture, many Americans mistake technological innovation and higher test scores for educational advancement. The pernicious foolishness of "top-down" school "deform" ensures that any cultural coming-of-age is retarded. Barone conceives of the teacher as an artist, someone who cultivates his or her individuality as s/he enables students to cultivate theirs. Invoking the notion of strong poet, Barone posits narrative as the moral means of subjective and social reconstruction.

Reconstruction is also on the minds of queer scholars. Published just before the assaults of the Bush Administration (and their conservative fellow-travelers), this collection criticizes what can now seem like political advances (or at least consolations), among them cinematic portrayals of "coming out" (such as in *In & Out*) or the abundance of (if not always supportive) gay and lesbian adolescent literature. Despite the setbacks of the past six years, one must always keep the heat on: some of us are now "queering straight teachers" (Rodriguez and Pinar 2007). One contributor cautions us against provoking the right-wing (and specifically the Christian fundamentalist segments of it). During the Bush Administration, provocation came from the conservatives themselves, as they scapegoated us in their crusade against gay marriage, conveniently timed for the 2004 election.

Despite the conservative catastrophe, democracy continues to be a mobilizing ideal in the U.S. In Chapter 13 I introduce a collection of essays dedicated to reaffirming the progressive association of democracy with education, here focused on curriculum leadership. We read analyses and examples of Schwab's notion of deliberation as well as of other important curriculum concepts, among them reflexivity and the mythopoetic (and the centrality of cultural criticism to each). For the editors of the collection – James G. Henderson and Kathleen R. Kesson – these concepts become meaningful in school settings, wherein educators grapple with everyday issues through dialogue with each other, their students, and others invested in the curriculum.

Along with James B. Macdonald and Maxine Greene, it was Dwayne E. Huebner who showed my generation what was possible. In the canon of curriculum scholarship, Huebner's *oeuvre* is required reading, as Chapter 14 makes clear. Huebner's scholarship represented a "turning point" in the intellectual history of the field, one that provided the conceptual tools by means of which the field was reconceptualized during the 1970s (see Pinar et al. 1995, Chapter 4). Huebner introduced political theory, phenomenology, and theology to U.S. curriculum studies, while reaffirming the significance of aesthetics and history. Structuring his scholarship was his simultaneous concern for classroom life and for the life of theory (see Anderson 2006, p. 3). As it is the case for other great scholars, Huebner's thought becomes more synthetical over the course of his career. In his final phase, focused on religion, we find a restatement of his 1959 reverence for awe and wonder (Huebner 1999, p. 8). His collected essays are canonical; no serious scholar can claim expertise in curriculum studies without studying them.

Honoring another great scholar – the philosopher of education Maxine Greene – is the task of Chapter 15. I work against the monumentalizing movement of such a motive by focusing on a specific event in which an eighty-year-old Maxine Greene emphasizes that she is "not yet." Not only does that phrase underscore the unfinished futurity of her career, it underlines the temporality of all scholarly work, its embeddedness in biography, in history, in circumstance. I liken Greene to the legendary New York public intellectual Susan Sontag. For both the mind is passion, an embodied means of political engagement through understanding the biographical and the historical. An inspiring demonstration of intellectual activism, Maxine Greene's philosophy of education extends efforts to understand curriculum as political, autobiographical, aesthetic text, to a curriculum field, like the legendary intellectual herself, that is "not yet."

Completing the canon key to the 1970s Reconceptualization of the U.S. field is attention, in Chapter 16, to the scholarship of James B. Macdonald. Junior scholars working in "the next moment" may take for granted a professional calling that, when Macdonald first envisioned it, was revolutionary. Grounded in "realpolitik" and in lived experience, one worked, Macdonald asserted, for social and subjective change. Macdonald defied the structure-of-the-disciplines movement of the 1960s (Pinar et al. 1995, pp. 159-168), criticized mid-century U.S. militarism and nationalism, pointed to the American substitution of technological for social improvement, all the while reaffirming what Freire once characterized as humanity's historical vocation: humanization (Freire 1968, p. 28). (The poststructuralist dismissal of humanism comes twenty years later, and is, I think, overstated, but that is a subject for another day.) Macdonald made plain that scholarship is never politically neutral, an idea others repeated as if it were their own. His analysis of the field provided the categories I borrowed in my initial mappings of the field (2000 [1975]). His critique of social engineering proved decisive for me (see 2006b, p. 109). His early 1980s scholarship on gender and for social justice presaged the predominance of those categories in subsequent curriculum scholarship. Like his friend and colleague Dwayne E. Huebner, James B. Macdonald appreciated the religious character of curriculum theory, characterizing it as a "prayerful." Like Huebner's and Greene's scholarship, Macdonald's contribution is canonical.

The mythopoetical strand of curriculum theory (see Leonard and Willis, in press) is also associated with James B. Macdonald. Mary Aswell Doll is perhaps the most prominent practitioner of it, bringing to this rich tradition her scholarly expertise in literature, theater, and myth (1988a, 1995, 1998, 2000, 2006). Eros, passion, and the body, loved ones and their dreams and death all preoccupy this sophisticated literary critic turned curriculum theorist. Like Maxine Greene, Mary Aswell Doll is devoted to the education of the imagination, a capacity realized by the delicate articulation of interpretation. Mary proposes a curriculum of dreams, in which her son's dreams and her brother's death trouble her teaching. Like a loved one awakening us from a deep sleep, Mary Aswell Doll focuses our attention upon the meaning of the morning.

In Chapter 18, I comment on the path-breaking scholarship of Ivor F. Goodson. In several areas – curriculum history, international studies, and life history research – Goodson has provided lasting leadership. In particular, his insistence that life history be grasped historically and politically gives lie to the Marxist nonsense that autobiography is only self-referential. Goodson's study of school subjects gives lie to the Marxist reductionism that ideology is main means of social reproduction. Correcting such errors constitutes a major intellectual service and contributes in crucial ways to the intellectual advancement of curriculum studies worldwide.

In Chapter 19, I conclude the collection with an introduction to Reta Ugena Whitlock's key contribution to southern curriculum studies. I lived in Louisiana for twenty years. (We moved to British Columbia three weeks before Hurricane Katrina struck the state.) I devoted a significant segment of my first years there to trying to understand where I was. Verticality and horizontality structured that endeavor, as I labored to connect what I saw and felt and heard to what I was studying about the history of the South. Reconstruction is the organizing concept upon which I finally settled. Reconstruction was resonant in three senses: 1) as that flawed and failed post-bellum effort to punish and re-integrate the Confederacy into the Union; 2) as the means of making experience educational; and 3) as the educational means of democratization. In Whitlock's work, the three senses of the concept conflate constructively.

The education of the public requires simultaneous subjective and social reconstruction, not only of the public, but, as I am arguing here, of the profession as well. The two are evident in Whitlock's work, as she narrates autobiographically what is at stake in reconstruction, a "working through" of the myths of the Lost Cause. In this work – one stunning example of scholarship in the "next moment" – several discourses are combined, among them the autobiographical, the political, the phenomenological, the theological, the racial and the gendered. Not only the future of U.S. curriculum studies depends on junior scholars such as Reta Ugena Whitlock: given the domination of U.S. Presidential politics by the neo-Confederacy, the fate of the nation may depend upon her and her generation.

ACKNOWLEDGEMENTS

In addition to graduate assistant Yoko Namita (for her assistance with the references), I wish to thank each of scholars whose work I have discussed here. Not a few of these are friends as well as colleagues: that fact becomes evident by the use of those colleagues' first names. Friend and/or colleague: permit me to acknowledge that not only the discipline of curriculum studies has been intellectually advanced by your work, I have been as well.

Almost no work is beyond criticism, of course, but accepting an invitation to introduce (or comment on) others' scholarship suspends the opportunity to criticize. In order to be faithful to that suspension, I accepted only those invitations requiring no misrepresentation: I agreed to introduce only work I admired. In edited volumes, there was one instance in which I disagreed with the argument of the chapter, and there I stated that disagreement, if parenthetically and somewhat indirectly, as you will note.

The "next moment" of U.S. curriculum studies is an intellectually momentous period. If we survive the assault on the profession (from outside and from within the university), the field is positioned to become even more sophisticated, more exciting, more important. To find our way to the future, let us study the past to understand the present.

THE LURE THAT PULLS FLOWERHEADS TO FACE THE SUN (2006)

[T]his heart of mine knows the world is alive and full of purpose.

David W. Jardine (2006, p. 84)

This is, as David Jardine, Sharon Friesen, and Patricia Clifford acknowledge, "the oddest of texts to grasp" (2006, p. xxxiii).[1] Actually, the text isn't odd; it's the present day that is and that makes this text seem odd. The present day is one of scarcity, demanding of us "sure-fire methods," the success of which is measured by standardized examinations, regularly administered. Such is, we are told, accountability. In the United States, politicians' calls for accountability seem reserved for the schools only. In the business sector – think of the Enron scandal, for instance – has anyone even heard of the word? Certainly it is a concept foreign to the Bush Administration. Complaints about the Bush Administration's incompetence in responding to the Hurricane Katrina disaster are dismissed as "blame-games." In such Orwellian times, David Jardine, Sharon Friesen and Patricia Clifford dedicate this book

> to the teachers and children who are suffering in the confines of a form of schooling premised on scarcity and impoverishment, and to teachers and children who have taught the three of us so much about what an enlivening and pleasurably difficult thing teaching and learning can be in light of curriculum understood as abundance (2006, p. xxviii).

Pleasure in difficulty? The curriculum as abundance? In the present day, these phrases sound odd all right.

Language creates as it decodes reality. Jardine, Friesen, and Clifford's vocabulary – drawn, in part, from Ivan Illich – functions likewise. "We therefore use the term 'abundance'," they tells us, "because of what it invokes, what it provokes, what it allows, the questions it supports, the language it encourages, the images and hopes and desires it brings" (2006, p. 9). As in poststurcturalism[2], language here is a passage to a world not evident in the present era of scarcity, but the world everywhere around us, in us, in classrooms.

This is hardly Jardine's first post-structuralist moment (see, for instance, Jardine 1992). His astonishing accomplishment has been grounded in phenomenology, and, more specifically, in radical hermeneutics, with its "decoding/creating" function always already restructuring its "original difficulty." In the present volume, phenomenology and post-structuralism become background to his and his colleagues' original point of view. Despite being distracted by scarcity, David calls us to return to our original difficulty, asking: "what is our real work as teachers and students?" (2006, p. 9). To answer, he reports, "we have been drawing upon three

1

interrelated disciplines in order to cultivate this imagining [of abundance]: 1) ecology, 2) contemporary threads of Buddhist philosophy, 3) hermeneutics" (2006, 7-8). These traditions are not prerequisites for understanding *Curriculum in Abundance*, but serious students will return to these traditions. Such study will permit a fuller and more nuanced appreciation of the scale of Jardine's scholarly accomplishment. There we discover "a great kinship between hermeneutics, ecology, and pedagogy" (2006, p. 277).

TO THE THINGS THEMSELVES

Understanding is thus not method: it is learning to dwelling in the presence of this riveredge ... and, under such witness, becoming someone because of it.

David W. Jardine (2006, p. 275)

The idea of abundance, we are told, emerged at the end of their last book, *Back to the Basics of Teaching and Learning*: *"Thinking the World Together"* (2003a). It that text Jardine, Friesen and Clifford suggested that "what is in fact basic' to a living discipline (and therefore a curricular inheritance entrusted to teachers and students in schools) is precisely its excessiveness" (2006, p. xxvi). Acknowledging that this idea is unimaginable during regimes of scarcity, Jardine explains that "understanding curriculum in abundance requires thinking and experiencing that is substantive, material, bodily, earthly, located, specific" (p. xxiv). To be understood, he insists, it must be practiced: "We have argued ... for the ways in which our thinking must find its thoughtfulness through the world work, in the face of the testy case that will slow thought down and test its resolve, its strength, its patience and its worth" (2006, p. 18).

David, Sharon, and Patricia experienced this abundance in public-school classrooms. There they heard not only the voices of students and teachers, they heard the sound of our calling. In the midst of children's bustling about, David hears his ancestors calling to him: "I like the experience of having my attention drawn, of being whispered to, of having a *calling*" (2006, p. xxiii). Having been called, we do not act as self-made men fantasize themselves exploiting the world's "resources," we listen and we respond. This is no unilateral assertion, but a dialogical, relational gesture of acknowledgement: "What abundance requires of teachers and students is a much more cultivated, much more deliberate and intellectually sound sense of the nature and limits of our own agency" (2006, p. 10). There is no politicized or psychologistic conception of agency here; indeed, Jardine underscores agency's passivity. Discussing the study of mathematics, he writes that the subject is a "living place, a living field of relations, and that to make our way into it requires a momentary sense of loss, of giving oneself over to *its* ways by 'letting'" (2006, p. 66). Prospective and practicing teachers won't hear such advice in many methods courses.

Still speaking of mathematics, Jardine appreciates that teaching is a meditative practice. It is, as Ted Aoki understood, a mode of being. He can "participate in the open space of mathematics," David tells us, "when my breath settles down and steps out paces of walking meditation: breaths and steps symmetrical and measured, seeking equilibration, oxygen filling up the longing spaces in patterns chemical precisions that return with exhalation" (2006, p. 85). This meditative sense of study – wherein an academic discipline seems simultaneously a spiritual discipline – calls us to go beyond issues of epistemology towards issues of ontology. Jardine explains: "Epistemology has to do with issues of what it means *to know* something – rooted in the Greek term *episteme*, to know. Ontology has to do with what it means *to be* something – from the Greek *ontos*, to be" (2006, p. 87). In my terms, academic study supports, indeed structures, self-formation; it recalls the German theory of *Bildung* (von Humbolt 2000 [1793-1794]).

Self-formation occurs through movement, as if on a journey (see Kliebard 2000 [1975]). Human experience, Jardine tells us, has "the character of a journeying... becoming someone along the way" (2006, p. 271). That some "one" is hardly alone – Jardine and his colleagues emphasize the relationality, the ecology, of human experience in the world – but there seems to me the suggestion of an apparently essential unified self, as least when they write: "Each variant *is* the original and therefore each stubborn particular must be read, somehow, in its wholeness, in its originary character. The simplest child's simplest utterance may itself be prophesy" (2006, 86). A western word, prophesy is not prediction (certainly in no social scientific sense), but a revelation onto times "not yet," as Maxine Greene is so fond of saying. The child's simplest utterance represents a call from beyond the apparently present moment in which we older creatures dwell, beyond yet not apart from it. Hongyu Wang (2004, p. 129) suggests

> The call from the stranger invites movement toward the beyond, but not beyond into absolute, essential, metaphysical truth. This movement toward the beyond is *with* the web of interconnections.... Only through her efforts to reach *out* can the deep connections within be touched, felt, and transformed. In a third space.

That is, she suggests, a third space in which Western distinctions among past, present, and future blur. There, our situation becomes discernible, and we can hear prophets among us.

Surely David Jardine, Sharon Friesen and Patricia Clifford are among them. Listening to them, "the dry and lifeless impoverishment of the curriculum guide version of the topic cracks open. A world begins to appear and we feel drawn into it" (2006, p. 41). There, responding to the call of the other is recoded into "learning styles" wherein one "constructs" the world according to cognitive schema; for Jardine and his colleagues, abundance is an ontological, not epistemological, fact. Responding to the call of the other requires, perhaps above all, the discernment of difference:

> [S]uggestions of multiplicity and diversity are not opulent educational *options* regarding how we might come to know topics that are in reality simple and manageable. Rather, multiplicity, diversity and abundance define

the way in which things *are*, and therefore, the great array of the ways of traversing a place that students bring to the classroom is *precisely what living things require if they are to be "adequately" understood in their abundance.* (2006, p. 88).

We may take epistemological paths to reach this place, but where we arrive is a living breathing place of being.

In this place – this curriculum - of abundance, not only people but ideas and images speak to us. "Images," David writes, "have a most peculiar sense of arrival. They seem to *arrive*, out of nowhere, often unexpectedly, with a clear feel of agency, of portend, of demand and deliberateness. This is phenomenologically undeniable" (2006, p. 91). The world does not wait for us act upon it, silent, defenseless; instead, this world of abundance is a meaningful place, alive with purpose. This vibrant world provokes our awe and wonder: "first is the question posed, not *by us* but *to us*" (2006, p. 91) Jardine emphasizes. "It pulls us into *its* question, *its* repose, *its* regard" (2006, p. 91). I am reminded of Rita Irwin's (2003) depiction of aesthetic surrender to the labor of creation. Such devotion does not mean relinquishing agency, but, as Jardine, Sharon and Patricia acknowledge: "What abundance requires of teachers and students is a much more cultivated, much more deliberate and intellectually sound sense of the nature and limits of our own agency" (2006, p. 10).

This is a nuanced, situation-specific, relational conception of agency. It would seem to acknowledge that agency requires recognition of the particular situation – its horizons, its meaning – so that we may act with precision, care, and tact (van Manen 1991). The agency of pedagogy demands, quoting Jardine, "deliberation" and "decision." The omnipresence – the worship – of technology does not alter this fact. "In fact," David, Sharon and Patricia emphasize, "the new technologies are aggravating and highlighting the necessity for deliberation and decision, a necessity that, strangely enough, was *there all along*" (2006, p. 51). Information does not obviate the necessity for ethical and intellectual judgment, as they are well aware: "Now that the Internet has broadened the boundaries of what we and our children *can* do, in our own work, the question of what we *should* do with these new arrivals arises anew" (2006, p. 55). We find ourselves in the midst not only of plenty, we are in the midst of "too much," and the pedagogical point is how to listen and, then, to respond to the call that then discloses the situation and the questions it poses to us.

CURRICULUM IN ABUNDANCE

We cannot do to children what we have not already done to ourselves.

David W. Jardine (2006, p. 184)

Where to start? As that last paragraph implies, we have already started, we are already "thrown" into the abundance of the classroom, already "beached" on a shore simultaneously familiar and strange. We are always already in the midst of a situation, to which we listen, in which we act. "When teachers ask us where to start," David, Sharon, and Pat tell us, "our only answer can be that they have to come to understand that they have already started because they, as well as their students, are already living in an abundant world" (2006, p. 98). Distracted by curriculum guides, we risk not seeing what – who – is in our midst, in whose midst we are. As Dwayne Huebner appreciated, the pedagogical question is also an ethical one: how are we to conduct ourselves?

Teaching within a curriculum of abundance cannot be reduced to technique. It is not tantamount to purchasing consumer goods from the shelf of curriculum topics, those "impossible, consumptive, isolated never really satisfying bits and pieces [of the curriculum] thus always leave us looking longingly for the last days when all will be redeemed and we can finally rest, assured" (2006, p. 274). Teaching the curricular abundance around us is less a behavior we "do" than "a way we carry ourselves in the world, the way we come, through experience, to live in a world full of life, full of relations and obligations and address" (2006, p. 100). It is a matter, as Jardine says, of ontology not epistemology, ethics not instrumental rationality, ecology not the exploitation of resources and assets.

Curriculum-in-abundance derives from "a deeply seated belief about how the world fits together in its deepest and most vigorous intellectual and spiritual possibilities" (2006, p. 100). Dwelling within curriculum-in-abundance supports, then, modes of being-in-the-world that enables us to experience the world, to recall the epigram with which I opened this foreword, as alive, indeed, purposeful. These modes of being do not just happen; they are not learning styles or pedagogical tools. "Experiencing the abundance of things must needs be cultivated" (p. 10), David points out. Moreover, "this process is often long and hard and full of its own dangers" (2006, p. 10). Does living amidst abundance render one abundant: passionately and profoundly engaged with the living compelled to live in scarcity? Is this why, as David discloses, "it is a little too easy for me to become rather zealous about this issue" (2006, p. 100)? Does abundance become

> quite literally a matter of life and death, of liveliness and deadliness, not only for myself but for the teachers and students I often witness laboring under the terrible burden of the belief in a world that doesn't fit gather and that must be therefore be doled out in well-monitored, well-managed, well-controlled packages, one lifeless fragment, one lifeless worksheet, one lifeless objective at a time. (2006, p. 100)

Full of life, one discerns the death in one's midst. Following Serres (1983), Jacques Daignault has warned us that "to know is to kill" (1992, p. 199), "that running after rigorous demonstrations and after confirmations is a hunt: literally" (1992, p. 198). As we will see momentarily, "literally" is also a kind of hunt that haunts the schools.

Those quoted lines from Jacques Daignault ascribe agency to us, but Jardine – true to his experience of a world that is alive and purposeful – ascribes agency to the world, in this instance, to the curriculum. Curriculum guides would seem to be themselves the hunters; they are, he knows, "defacing," precisely because they

5

decline to recognize the faces of those who encounter them. Moreover, he reminds us, "they will not listen. They already know ahead of time anything worth saying. They only speak and those who approach must only listen" (2006, p. 105). Curriculum guides ensure that "nothing happens" in the classroom that is not planned. There is little support for improvisation (Aoki 2005 [1990], p. 367). Instead of music,

> we inundate our children with relentless streams of one activity after the other and excuse it by referring to their short "attention spans," never once suspecting that many of the things they are inundated with in schools are *not worthy of attention*, because they have been stripped of their imaginal topographies (their living "ecologies," we might say). (2006, p. 274)

The employment of knowledge to monitor, control and distribute the world's abundance not only engenders "defeat" and "bewilderment." It leads, Jardine (2006, p. 101) suggests, to "exhaustion, paranoia and, I suggest, eventually violence." It leads not only to psychological violence; it has led, on occasion, to spectacular school violence (see Webber 2003).

A CURRICULUM OF SCARCITY

> There is no use hiding this fact: once curriculum is experienced in abundance, sometimes continuing to live in some schools becomes unbearable.

David W. Jardine, Sharon Friesen, Patricia Clifford (2006, p. xxvi)

The violence of the school system is a curricular issue as well, as Dwayne Huebner once pointed out during conversation (just after the Columbine murders) at Louisiana State University. By including this book in courses for prospective and practicing teachers, teacher educators can critique the culture of scarcity within the curriculum of teacher education. The subject should be included in the secondary school curriculum as well. Why would students be kept from studying what they themselves are undergoing and see around them? If teachers regain relative control of the curriculum they teach – a prerequisite, I argue, for practicing our profession (Pinar 2006c) – there are those will choose to offer courses on violence, including school violence. Courses might be offered not only on the history and gender of violence, but on its educational institutionalization in curriculum guides.

There is also violence in the theory of constructivism, Jardine implies, wryly. "Charmed by constructivism," he opines, "we don't quite know how to deal with the fact that the orderliness and ways of the pine tree outside of my window has disappeared into appearances of my own ordering" (2006, p. 129). Here he fells not only the savagery of solipsism, but the eeriness of equilibrium, at least as that concept has established itself as the center of gravity in developmentalism. David offers to invite "the old man home," (2006, p. 75) but the invitation is, it appears, for a tongue-lashing, as he complains that, thanks in part to Piaget, development is construed as "a succession of structures oriented towards steadily increasing stability and inclusiveness" (2006, p. 132). Despite its apparent biological underpinnings (see Doll 1993), such confidence seems cultural and, even, compensatory.

It would seem to be colonial as well. There are several gestures of genius in this book, and this is, it seems to me, one of them. David links developmentalism and "the images of maturity that it portends" to "the old colonialism" (2006, p. 134). A culture of incalculable confidence would seem to serve as the bridge between the two. "With colonialism," Jardine explains,

> we were able to believe that we stood in the midst of the world as the best – the freest, the most reasonable, the most civilized. With developmentalism, we get a new twist on the modernist spirit of universality and necessity ... we not just "the best" ... we are that towards which the world is heading in its progress toward maturity (2006, p. 134).

The old colonialism – and the culture it reflected and promoted - was also gendered and racialized (Stoler 1995). David appreciates the simultaneity of historical events: "At the same time as the rise of objectivism in modern science, Europe underwent the systematic witch-burning purification quackery crones who bore odd and bloody wisdoms in their breath and bones" (Jardine 1997, p. 164). The culture of scarcity is gendered masculine; in racial terms, it is white.

The assault on the earth is also gendered and racialized; like C. A. Bowers, Jardine focuses on the culture of this violence. For him, the ecological catastrophe would seem to be, in part, a consequence of how we live, how we are educated. Like Jardine, Bowers (2006) also considers constructivism as a symptom and cause of this cultural problem. Jardine focuses on environmental education to make the point:

> I believe that "environmental education" should not be a subdivision of schooling, but should describe the way we educate *altogether....* *All of the topics* entrusted to teachers and students in school can be understood as living fields, living inheritances, living places with ways and relations ands interdependencies, *including* (but not restricted to) those topics that usually fall under "environmental education" currently in schools (2006, p. 144).

The social and curricular fragmentation a market-economy of education institutionalizes accompanies and supports the exploitation and degradation of the biosphere. "What would happen," Jardine asks, "if we imagined children, not as consumers and producers of constructed products of our own making, but as inhabitants in a world that is more abundant than I make of it" (2006, p. 147)?

The answer to that question is, in part, that we would devise not a fragmented, specialized curriculum to be "covered," not only traversed (at one point Jardine plays with the idea of surfing, warning us that if we slow down we sink), but "covered over," its abundance buried deeper, it sometimes seems, than six feet under. (Curiously, that TV series testifies to Jardine's point that confronting death invigorates life.) "When the idea of scarcity insinuates itself into how we imagine the curriculum topics entrusted to teachers and students in schools, " David, Sharon and Patricia point out "those topics become necessarily bounded in ways that make it possible to control, predict, assess, and monitor their production, distribution" (2006, p. 4).

In unbinding curriculum topics and allowing them to circulate amidst the life in our classrooms, we create "an integrated curriculum that is a lived (in) place where we can "understand ... the full, living breadth of its Earthly interdependencies and kinships" (2006, p. 174). This is no curriculum we can imagine as entrapping us in an ivory tower; it is a curriculum whose endless hair enables us to move. "An integrated understanding," David Jardine (2006, p. 174) advises, "neither 'constructs' nor 'consumes' its object but delicate sustains that object while drawing from it; as ecology maintains, the living source must be protected so that we can return." At "home" we are not dispersed amidst the fragments scattered before us as "curriculum topics," bulletin boards and sound bites, lacerating our uncovered skin.³

Assault guarantees the inability to focus. Curricular fragmentation, Jardine, Friesen and Clifford appreciate, risks subjective fragmentation. The obsession with covering curriculum, with constructing knowledge (preferably "collaboratively" in groups) by constant activity, produces hyperactivity. Dispersed amidst curricular fragments, is it any surprise that, in Jardine's phrase, "attention starts to skitter" (2006, p. 178)? It is a circular and compounding process: "skittering attention leads to the belief that the world is fragmentary" (2006, p. 178). The ecological crisis is also a cultural crisis.

> It is fascinating to consider how, in these ecological desperate days, just as ecology is heralding the need for a continuity of attention and devotion, our schools are, in so many cases, full of attention deficits (itself wonderfully co-opted marketing term along with its dark twin, "paying attention"). (2006, p. 181)

Embedded in the monetary images a business-model of education sells is an explicitly political discipline.

This political discipline – the indebting of attention – is hardly new: Foucault associates the rise of the disciplines with the end of monarchy (Ransom 1997). One hundred years ago the American progressives were asserting the centrality of interest – and the apparent autonomy of attention such an educational concept implies – as key in the continuum between child and curriculum. Progressives' emphasis on the autonomy of attention occurs, Jonathan Crary (1999, p. 63) points out, at a time when technologies and institutions, including the school, were being mobilized to command the attention of mass populations. Crary implies that the American progressives – Crary is thinking of William James in particular - were consciously contradicting the influential work of William B. Carpenter, work done in the 1870s in which attention is described as an element of subjectivity to be externally shaped and controlled:

> It is the aim of the Teacher to fix the attention of the Pupil upon objects which may have in themselves little or no attraction for it.... The habit of attention, at first purely automatic, gradually becomes, by judicious training,

suggestion of appropriate motives, whilst taking care not to overstrain the child's mind by too long dwelling upon one object.

(Carpenter 1886, pp. 134-135; quoted in Crary 1999, p. 63)

In our time, we strain to keep the child's mind by covering curriculum topics quickly.

If we lose momentum as we surf along the surface of curriculum, Jardine points out, we're sunk. We lose our very being, and not only our subjective being, but, at the same time and predictably so, the biosphere in which we dwell. The warning signs are all around us – yes in global warming and in intensifying hurricanes - but in our children. In particular, Jardine thinks of the "ADD kids" as

canaries in a mine shaft – warnings, portents, heralds, like the monstrous, transgressive child often is … that airs have thinned and sustaining relations have been broken and need healing. Perhaps they are signs that education needs to become a form of ecological healing. (2006, p. 182)

Like Crary's progressives one hundred years ago, Jardine is attempting to contradict – through education - the primary tendencies of our day.[4]

The primary of these is the political imposition of the business model accompanied by increased accountability and curricular fragmentation, all of which is accomplished through the uncritical acceptance of new technologies and their presumed centrality to teaching and learning. In the United States, technology – and the utopian fantasies marketed around it – functions politically to distract citizens from the political and cultural problems political conservatives' embrace of business and religion have only aggravated. Presumably, technological advancements will solve the educational problems that political conservatives' assault on the poor and lower middle class have intensified.

Jardine questions the new information communication technologies (ICTs), focusing our attention on why "we want information" and on what "we wish to communicate." These questions – why and what we want to know – are, indeed, curricular questions, and Jardine appreciates that ICTs cannot answer them. While "ICTs cannot help us with this, at the same time, they are radically transforming both what and how we think about curriculum topics themselves" (2006, p. 205). Like Theodore Sizer (see 2004), Jardine focuses on the world youth already inhabit, pointing out that

Our students are already experiencing a world that is much richer, much more difficult and challenging, much more alluring and full of adventure than the version of the world made available made available in many classrooms. (2006, p. 23)

For Sizer, this fact means the school building - as the only or even primary site of education - is antiquated. For Jardine, this fact underscores the intergenerational character of public education: "Young and old thus deeply *belong together*" because "*inquiry is a necessarily intergenerational enterprise*" (2006, p. 208). The educational point is for young and old to understand together, and from their generationally situated subject positions, the present "version of the world."

LIVING IN THE WORD

Let's reclaim the word. This *is* research.

David W. Jardine (1997, 165)

A culture of scarcity is a culture of literalism. It is no accident that biblical literalism – and the religious zealotry it reflects and supports – accompanies political conservatism and consumer capitalism in contemporary America.[5] Abstract ideals become commodities: the American dream is no longer democracy but wealth, a fantasy compensating for those massive transfers of economic assets from the poor and lower middle classes to the upper classes during these last forty years of Republican Party rule. Lives of literalism are so miserable for so many – misery intensified by the discrepancy between the fantasy that is the American dream and the reality of minimum wage jobs the market economy creates – that they flee to the American versions of the Taliban. Like the Taliban, U.S. religious fundamentalists and political conservatives (the so-called Christian Coalition, for instance), claim the moral high ground (no abortion, no gay marriage, no drugs) based upon the literal Truth (God's word). It is an ideology of literalism.

Educationally, such literalism takes the form of curriculum guides to be covered as if they were so many Internal Revenue Service (IRS) or Revenue Canada income tax regulations and procedures. Indeed, the curriculum is to be audited (English 1999). This is anti-intellectualism at its most extreme, accountability covering up political manipulation and scapegoating. With the curriculum alienated from those who study and teach it, is it any wonder millions suffer from "attention deficit disorder"? There is assessed learning but no study (Block 2004), no pleasure, only misery:

> If, however, we begin within the scarcities of dryness and impoverishment of those very same curriculum guides, this will never necessarily lead us to the deep intellectual pleasures of learning, the deep intellectual pleasures to be had in our living in the world with children. The movement between the mandated curriculum and the disciplines and the beauties of the world it bespeaks is a one-way-street (2006, p. 227).

As the road sign announced at the start of our street in Baton Rouge, it is a Dead End.

What's in a sign? It is an indication of realities beyond itself, realities to which it points. Only in a culture of scarcity and literalism is the sign self-enclosed, pointing only to itself. As David, Patricia and Sharon appreciate: "literalism is indicative of precisely the sorts of closure regarding what can be said, written, spoken, heard or imagined that healthy, living systems do not display" (2006, p. 160). The American Taliban claims eternal life for its adherents but displays none of the earthly kind, except through the occasional but regular sex scandal. Jardine prescribes inversion (I can't help but hear the nineteenth-century echo) to medicate the sickness of literalism:

> Let's invert this, then: interpretive inquiry is directed toward the causing of dis-ease in such moments of closure. It is deliberately provocative, playful, audacious, and, too, petulant sometimes. But its provocations are on behalf of something: re-enlivening, finding the life in what has become morose

(Jardine, 1997, p. 165).

Such inverted inquiry may not be the second coming, but it holds the promise of resurrection after educational death.

Judaism, not Christianity, provides Jardine the imagery for our time of scarcity and literalism. He thinks of an empty chair, the place left vacant with bread and wine at the Seder table. We are waiting for Elijah to arrive. This empty chair does not, David tells us,

> bespeak someone who has *left* but someone who is *coming....* This empty chair now stands for *a future which has yet to come.* The futurity represented by the empty chair is not a given, not "frozen" but "yet to be decided." What will become of me, what will become of this work I am producing – all this is still coming, is not yet settled, and no amount of hurry or anxiety or effort will outrun this eventuality (2006, p. 219).

David is speaking of himself, and of schools as well. Hurry and anxiety structure the culture of scarcity. In Malachi 4:5-6, we are promised: "Behold, I am going to send you Elijah the prophet before the great and terrible day of the Lord. And he will restore the hearts of the fathers to their children, and the hearts of the children to their fathers, lest I come and smite the land with a curse." Can you hear Elijah through the words of this sacred text, the book you are about to study?

Moving from an empty chair to emptiness, from Judaism to Buddhism, David tells us "the idea of abundance leads to a deep experience of the limitedness of human life, this life, my life" (2006, p. 265). Paradoxically, this experience of limitation leads to fullness. The nearing of death intensifies one's remaining days. Collectively, the emptiness of the present enables us to experience the fullness the future portends. There is

> something the three of us have just recently named and can't quite follow up yet with any words – that this experience of the "letting go" of a topic out of its self-containedness and fragmentary and impoverished isolation - its "empyting" in the Buddhist sense, into the abundance of things – seems to ask us to experience a sort of death (2006, p. 268).

It is the death of that isolated ego regimes of scarcity and literalism produce; it is a welcomed end to "the venerated Protestant-Eurocentric-Neo-North American Loneliness of Individuality, of one's self existing estranged of all its relations" (2006, 267). Following, in the same sentence, David adds a compelling capsule summary of that accursed episteme: "like some independent, immortal soul caught through some awful accident in the messy, bloody, dependent squalors of the flesh" (2006, p. 268).

ENDBIT

Perhaps the greatest and most fearsome is the moment of knowing I am this Earthbody *and nothing besides.*

David W. Jardine (2006, p. 270)

Let us embrace the "dependent squalors of the flesh" (2006, p. 268). They are what drew me to New Orleans twenty years ago; they are what sustained me during my sojourn there. The sin of Hurricane Katrina was not, as the televangelists were quick to proclaim, New Orleans'. The sin of Hurricane Katrina was the Bush Administration's. From the treasonous ineptitude that allowed the September 11, 2001 attacks to occur, to the lies rationalizing the invasion of Iraq, to the immoral ineptitude that produced the disaster following Katrina, the Bush Administration personifies and institutionalizes what Jardine and his colleagues name as a "self existing estranged of all its relations" (2006, p. 268). Given its moral emptiness, it is no surprise, then, that the Bush Administration's *No Child Left Behind* legislation is designed to accomplish precisely that, to entrap teachers and students in a competitive culture of scarcity and literalism in which many children and teachers must necessarily be left behind. Like those stranded in a flooded abandoned city, huddled together on rooftops holding scribbled signs "HELP US," children huddle in "youth cultures" where (no canaries here) they suffer no "attention deficit disorders."

Study *this* sacred text, dear reader. Allow yourself to experience "the lure that pulls these flowerheads to face the sun" (2006, p. 270). Join David Jardine, Sharon Friesen and Patricia Clifford as they are "pulled now, beyond ... wanting and doing, into an effort, these words, at airbubble rockcast riversinging" (2006, p. 270). No false prophet he, Jardine invites us to join him, Sharon, and Patricia in acknowledging that, yes, educational experience involves suffering; it "involves opening ourselves to the open-ended sojourn of things, their ongoingness and fragilites and sometimes exhilarating, sometimes terrifying possibilities and fluidities" (2006, p. 271). In the suffering of study we can experience redemption:

[E]xperience is not something we *have*: it is something we undergo, and, to put it more intergenerationally, something we just might *endure*. It therefore has to do with duration, with what lasts, and therefore with what can be cultivated, taken care of: experiences worthy of the name are not [only] interior mental events had by a self-same subject, but are more like places that hold memory, topographical endurances (like these riveredges) full of ancestry and mystery and a complex, unrepayable indebtedness. Full of dependencies, full of "it depends," full of dependents. And more, experience therefore links with my own abundance, what I can live with, which, in part, means were I need to be, in what "space," (in what relations) to endure. (2006, p. 271)

It is not by refusing the squalors of the flesh, but by embracing them, embracing our worldliness, our being-in-the-world, that we can experience *abundance*. We can experience abundance now, not in an after-life. It is here, even in classrooms, especially in classrooms where we dwell in the curriculum of abundance that we can *live*, in *this* world, the world now being destroyed before our eyes.

The "hidden chapter" (Britzman 2003) of *Curriculum in Abundance* is, I am suggesting, a political chapter. The clues, I submit, are everywhere, lodged among the ancestors, the prophets in our classrooms, the living knowledge disguised and degraded as curriculum topics. These clues point to an unwritten chapter on politics, a chapter calling us to outrage: moral, generational, professional. What has happened to the schools, what (for us Americans) has happened to our country, what is happening to the planet, yes, it is a crime: a crime against children, against America, against Life. Full of life, living amidst abundance in these terrible sites of scarcity, we might steady ourselves through study. So steadied and made strong, "[w]e must also," David Jardine, Sharon Friesen, and Patricia Clifford remind us,

cultivate in ourselves the ability and the desire to adamantly refuse some inheritances, those that toy with impossibility and despoil our ability to dwell in the suffering of things.... We must refuse the leveling that violates the deeply ecopedagogical repose of things (2006, p. 277).

We must face the sun. Join us.

"WHAT SHOULD BE AND WHAT MIGHT BE" (2005)

The sound of silence breaking is harsh, resonant, soft, battering, small, chaotic, furious, terrified, triumphant.

Janet L. Miller (2005, p. 68)

Janet Miller and I go back a long way. It has been more than thirty years since we met on the campus of the University of Rochester. Our friendship – and our professional partnership – took root in the snows of upstate New York, and grew (yes, rhizomatically) in Ohio, Virginia, Louisiana and in New York. There is a "worldliness" to our friendship, grounded as it is in shared commitments to and lived experience of the academic field curriculum studies, commitments first enacted and experienced perhaps most intensely during the field's reconceptualization, a decade-long event that was simultaneously intellectual, political, and personal, as this collection testifies (see chapter 4, Pinar et al. 1995).

Winter 1978 found me in Berkeley, California, where I was a visiting scholar and a visiting Dad. In Columbus, Janet was working at Battelle Memorial Institute. We spent hours on the telephone, planning the new journal and the conference its editors would sponsor: *JCT* and what would later become known as "Bergamo" (see Pinar 2006b, pp. 153-162). In those conversations we imagined together *"what should be and might be."* These imaginings were never fixed, always in motion, and they ranged from the theoretical to the practical, the professional to the personal. As Miller (2005, p. 19) points out:

> In fact, I think one big reason why the conferences sponsored by *JCT* over the years drew a loyal following was that the reconceptualization was itself about understanding curriculum as intersections of the political, historical, the autobiographical.

It seemed we were always at intersections, junctions (*JCT* as the road-signs signal) where diverse ideas met, sometimes clashed, sometimes conjoined and created something new.

Janet Miller and I were together often in those years, and not only over telephone, but at conferences, at Paul Klohr's house on Walhalla, at Janet's place on North High Street (and, later, on South Lazelle in the German Village) all in Columbus, in Norfolk, Virginia, on Long Island, in Manhattan, in Baton Rouge. In gay discos. With Janet (she is referring to this collection) I say: "You won't hear the roar of silences breaking here." But I will tell one secret: Janet is one of the best dancers in the world. During the late 1970s and early 1980s, we danced and danced. Some of you know the music (Donna Summer, Thelma Houston); perhaps a few of you even remember those damned disco balls, glittering, splintering kaleidoscopic, lighting crowded dance floors. If there is one image of you that remains with me more than any other, Janet, it is of you dancing, gliding, arms outstretched, smiling, moving to the music. We were in sync on the dance floor.

And off. Not that we were fused, of course; we spoke, as Janet notes about herself, "through multiple and changing autobiographical voices." The work of reconceptualization was "sometimes noisy, sometimes quiet work," but, as Miller underscores, the intellectual and organizational work also spoke "to the daily need of reinventing our selves through and in these processes" (2005, p. 6). These were simultaneously subjective and social processes, as we rejected the bureaucratic roles fashioned for us by the past. As Janet acknowledges, our generation declined "to pass on its 'received heritage' – a heritage that framed curriculum as an administrative designation" (2005, p. 62).

Solitary and in solidarity with others, Janet remembers her participation in the field reinventing itself. "My memories here," she writes, "attempt to honor the connectedness that informs and impels my own work as well as the work of others long involved in this project called reconceptualization" (2005, p. 40). As she will suggest about school reform, this "memory text" (as Marla Morris [2001, 8] might characterize it) is very much situated: "[T]he brief history I've reviewed here speaks of, as well as constantly questions, my partiality in terms of remembering, interpretation, and attachment" (2005, p. 40). Acknowledging, then, the situatedness of memory, interpretation, and its social relationality, Janet declines to "generalize from my middle-class, white woman enactment of U.S. curriculum theory professor" (2005, p. 157). She speaks her situated singularity and, in so doing, calls us to ours.

Janet Miller may not generalize from that situated singularity, but she is hardly hermetically sealed within it. From the outset, Janet always

struggl[ed] to create spaces within reconceptualized versions of curriculum theorizing that could enable me to explore, for example, "the personal" and "the political" not as a binary but rather as reciprocal, interactive, constantly changing and (re)constructing influences on my own and other teachers' conceptions of curriculum, pedagogy, and research (2005, p. 137).

These "spaces" were simultaneously subjective, social, and political: imbricated, interwoven, in-between.

Such spaces were discernible in the work of Maxine Greene. "I first read some of Maxine Greene's writing when I was studying for my master's degree at the University of Rochester in 1973 and 1974," (2005, p. 45) Janet remembers. "I immediately was drawn to Maxine Greene's compelling philosophical and political analyses of curriculum as project – and to her uses of literature as means of engaging in such analyses" (p. 46). At Ohio State with her mentors (and mine) – Paul Klohr (see Pinar *et. al* 1995, p. 183) and Donald R. Bateman (1974) – Janet Miller (1977) wrote her Ph.D. dissertation on the significance of Maxine Greene's philosophy of education for the fields of curriculum theory and English education.

That work held specific significance for Janet as a feminist theorist. Janet attends to a chapter of Maxine Greene's (1995) on "the shapes of childhood recalled," (2005, p. 48) precisely "because it evokes provocative tensions in the doing of educational autobiography that resists closure or paralysis around issues of identity and agency" (2005, p. 49). Maxine Greene provides, Miller (2005, pp. 48-49) observes,

> glimpses of contradictions, disjunctures, and ambivalences, the "incompleteness" that she experiences within and toward her "self" as a woman who desires both to "merge and to be outside" as an academic who dares to do educational philosophy in unconventional ways, and as a scholar who reads imaginative literature as one way of disrupting and questioning any one final version of her self and world. (the quoted passages within Janet's sentence are Greene's)

At the same time, Miller (2005, p. 49) continues, "Maxine gestures toward possibilities of taking action against unjust and inhumane conditions even as individuals face the 'incompleteness' and 'unfinished whole' of their actions, their knowledge, their 'selves,' and their lives." In this convergence of subjective meaning and social significance resides the project of reconceptualized curriculum theory.

In disciplinary terms, it is a convergence of literary and social theory, of literature and politics. In the spaces in-between those apparently disparate disciplines Janet locates autobiography as one key form of educational inquiry. It is not to be regarded as literature, per se, but she does wonder "what might happen to the forms and purposes of autobiography in education if they assumed the potentials of imaginative literature to disrupt rather than reinforce static and essentialized versions of our 'selves' and our work as educators" (2005, p. 54). Janet quotes Maxine Greene to show how such "defamiliarization" and "revising" can enlarge our capacities "to invent visions of what should be and what might be in our deficient society, on the streets where we live, in our schools" (2005, p. 54). "In fact," Miller (2005, p. 54) concludes, "this may be the only reason to use autobiography as a form of educational inquiry ... [to] call into question both the notion of one "true," stable and coherent self and cultural scripts for that self." Such calling into question occurs constantly in this collection.

AUTOBIOGRAPHY

[A]n educator who conceives of autobiography as a queer curriculum practice doesn't look into the mirror of self-reflection and see a reinscription of her already familiar, identifiable self. She finds herself *not mirrored – but in difference.*

Janet L. Miller (2005, p. 224)

In Janet Miller's autobiographical voice we can hear the "sound of silence breaking" (2005, p. 61). It is that courageous voice that names "heretofore unspoken connections among gender, sexuality, and curriculum" (2005, p. 62) that, in the late 1970s, were then just "emerging as central issues within the field of education, in general, and curriculum studies, in particular" (2005, p. 62). As Miller (2005, p. 62) understood: "Curriculum and feminist theories have moved into areas of inquiry that may break that unnatural silence." It would be through Janet's autobiographical voice that the social terrain of gender and sexuality would be redrawn, where she would see herself, and where I would see myself, not mirrored, but in difference.

It was during a session at the Bergamo Conference that Janet found herself writing, not for the first time, on legal yellow writing paper. She entitled the piece she wrote for the session "Yellow Paper," and in it she described the writing, in the mid-1970s, of her dissertation in longhand, on the same type of legal yellow writing paper that she had grabbed that afternoon. In the last part of "Yellow Paper," Janet spoke of breaking a silence, of "my desiring to share those words with the woman I love" (2005, p. 218). It was, Miller (2005, p. 219) explains,

> My ongoing work in autobiography thus provided an incentive and a reason, in the conference session, to tell how my life, my "identities," and my love exceeded the very academic and social normative discourses and frameworks that tried to contain them. That extensive and long-term autobiographical work also provided a backdrop against which, at that point in my life, I could queer both the subject and the forms that autobiography typically took in educational settings. I was interested not only in pointing to the "undesignatable field of differences" within identity categories of lesbian, woman, teacher, and researcher, for example. I was also interested in exploring uses of autobiography that addressed and even exemplified performativity, the power of discourse to produce, through reiteration, an "I" that is always coming into being through social and cultural constructions of gender identity and, simultaneously, failing to cohere.

In this paragraph – you are able to read the entire essay in this collection – Janet Miller is working several tensions. Ted Aoki would suggest, I think, that the paragraphs discloses Janet's dwelling in a "generative tensionality" (see Pinar and Irwin pp. 161, 164, 211).

First, Janet is working the tension between the subjective meaning and social significance of her professional persona and scholarly work. Janet is participating in a public event where her long-term study of autobiography is well known, as is her key role in the reconceptualization of the field. This present – simultaneously a social fact and a subjective reality – provides a passage to a future where she acknowledges, in public, her love for Elizabeth Ellsworth. That public acknowledgement of a private relationship would revise many participants' perception of Janet's professional persona and of her work. I suspect it did so for Janet as well; she was exceeding the discourses and the voice(s) those discourses expressed and contained, creating new space and finding new voice.

For me, this "performance" of autobiographical voice and professional identity reveals how working the past autobiographically enables one to "midwife" the future and, in so doing, reconstruct the public space in which identity is reiterated. That future – itself a convergence of subjective meaning and social significance – is a shared and public space, a kind of civic square. It is, as well, a room of one's own. As an established scholar, Janet Miller created herself as she was created by others. Interpellated, then, in social terms as autobiographical and feminist curriculum theorist, Janet's public persona no longer coincided with her private reality. Janet exceeded that public identity through its discursive rewriting. It is as "text" – writing on a yellow writing pad – that Janet Miller moves from 1970s Ph.D. student, studying the existential-political philosophy of education Maxine Greene had formulated, onto her present as autobiographical and feminist curriculum theorist, into a conference session (a classroom for colleagues), wherein she queers autobiographical curriculum practice and, in the process, her professional persona as well.

While the social and the subjective are inextricable, the two can, sometimes must (when in tension), be worked separately, as that paragraph illustrates. It is through working the past, in this instance recalling the 1970s work, evoked through the artifact (the yellow writing pad), that Janet's subjective space – the room of her own – exceeds the public space and becomes disjunctive with it. Subjectively "larger" than the persona interpellated (however understandably) by her fellow conference-goers, Janet dwells in the disjunction between private and public self. No longer identical with the interpellated self, one is able to reconstruct that public space through discursive means, in this case, by reading writing aloud the private reality. By working the tension between the autobiographical and the social, Janet Miller reconstructs both.

In that Bergamo session, Miller not only queers autobiography (see Miller 1998) thematically, she also queers it structurally, in her rewriting of and dis-identification with herself: "[W]hen autobiography is conceptualized as a queer curriculum practice, it can help us to dis-identify with ourselves and others" (2005, p. 220). Such a practice creates a disjunction between the self that is and the self that might be; one finds oneself "*not mirrored – but in difference*" (2005, p. 224). Such practice challenges that "humanist educational research and practices that normalize the drive to sum up one's self, one's learning, and the other as directly, developmentally, and inclusively knowable, identifiable, 'natural'" (2005, p. 223). Reconstructing the public sphere in curriculum and teaching requires reconstructing the private sphere as well.

Such reconstruction – "*strategically* producing a difference out of what was once familiar or the same about what it means to 'be' a teacher or student or researcher or woman," (2005, p. 220) as Janet succinctly puts it - cannot occur if "telling my story" (2005, p. 220) reinscribes the "self" already hailed into existence by others. Nor can strategically producing a difference occur if such difference is understood as only – here Janet quotes Maxine - "binary and oppositional rather than nuanced, plural, and proximate" (2005, p. 220). To democratize the subjective sphere – in Janet's words "addressing 'self' as a "site of permanent openness and resignifiability" (2005, p. 220) – requires "*queering* autobiography, for speaking and writing into existence denaturalized ways of being that are obscured or simply unthinkable when one centered, self-knowing story is substituted for another" (2005, p. 220). It is the structure as well as thematic contents of the "self" that are reconfigured in queer autobiographical practice.

Such subjective labor cannot be conducted effortlessly, nor without troubling a life carefully composed and socially stable. In all likelihood, there will be discomfort in "strategically producing a difference" (2005, p. 220) between the self that is and the self that might be. "Autobiography as a queer curriculum practice," Miller (2005, p. 223) points out (after Britzman), "also compels us to consider 'tangles of implication,' how we are implicated in our desires for enactments of, as well as in our fears and revulsions toward, those identities and practices that exceed the 'norm.'" Again, this work is hardly self-enclosed: such subjective reconstruction creates "more space for and recognition of the various actions and 'selves' performed daily in a social landscape blinded and hostile to variety" (2005, p. 221). Too many schools are indeed "blinded and hostile to variety." After thirty years of right-wing school "deform" schools are *required* to be blinded and hostile to variety.

Schools are the specific social landscape Miller has in mind, wondering if the queer character of the first wave of autobiographical work (during the 1970s) disappeared because it "invited too many denaturalized stories" (2005, p. 224). These were stories that "many educators could not or would not want to hear," in part, because "official school knowledge, identities, and visions of revolutionary educational practice were exceeded by heretofore unimagined or at least unarticulated constructions of students, teachers, and curricula" (2005, p. 224). As L. L. Langness and Gelya Frank (1981, p. 93) have observed, "[a]utobiography can be a revolutionary act."

Not only taken-for-granted conceptions of school are challenged by the queerness of autobiographical practice, Janet suggests, so too are "developmental and incremental notions of both learning and autobiography" (2005, p. 224). Indeed, "queered versions of autobiographical work" threaten those dominant and taken-for-granted developmental narratives "in which one, through linear learning of official and predetermined curricula, passes from ignorance to knowledge about both 'self' and 'other'" (2005, p. 224). As we know from Bernadette Baker's careful and ground-breaking work, the very concept of developmentalism is historically continent, appearing "in the vicinity such fears [of racial amalgamation in the late nineteenth century] (2001, p. 463)." It was also, as I suggest and as Janet suspected, queer (see Pinar 2001, chapter 6).

FEMINIST EDUCATOR

Curriculum and feminist theories have moved into areas of inquiry that may break that unnatural silence.

Janet L. Miller (2005, p. 62)

As teachers we are both subjective and social creatures, conceived by others, struggling to create ourselves, inviting our students – through study - to do the same. We are burdened by the psycho-political history of our profession; as Janet points out, "U.S. educators throughout the nineteenth and into the twentieth century internalized the notion of subordination as a primary framework for behavior within the classroom" (2005, p. 72). This is, as Janet suggests, a gendered notion of social control, in which our "subordination" is a gendered subordination. Because the profession is imagined as female, mostly male legislators and administrators have assumed they are entitled, indeed obligated, to direct it. The subordination of U.S. educators is a form of what Southern Baptists imagine as the biblically-ordained "gracious submission" of wives to husbands.

Such submission becomes, as Janet knows, internalized; there is no firewall between "teacher" as social identity and "teacher" as subjectively lived. Janet knows this fact from her own lived experience: "I had, without thinking, and without questioning, transferred an expectation of myself as a woman, which largely was a societal creation and well as perhaps a psychologically based developmental need, to my professional role" (2005, pp. 73-74). Because she understands that interpellation – her professional role - is simultaneously subjective and social, "I encourage my students, men and women who themselves teach, to explore underlying assumptions and expectations that frame their conceptions of themselves as teachers" [2005, p. 75). Such "underlying assumptions and expectations" (2005, p. 75) comprise social sedimentation in which the self is submerged, and from which it can separate. As Ewa Plonowska Ziarek (2001, p. 39) points out:

> Yet, it is the tear, or the separation of the self from its sedimented identity, that enables a redefinition of becoming and freedom from its sedimented identity, that enables a redefinition of becoming and freedom from the liberation of identity to the continuous "surpassing" of oneself.

The exploration Janet Miller encourages, then, enables students to separate from others' expectations of them, especially as these have been internalized, turned into psychic sediment.

Miller (2005, p. 99) performs this self-reflexive self-separating labor herself, remembering that "in the summer between fifth and sixth grade, I spent a lot of time hoping that I would get Mr. Brucker as my sixth-grade teacher." That hope may have been structured by the power of patriarchy, but such abstractions fail to convey its subjective meaning:

> But to have a man as a teacher, in that last year of elementary schooling that still sanctioned childhood play even as it prepared us for the grown-up demands and rigors of junior high school, supposedly guaranteed for us the rites of passage into the rules, content, and structure of the disciplines (2005, p. 100).

In psychoanalytical terms, the male subject here functions as a transitional object, and not only for the transition from "play" to "work," but from childhood to adolescence, from the projects and interest centers of elementary school to the disciplinary vocationalism of secondary school.

It turns out Mr. Brucker also functioned as a transitional object from traditional to more contemporary conceptions of femininity and womanhood. "[I]n our unit on careers," Miller (2005, p. 101) remembers,

> Mr. Brucker [discussed] possible jobs that we girls might want to consider. He didn't just assume that we or our mothers would want to stay at home.... He challenged us girls to move beyond stereotypical images of ourselves that we reinforced every recess in our jump rope and hopscotch play, for example, by insisting that we be part of the class kickball team.

Mr. Brucker demonstrated that teachers are not inevitably agents of reproduction.

Perhaps it is "giving back" to teachers past that inspired Miller to "spending a portion of my time in the schools, working directly with teachers and students" (2005, 147). Such work is hardly unproblematic, Janet understands, "for, as a woman teaching in the university, I still feel the pull of internalized expectations for myself either as distanced 'expert' and 'conveyor of knowledge' *or* as nurturer and caretakers of my students' needs and interests" (2005, p. 149). Thinking of teaching young children, Janet is acutely aware that "such work is historically grounded in social expectations and school structures that rely on women's accustomed roles as subservient, genteel, and docile reinforcers of the status quo" (2005, p. 148). That problematic becomes concretely clear in her narratives of Georgette, one of the teachers with whom Janet worked collaboratively for several years, the first three years of which Janet reports in *Creating Spaces and Finding Voices* (see Miller 1990).

"OUR WORK TOGETHER"

> Memoir, like autobiography, must recognize its own social construction and cultural conditioning.

> Janet L. Miller (2005, p. 202)

Perhaps more than any other autobiographical curriculum theorist, Janet Miller (2005, p. 136) has focused upon "our work together." In mid-summer of 1986, Janet tells us, "I joined five graduate students in a picnic lunch to celebrate the end of our coursework together" (2005, p. 135). But, it turns out, this picnic was not to be the end of it, but, rather, another beginning: "By the close of the afternoon … we agreed to continue our conversations in an informal and unofficial way" (2005, p. 135). And not for a few weeks, or, even, months: "At present, we have been meeting and talking together on a regularly scheduled basis for six years" (2005, p. 135). This remarkable, probably unprecedented, fact testifies to the power of "our work together" (2005, p. 136). What became increasingly clear was that, despite the collective commitment to collaboration, willing participants could [not] easily avoid the circulations of power that attend any human interactions, or could "progress" in seamless and transparent ways, with all participants moving as a collective through the collaborative work in similar ways and at identical times (2005, p. 138).

Georgette was a case in point.

In the collaboration with Georgette, Janet focused on how "stereotypic and essentialized notions of women teachers as only caretakers and nurturers" can foreclose opportunities for becoming "creators and examiners of our own as well as others' constructions of knowledges and practices" (2005, p. 150). Through her work with Janet and other members of the group, Georgette described "her journey through our collaborative attempts thus far as one of 'becoming vocal'" (2005, p. 153). A first-grade teacher, Georgette became clear about the "ways in which historical and social constructions of teaching as 'women's work' have framed and constrained her own expectations for herself as early childhood educator" (2005, p. 153).

While such work is solitary, it did not occur in isolation. Supported and, no doubt, inspired by others' self-reflexive labor, Georgette's work inspired others in the group, including Janet: "Georgette's struggles have provided me with incentives for parallel analyses of my own expectations and internalizations of caretaker and responsible leader roles without our research group" (2005, p. 157). And not only Georgette inspired Janet to examine her interpellation as group leader; so did Beth, who asked: "What are we going to do?" (2005, p. 139).

Beth's question, Miller tells us, was only "the first of countless questions that have emerged throughout our ongoing collaboration" (2005, p. 141), questions concerning the "tangled intersections of theory and practice" (2005, 144), abstractions expressing "the permeable boundaries of their - and our – relations with and to one another" (2005, p. 144). Janet notes: "It is our daily challenge, our daily work" (2005, p. 144). It is work that positioned Janet not only as "leader" but as "student" as well:

As we continue our meetings, discussions, and individual as well as dialogical journal writing, I am acutely aware of just how much I have been influenced in my teaching, research, and curriculum theorizing efforts, by our interactions, reflections, and confrontations with one another (2005, p. 135).

For me, this is the subject position prerequisite to study (see McClintock 1971; Pinar 2006b, pp. 109-120).

Studying the gender of teaching (as "women's work"), including participants' internalized expectations and assumptions of that work, led to study of "our 'selves' as white Western women who are trying to raise questions about how we 'perform' ourselves as women teachers, how we might address the provisional and political nature of identity construction" (2005, p. 157). Such identity is no simple or obvious matter of empirical representation, it exists in the social imaginary. School "reform" of the last thirty-five years positions teachers as "wives" in "gracious submission." Despite the gendered (and racialized: see Pinar 2004a) politics of school "reform," Janet Miller (2005, p. 144) and her colleagues proceeded with their important work:

> So, we take heart in the fact that we can analyze, critique, and work to change our habitual responses to static and limiting constructions of our work and our educational identities.... It's a form of local and contingent "emancipatory" work, if you will, and it what we can do to continue the slow but crucial to understanding and, if necessary, change the nature of our own and perhaps our students and colleagues' educational experiences.... As we continue to meet on back porches and living rooms, still juggling coffee mugs, bagels and conversations, we still ponder the discrepancies in our expectations as collaborative group members as well as members of various educational communities.

That is the power of working from within, together. As Georgette testified: "I know I have changed as a result of our work together, changed from an accepting, docile teacher, to a questioning, challenging person" (2005, p. 155). Such transformation is not exactly what politicians have in mind when they demand "school reform."

SCHOOL REFORM

> The longer I engaged in these reform studies, the more I worried about large-scale attempts to implement versions of whole-school "reform."

> Janet L. Miller (2005, p. 170)

Noting, with understatement, that "some school reformers during the past decade have assumed that particular conceptions of school reform could be implemented in similar ways across diverse classrooms in the United States," (2005, p. 165). Janet Miller discovered that many teachers declined to position themselves in "gracious submission." Indeed, Miller (2005, p. 167) found that

> [m]any of the teachers I have observed and interviewed responded in ways that disrupted, called into question, subverted, divided, or re-formed what had been presented or agreed upon as "the ways" to proceed in their school reform projects. And I, as a researcher of these school reform efforts, also responded in ways that sometimes disrupted the generalizing intentions and design of the research projects in which I was participating.

Despite the fact that "students' raised achievement scores would be *the* criterion used to measure 'successful' reform efforts" (2005, p. 169), there were teachers, Janet discovered, who exhibited a more subtle and sophisticated sense of "reform."

Informed by her experience and understanding of "our work together," Janet formulates a concept of "situated school reform" (2005, p. 165) that "disrupts any essential or generalized notion of school restructuring processes or goals" (2005, p. 165). Indeed, situated school reform "draws attention to how these processes and goals constantly are re-written within specific school cultures and by particular individuals" (2005, p. 165). School reform is not raising test scores to establish bragging rights for politicians; it is the subjective labor of self-understanding:

> A notion of situated school reform and research thus refocuses my work so that I might look for ways that particular situations might enable both teachers and myself to re-write, to re-work any discourses of reform and educational research that would generalize, universalize, standardize, and reify teacher or researcher identities. (2005, p. 176)

This is, I submit, the subjective labor of self-reconstruction, labor enabling the reconstruction of the public sphere in curriculum and teaching.

Acknowledging that "some school reform movements *do* encourage administrators, teachers, students, and parents to consider carefully their particular schools organizational and social cultures as they arrive at their own interpretations of school improvement tenets" (2005, p. 166), Miller appreciates that school reform is local, singular, situated:

> I believe that *a* focus on teachers' actual responses to and engagements with school reform efforts might point toward "more lucid understandings" of the need for school reform conceptualizations that take into account the constantly changing nature of teaching and learning within particular classrooms and school settings (2005, p. 167).

Situated school reform is, then, lived. It engages the processes of self-formation, especially as these are structured through study, through the juxtapositions of lived and embodied ideas, juxtapositions producing "excessive moments."

JUXTAPOSITION AND EXCESSIVE MOMENTS

> The strategy of juxtaposition is one that invites inconsistencies, ambiguities, ambivalence, and foregrounds the fact that there will always be "unspoken themes" that cannot or will not be interrogated.
>
> Mimi Orner, Janet L. Miller, Elizabeth Ellsworth (2005, p. 114)

> Excess is a symptom of histories of repression and of the interests associated with those histories.
>
> Mimi Orner, Janet L. Miller, Elizabeth Ellsworth (2005, p. 111)

The concept of "excess" enables Janet – in collaboration with Mimi Orner and Elizabeth Ellsworth - "to call attention to the relation between particular educational discourses and repression" (2005, p. 111). What is "contained" by an educational discourse and "what becomes excess or excessive to it" is, they suggest, "no accident" (2005, p. 111). Indeed: "Excess is a symptom of histories of repression and of the interests associated with those histories" (2005, p. 111). Excessive moments are like epiphanies, enabling s/he who experiences them to discern the repression of which they are symptomatic.

It is a significant contribution to our understanding of educational experience to appreciate that such moments are related to repression, that they represent, in a sense, shifts in the plates of repression, versions of psychic earthquakes. Like earthquakes, they occur without prediction, precipitated by pressures building from the contradictions of lived experience and our self-reflexive study of it. Unlike earthquakes, they can be encouraged pedagogically. Orner, Miller, and Ellsworth suggest a strategy for producing such "excessive moments" by deliberately shifting or juxtaposing the "plates" of understanding. As they read their sections to each other in preparation for presentation at the Bergamo Conference, "the more the juxtaposing of educational discourses not intended to be read together created for us meanings that exceeded the norms of the discourses that informed our separate texts" (2005, p. 112). Repetition produced difference; juxtaposition produced excess.

Orner, Miller, and Ellsworth's individually composed sections were not written, then, "to engage each other directly or linearly" (2005, p. 113). The "fault line" (in my analogy) is "the relation we construct among moments, narratives, and authorial voices" (2005, p. 113), and it is one of "*juxtaposition*." It is this "strategy" the three theorists employ as a means "of foregrounding and negotiating the fact that there are no simple, linear, cause-effect relations between official forms of education representation and the moments in theory and practice that exceed them" (2005, p. 113). Orner, Miller, and Ellsworth explain:

> Juxtaposition, as an aesthetic device in postmodern art and as rhetorical device in postmodern theory and writing, provokes viewers and readers to make associations across categorical, discursive, historical, and stylistic boundaries – associations never intended or sanctioned by the interests that construct and require such boundaries (2005, p. 113).

Their formulation precedes my own employment of the practice in *The Gender of Racial Politics and Violence in America*, in *What Is Curriculum Theory?*, in *Race, Religion and a Curriculum of Reparation*, and in *The Synoptic Text Today and Other Essays*.

In those studies I juxtapose paraphrased works of others; in Orner, Miller, and Ellsworth's practice of the concept the emphasis is on the disruption of repression and the "eruption" of "excessive moments." The juxtaposition of sections in their conference presentation, now a chapter, "invites readers to explore notion of performance and the performative across various moments of education research, writing, and teaching" (2005, p. 114). The three scholars suggest that "juxtapositioning also invites readers to allow what happens in one of the three texts to spur images from that text to the others, and on to the reader's own contexts and practices" (2005, p. 114). This example speaks to what is for me the very definition of educational experience, namely the intertextual reverberations of ideas from one text to other texts, including scholarly as well as subjective and social texts, experienced by the embodied, self-reflexive, historical individual.

"WORKING DIFFERENCE"

We use "working difference" here, then, to refer to the possibility of engaging with and responding to the fluidity and malleability of identities and difference, of refusing fixed and static categories of sameness or permanent otherness.

Janet L. Miller and Elizabeth Ellsworth (2005, p. 181)

For at least two decades, Janet and Liz point out, several disciplines have devoted themselves to the "reconsideration of relations among subjectivity, power, and difference" (2005, p. 180). The two scholars invoke the notion of "working difference" to point to "the possibility of engaging with and responding to the fluidity and malleability of identities and difference, of refusing fixed and static categories of sameness or permanent otherness" (2005, p. 181). While not discussed in this same chapter, it seems to me that it is, in part, this tendency toward categories of sameness discernible in many autobiographical curriculum studies that compels Janet Miller's commitment to "working difference." As she points out, too many such studies – the evocation of "teachers' stories" – tend to

offer unproblematized recounting of what is taken to be the transparent, linear, and authoritative "reality" of those teachers' "experience." And their "teachers' identities" in these stores often are crafted as unitary, fully conscious, universal, and non-contradictory (2005, p. 51).

"Working difference" cracks the surface of "experience," exposing those genealogical and sedimented layers of repression interpellation necessitated.

It is hardly the replacement of one static identity with another that "working difference" effects. Janet and Liz emphasize that "working difference" foregrounds the possibility and significance of reading and performing difference as "work-in-progress" (2005, p. 182). Nowhere is that more pointed than in Miller's discussion of Toni Morrison's (1992) *Playing in the Dark*. That "powerful work compels us," Janet writes, "to work with our students to identify what Morrison (1992, p. 18) calls a 'willful critical blindness' – those 'habits, manners and political agenda' (1992, p. 18) that have contributed to an objectified Africanist persona as 'reined-in, bound, suppressed, and repressed darknesss' (pp. 38-39)" (2005, p. 228). Specifically addressing English teachers and English educators, Janet calls us to monitor our classrooms and the literature we teach for "willful critical blindness" (2005, p. 228). That work cannot proceed unless we are also "aware of the places where our own pedagogical imaginations may have been sabotaged as well as sabotage, may have been polluted and pollute our visions of what it could mean to read and write, teach and learn across social and cultural difference" (2005, p. 228). Such pedagogical action requires autobiographical study.

Sedimented subjectively, "willful critical blindness" also follows from, as Miller (2005, p. 228) observes, from the "external presses for standardization and accountability that current characterize the teaching of English/language arts and the field of education, writ large." Likewise, Linda McNeil (2000, p. 7) has pointed out: "[t]he conservative transformation of American public education [has occurred] through the use of technicist forms of power." Still thinking of the teaching of English but speaking to all educators, Miller (2005, p. 228) notes:

> [I]n the press for standards, accountability, and standardization of curriculum and teaching, we easily may lose sight of ways in which reading and writing in the English classroom and teacher education sites in fact can challenge static and stereotypic constructions of "literary whiteness" and "literary blackness," for example.

I suggest that "accountability" is a racialized and gendered form of power in which teachers are reduced to positions of "gracious submission" to mostly white male politicians (see Pinar 2004a; in press).

Such positions of submission smash teachers and students onto the social surface, but, despite this shattering of "our multiply inflected and constructed identities as gendered, raced, classed selves" (2005, p. 229) (as Janet appreciates), self-reflexive educators remain torn by conflicting demands. Confined to "sites of disunity and conflict, unfinished and incomplete" (2005, p. 229), we teachers are torn "in part because we must respond to differing and disunited contexts, individuals, and historical moments at the same time that we often are required to respond to normative demands for similar and 'acceptable' performances of our students' and our own selves" (2005, p. 229). Behind enemy lines we still signal to others that this (standardized) world is not *the* world. "We are," Janet reminds us, "in-the-making" (2005, p. 229).

"EDUCATION-IN-THE-MAKING"

> I use autobiography as also in-the-making, as one means of grappling with multiple versions, and questions about various versions in constructions of my identities "as" English teacher, teacher educator, researcher, curriculum theorist, writer, partner, feminist, woman who struggles to not close down, in the press for standardization, around "certainty."

Janet L. Miller (2005, p. 233)

Not unlike Ted Aoki's (2005 [1990], p. 367) concept of "improvisation," Janet Miller's notion of "in-the-making" emphasizes our "incompleteness – the open question, perhaps – that summons us to the tasks of knowledge and action" (Greene 1995, p. 74). So summoned, we – teachers and teacher educators – must attend to issues of "risk and safety" (2005, p. 229) in our "constructions and deconstructions of meanings and identities in classrooms" (2005, p. 229), as we are implicated in the very discursive structuration of knowledge as action. Attending specifically to English education-in-the-making, Janet notes that teaching "calls attention to those very constructions of meaning as always situated in language that unwittingly writes us" (Felman 1993, p. 157). Such situatedness also calls attention to understanding curriculum as autobiographical text, to autobiography as a textual pedagogical practice.

In "autobiography in-the-making," Miller (2005, p. 231) tells us, "I push my students to tell situated and multiple stories of our educational experiences of teaching, learning, and research." Informed, in part, by the work of Madeleine Grumet (1988) and Jo Anne Pagano (1990), Miller extends and complicates our understanding of autobiographical practice by emphasizing the disjunction among internalized and discursive as well as cultural and historical constitutions of the "self." Always attentive to interpellation as simultaneously subjective and social, Miller (2005, p. 232) advises:

> So, if we do write multiple and situated stories of ourselves as educators and immediately call those into question, rather than try to create just one summarizing "true" autobiographical rendering, we also might wrestle with those normative meanings and identities that society, history, cultural conditioning and discourses have constructed for us as well as those that we have constructed or perhaps have unconsciously assumed.

Embedded in language, constituted by history, how do I create subjective spaces – Janet characterizes them as "cracks" in the official curriculum - in which I can act, informed by that self-reflexive knowledge and ethical conviction autobiography "in-the-making" enables? How can we teach such conviction in a postmodern age? (see Slattery and Rapp 2002)

These are vexing questions, questions closed down by disingenuous demands for "accountability," by "willful critical blindness" (2005, p. 228), by repression, simultaneously political and psychic. Through study one summons oneself to question, to become "in-the-making," to take action in the public world that is the classroom understood as civic square. Autobiography becomes the practice, oneself the provocation, and the classroom the site to reconstruct the private and public spheres in curriculum and teaching. Janet Miller (2005, pp. 232-233) calls us to undertake such pedagogical action:

> Autobiography in-the-making, then, includes multiple tellings, multiple questionings of those tellings, and multiple angles on representations of "self" that give strategic leverage on two central questions that frame a notion of English education-in-the-making: 1) as a teacher, as a teacher educator, how *will* I respond to students' and colleagues' identities and responses that deviate from the "norm," and/or that are different from "mine? And 2) how *will* I respond to educational discourses and practices that function to position some as permanently "other," knowing that, at the same time, I am always caught up in and by the very languages and resulting practices that I wish to challenge?

Too sophisticated to be seduced by social engineering, Miller replaces ends-means calculations with ethical questions requiring pedagogical action. Such action is "performed" with the humility that accompanies the realization that, as Miller (2005, p. 238) notes, "the teacher or researcher can never fully know her 'self' nor her students nor what she teaches or researchers, and can never fully control or predict what is learned." She quotes Ellsworth to emphasize her point: "At the heart of teaching about and across social and cultural difference is the impossibility of designating precisely what actions, selves, or knowledges are 'correct' or 'needed'" (Ellsworth 1997, p. 17).

This frank acknowledgement of uncertainty is coupled with the recognition that educational experience is not always observable and measurable. Despite the teacher scapegoating tactics of those who insist it is (see, for instance, Hirsch 1999), Miller points out that

> There may be no raised achievement score, no journey entry, no completed homework assigned, no worksheet completed, no behavioral objective met, no Regents exam successfully passed, no certified "excellent student" as a result of a particular teaching and learning experience. And yet something of value has happened in that classroom (2005, p. 239).

Indeed, the observable and the measurable are often the trivial.

Educational experience that is subjectively meaningful and socially significant does not occur readily through curriculum connected to standardized examinations. Especially in the nightmare that is the present, "the 'sweaty fight for meaning and response-ability' is an always-new struggle.... It's difficult, challenging, exhilarating, discouraging, numbing, mandatory, and exciting work – daily work that's always in-the-making" (2005, p. 242). This is the everyday subjective labor of enabling our students to reconstruct the classroom as civic square *and* as a room of one's own.

CRACKS IN THE CURRICULUM

> Thank goodness there were cracks in the official curriculum and predetermined objectives through which my students and I could connect words that we were studying ... to our selves, to one another, and to the world around us.

Janet L. Miller (2005, p. 234)

"As a beginning high-school English teacher," Janet Miller (2005, p. 233) remembers, "I felt constrained to teach for the test, to cover the curriculum, to fill in the blanks – in short, to prepare my students for what was coming next rather than to respond to what was happening to and for them in our classroom." This is a succinct statement of teachers' subjugation in the regime of "accountability." Without academic – intellectual – freedom to influence what and how they teach, without the discretion to choose how to assess student study, teachers are disabled from practicing their profession (see Pinar 2006c). Janet acknowledges: "Confronted by this officially mandated, test-driven, and dissected approach to subject English, I tried to justify my distancing from my own passions for learning in order to sustain a curriculum and pedagogy that kept students from theirs"

(2005, p. 233). Teachers *and* students have been forced into positions estranged from their lived experience of intellectual work.

Millers remembers that the present nightmare – in which teachers have lost control of the curriculum they teach and the means by which they assess students' study of it – began after Sputnik, first with the 1959 Woods Hole Conference, followed by the Kennedy Administration's national curriculum reform movement. Despite the Dartmouth conference and others like it, politicians intensified their scapegoating and control of teachers' professional practice. Despite these outrageous unjust conditions, many in the profession proceeded, insisting, in our time, on "best practices" that are often at odds with the right-wing agenda of cultural authoritarianism. Janet remembers that her own sense of being an English teacher was formed in a time before Sputnik:

> My own perceptions of what English teaching could be were fueled by my love of reading and by my senior-year high school English teacher, Miss Biedle, who engaged us in student-and-response-centered activities before they were ever deemed "best practices." (2005, p. 233)

Left to their own devices, individual teachers have often devised "best practices" according to the specificity of their school situations.

It is, as we know, the specificity of schools and of classes within schools that stymies efforts to devise such practices. Superb teachers are not superb in every setting, on every day, with every group. Nor are they superb in the same way. Teaching is context specific, as Miller testifies. Among her assignments was a class of mostly working-class students, insensitively labeled 12D. "D is for Dumb, John D. announced to me on my first day in that class" (2005, p. 236), Janet recalls. With such administered self-defeat, what is a student, what is a teacher, to do?

> [I] was stymied by the relational and experiential tensions between the plant managers' kids who lived on Mortgage Hill and who were students in my modern literature classes, and the plant workers' kids who lived at the bottom of that hill, or on the Mohawk Indian Reservation six miles down the road, who were my students in English 12D. (2005, pp. 236-237)

First a student of literature, Miller had to face the effect of such classification schemes on her sense of herself as a teacher. "So, daily," she recalls, "between sixth and seventh periods, in the momentary lull that signaled the modern literature students' departure and the English 12D students' entrance into my classroom, I had to face the bifurcated English teacher I denied I could ever become" (2005, p. 238).

Despite the odds against us, despite class conflict, "willful critical blindness" (2005, p. 228), despite the gendered and racialized politics of school "deform," we teachers still find ways to practice our profession: "Yes, in some ways I taught within and between the cracks of mandated ... expectations" (2005, p. 238). Such "cracks" become discernible from certain "subject positions," certain shared and situated terrain: "But I was able to pry open those cracks more readily for the students with whom I shared social, cultural, and academic backgrounds" (2005, p.

238). This is no argument for cultural homogeneity, but a frank and welcomed acknowledgement that the practice of teaching is situated in culture, in race, in gender, in class, in historical moment: it is no surgical incision that can be practiced on everyone everywhere always the same. Is not the fascination – obsession - with the educational potential of "technology" the fantasy that computers can somehow clean up the mess left by history, culture, and politics without ever having to work *through* culture, history, and politics? Is not technology fantasized as education's surgery?

"WHAT'S LEFT IN THE FIELD?"

If conceived and enacted as a recurrent and yet always changing project, curriculum studies would entail both recognizing and welcoming the need to constantly un-make and re-make the field.

Janet L. Miller (2005, p. 201)

Janet Miller subtitles her American Educational Research Association Vice-Presidential address "a memoir." Like this collection itself, this "memoir makes no pretense of replicating a whole life" (2005, p. 201). A memoir is a collection of self-reflexive "musings," Miller (2005, p. 202) explains, "on themes or puzzles" that have run through one's life, musings on one's narrative reconstructions of that life. She quotes Judith Barrington's (1997, p. 88) characterization of memoir: it is a "track of a person's thoughts struggling to achieve some understanding of a problem" (2005, p. 201). In this sense, a memoir is a recasting of one's "theoretical relationship" with oneself, a Marxian idea of interest to Louis Althusser (1993, pp. 169-170): "I was greatly struck and still am by something Marx said to the effect that the philosopher expressed in his concepts (in his conception of philosophy, that is) his 'theoretical relationship with himself'." That "theoretical relationship" with oneself can be explored and recast through autobiographical reflection:

My first thoughts about linking those readings [of the phrase "what's left in the field"] to a "curriculum memoir" segment focused on tracing my feminist commitments to autobiographical explorations of connection, collaboration, and curriculum that calls into question any seamless, unmediated, power-neutral, static version of "self," content, relationship – or curriculum field. (2005, p. 202)

In that succinct statement we glimpse how far and how fast the field traveled from Tyler's Rationale.

Not everyone took the journey, and even those who did, did not travel in the same way or to the same destination. At the outset of *Understanding Curriculum*, William Reynolds, Patrick Slattery, Peter Taubman and I acknowledged this fact (with an auditory rather than spatial image) in our likening of the contemporary field to "a cacophony of individuals' voices ... [a] complicated symphony ... what will sound to some as excessively contrapuntal" (1995, p. 5). Janet Miller lived through the collective composition of that "symphony," those sounds of silence breaking. What her "nerves and skin remember" (2005, p. 202), she tells us, is framed by what Maxine Greene wrote in the *Educational Researcher* just after her election as President of AERA. "There ought to be controversy among us," Greene (1981, p. 6) pointed out, "open debate, an ongoing conversation." Maxine Greene was clear we work in a field that needs reminding.

The post-reconceptualization period – the last twenty-five years – has been framed, on the "outside," by an ever-increasing savagery from the political right, scapegoating and political subjugation disguised as calls for "accountability" – what Miller rightly terms "the, narrow, technocratic, prescriptive version of curriculum work" (2005, p. 204) – and, on the inside, by continuing complaints by those still at the station, those who still see something of value in Tyler's Rationale, those who still insist that it's our job to tell teachers what to do. "Maxine Greene's visions for educational research remain unfulfilled" (2005, p. 203), Janet rues. "I could surmise that there's nothing in the field but posturing, fiefdoms, and self-interest. Perhaps there's nothing ethically left in the field" (2005, p. 203). Who has not felt such a moment of discouragement?

Integrating the relative speed and complexity of the Reconceptualization would be arduous enough, even if the public world around us were not antagonistic. The combination of the two, I worry, has "shut down" some in our generation, even though many of us are still a decade or more from retirement, even though the historical moment requires that we mobilize, create infrastructure (such as the American Association for the Advancement of Curriculum Studies, of which Janet Miller served as its first president: 2001-2007). Despite the speed, despite the complexity, despite the fatigue (physical and emotional), we must mobilize to continue the intellectual advancement of the field of curriculum studies.

There is second sense of "what's left in the field." This second sense conveys what Miller suggests "is departed, what is no longer present, in our work in curriculum studies" (2005, p. 204). What is missing are the teachers. They have not been permitted to travel with us on the journey of reconceptualization. Rather than an occasion for impotent and misdirected rage, Janet finds this fact an occasion for mourning:

> But Katherine, the first-grade teacher, decided at the last minute not to attend the [Bergamo] conference. She told us she had to withdraw because she felt torn apart by the active questioning and discussion at Bergamo.... There was too great a discrepancy, she said, between the kinds of curriculum studies represented at the conference and the passive, submissive atmosphere and pre-determined content that was mandated in the elementary school where she taught. (2005, p. 205)

The scapegoating of teachers, their increasing subjugation by legislation (such as *No Child Left Behind*) that disables them from practicing their profession, has left us looking at each other from a distance.

Caught in a world not of our own making, we are under assault from circumstances both exterior and interior to the field. We have not chosen the balcony; we prefer the dance-floor, from which we have been barred. Given these facts, the "build it and they will come" fantasy that has, in part, inspired the Curriculum and Pedagogy movement requires, like the movie with which the phrase is associated, a taste for magical realism (see Pinar 2004b). "[W]e remain," Miller (2005, p. 206) concludes, sadly, sagely,

> in a crisis of identity precipitated by … the reconceptualization…. Perhaps what's left in the field is the work that it will take to address one another, not to merely "mend" or to "make the field whole," but to engage one another with "openness with regard to the social consequences of what we do" (Greene 1981, p. 6).

As Janet appreciates, the future of the field depends on our capacity for such engagement.

FIRST RECONCEPTUALIZATION, NOW INTERNATIONALIZATION

> What new disciplinary, interdisciplinary and transnational pedagogical and curricular practices might infuse and bring fresh life to what some see as a bifurcated and balkanized American curriculum field?
>
> Janet L. Miller (2005, p. 248)

Janet Miller's question is mine as well. One of my motives in asking Janet and others to participate in the internationalization of U.S. curriculum studies – in part through joining me in founding the International Association of Curriculum Studies and its U.S. affiliate, the American Association for the Advancement of Curriculum Studies – was my hope that by focusing outward we might be enabled to stabilize the field internally. Such a moment of consolidation has not yet occurred. While hardly limited to the academic field of curriculum studies, interrupting American narcissism is proving (as of this writing: January 2004), even more difficult than I feared.

Janet Miller and I share a second and much more important motive for internationalization, a motive she has articulated more eloquently, more profoundly, than have I. That motive concerns what we see as the curricular imperative to attend, as Miller (2005, p. 249) phrases it, to "the worldliness of American curriculum studies." From the essay so entitled, it is clear that Janet is thinking of September 11, 2001 (an event, living in New York City, she experienced in a direct way those of us outside New York cannot fully imagine). Janet is also thinking of the Bush Administration, of high-stakes testing, curricular standardization, and of "accountability." In one succinct statement, Miller (2005, pp. 245-246) synthesizes the multiple motives for attending to the "outside" of the U.S. field:

> If we can conceive of the curriculum field as text, … then one major obligation is to also work the tension to which [Edward] Said alludes: how might we construct a field of American curriculum studies that does not leave

it hermetically sealed cosmos with no connection to the world, but which also avoids reducing that text to its worldly circumstances?

It is a field in-between, occupying what Hongyu Wang (2004) theorizes as space in-between: intercultural, intrasubjective, dialogic. Janet Miller (2005, p. 246) describes this "third" space as "intertextual," as "working in and with this tension."

The field is not in that space now. It remains sealed – if divided - within the borders of an "imagined community." Like the nation, U.S. curriculum studies seems even more withdrawn, more self-absorbed, as if still in shock, uncertain, the future in doubt. Like the nation, the field risks reacting to external assault and internal complexity by its own version of right-wing reactionary politics, by the denial of diversity, by nostalgia for a past that never was. Such a reaction represents, Miller (2005, p. 247) understands, a flight from worldliness:

[O]ne danger of our field, I believe, is that the tragic events of September 11, the most recent war against Iraq, and further re-shapings of the world through effects of globalization, ecological crises, bioethics debates, instant and constant interconnection through the internet, and new waves of immigrants and refugees could compel those of us engaged in American curriculum studies to focus more exclusively than ever on a narrow, standards-centric version of our worldly circumstances. Or, these same events and situations could persuade us to retreat into what seems to be our field's own version of a hermetically sealed cosmos that encapsulates endless and often un-worldly debates about functions, purposes, and the varying discourses used to frame conceptions of our work in American curriculum studies.

The difficulty of the present makes the difficult decade of Reconceptualization seem, in retrospect, effortless.

"The U.S. curriculum field," Miller (2005, p. 247) is clear, "especially given these most recent world events, necessarily must … confront the implications of curriculum as international and global text." Such text is, she underscores, simultaneously local and global, as each is embedded in the other. "To understand curriculum studies globally," she writes, "means to understand our work as potentially embedded in multiple local contexts of use, not only *around* the world but also *in* the world" (2005, p. 247). Employing Deleuzian language, Janet Miller (2005, p. 250) sets the agenda for the next decade of internationalization:

We must work to understand how we are implicated in that worldliness – implicated not only in the sense of our vested interests but also in how American curriculum studies folds in, on and around other cultures, knowledges, and identities, and how those, in turn, now enfold American curriculum content and practices. To address such implications requires proliferating, in multi-variant ways – not containing in a hermetically sealed cosmos – the discourses and practices that comprise our work in curriculum studies. Thus, I propose that we now ask, in light of the pressing social, cultural, and historical conditions that necessarily frame our work: how will we rethink curriculum studies, yet again, as text that is fully implicated in its unavoidable worldly circumstances?

It is a question we must ask and answer individually and collectively.

We can make opportunities to do this work. The establishment of new professional associations provides infrastructure acutely needed in this nightmare time, providing (a relative) refuge from political assaults from the outside, creating safe – in-between – spaces of complicated conversation within. Social reconstruction requires subjective mobilization. With Ellsworth, Miller elaborates:

> [C]onstructing and disrupting fixed meanings of difference is profoundly situational, and often tedious. It is also personal and social at the same time, risky, never predictable, and requires imagination and courage of the intellect as well as of the heart.... And, as [Patricia] Williams reminds us, working difference is life work. "Nothing is simple. Every day is a new labor" (1991, p. 130; quoted in 2005, p. 193).

In a footnote, Miller and Ellsworth (2005, p. 195 n. 2) emphasize: "[W]e argue for a politics that is responsible to rather than repressive of difference."

Socially and subjectively we might undertake such responsibility by becoming internationalists, a concept once influential on the left. As Michael Hardt and Antoni Negri (2000, p. 49) remind us: "There was a time, not so long ago, when internationalism was a key component of proletarian struggles and progressive politics in general." May it become so again. With Janet Miller's participation and leadership, reconceptualization will be followed by internationalization.

GUERNICA

> [T]he force of my response to one particular painting eventually would point to my efforts to understand some possible connections among curriculum, the arts, my work as an academic, and my life.

Janet L. Miller (2005, p. 209)

Internationalism was at its most fervent during the 1930s, a terrible decade of economic depression, the rise of fascism, the outbreak of war, most devastatingly World War II on September 1, 1939 but, earlier, the bloody Spanish Civil War. Picasso painted a depiction of that savagery, a powerful painting he entitled *Guernica* after that city was bombed by fascists on April 26, 1937. "My nerves and skin remember a work of art," Janet tells us,

> a curriculum if you will, that was created where it was needed, within and because of massive and horrific social, political, and cultural disjunctures and tensions. That work of art, Picasso's *Guernica*, influenced and ultimately impelled me to consider the possibilities inherent in conceiving of both curriculum and teaching as human projects, where "ongoing conservation" and "new stories can root." ... And that viewing inspired in me a conception

36

of curriculum as never-ending but, at the same time, potentially transformative human project. (2005, pp. 208-209)

It was an "excessive moment."

Janet first saw Picasso's *Guernica* when she was a junior-high school class trip to New York City. "I felt frozen by this painting," she remembers, "unable to speak even after I had backed away from the canvas, in retreat from the pain that emanated from Picasso's vision of the wanton destruction of war" (2005, p. 209). It was as if "all the color had been drained from the world" (2005, p. 209). Janet remembers speaking about the powerful experience of confronting the painting with Miss Biedler and her classmates about their reactions to *Guernica*. (This was the same Miss Biedler Janet remembers as she teaches high school English, wondering "how Miss Biedler had found the room in her curriculum to even mention the connections she saw among music, art, and the literature we were studying at the time" (2005, p. 211).)

That wasn't the end of it. Janet was haunted by the painting. She read more about the Spanish Civil War and tried to figure out Picasso's political stance by studying more about the historical and political circumstances in which Picasso painted *Guernica*. Such study did not contain the experience of encountering the painting. Nor did it render the experience less compelling: "[U]ltimately, *Guernica* shattered my learned and limited ways of seeing, forced me to consider new ways of looking at life and death, demanded that I encounter, confront, and, most importantly, respond to and take action in and on competing visions of the world" (2005, p. 211). It is this imprinting educational experience that informs Miller's wise counsel:

> While the "controversies among us" in the curriculum field are *not* in any way analogous to the inhumanity that provoked Picasso's shattering images, our controversies in fact may be precisely what necessitate and ignite creative and imaginative acts of curriculum construction and reconstruction – visions of what "should be and what might be" in the curriculum field as well as in our schools. Intractable humanness and always changing circumstances, with their accompanying potentials for "acts of imagination" and new beginnings provoke us to engage one another. (2005, pp. 211-212)

Let our civil wars conclude and new coalitions assemble in those in-between spaces where, against the odds, complicated conversation continues.

Just as *JCT* and Bergamo – a journal and conference in which Janet Miller played key roles – provided necessary infrastructure for the Reconceptualization, the American Association for the Advancement of Curriculum Studies – a comprehensive and inclusive professional association, sponsoring a conference and a journal, an association in which Janet Miller is also playing key roles – provides key infrastructure for this present moment, a time of consolidation and internationalization, in which the latter engenders the former and the former animates the latter. "We haven't done it right the first time," Miller (2005, p. 213) suggests. "We will need to do it again. What's left in the field is the need to remake our work, and our selves, again and again. And that we have the opportunity to do so is both the challenge and the gift" (2005, p. 213). The balkanization and fragmentation of contemporary curriculum studies are not end-states, she is admonishing us to remember, but, rather, a "challenge" and "a gift." "What's left in the field," Janet Miller (2005, p. 213) reminds us,

> are people with nerves and skin, whose memories, representations, and connections with one another are full of "systemic errors, of holes that connect like a tangle of underground streams." Thus we must work our relationships to one another if we are to construct and reconstruct the curriculum field as an on-going and human project, incapable of closure yet dedicated to taking action in order to create "what should be and what might be."

We are admonished to begin our work together, again, now.

Janet, your work has been and continues to be a challenge and a gift. Challenging us intellectually, ethically, and subjectively, your gift commemorates the past, complicates the present, and commands us to reimagine our future. Like *Guernica*, your work's power and beauty, framed in this collection, will engage those who see it. May many be moved, as I have been, by what you have painted.

"A LINGERING NOTE" (2005)

"But on this bridge, we are in no hurry to cross over;
in fact, such bridges lure us to linger."

Ted T. Aoki (2005 [1996], 316)

There is a problem with an American doing this work. Aoki is a Canadian scholar, uniquely so. To be grasped in terms of Canadian intellectual life, his work must be situated within Canadian history and culture, specifically, within Canadian curriculum studies. I lack the expertise for such a project, nor am not appropriately situated to undertake it. (I am not reiterating the view, held by some in cultural studies, that subject position is a prerequisite for expertise.) I think Aoki's work is extraordinarily important for American as well as Canadian curriculum studies, as I trust the attention I gave to it in *Understanding Curriculum* testifies. In that textbook, I focused on Aoki's intellectual leadership in the effort to understand curriculum phenomenologically. While acknowledging there the movement in his work from phenomenology toward poststructuralism, I confess I did not grasp the full extent of it.

Why? I attribute this lapse in judgment to the fact that, while I had access to a number of Aoki's essays, I did not have access to them all. A number were in fact unpublished; and many were published in journals not readily accessible in the U.S. Several of the most brilliant, in fact, I had not yet read when I composed the passages on Aoki's work for *Understanding Curriculum*. Now, thanks to Ted Aoki and to Rita L. Irwin, I have (and you have: see Pinar and Irwin 2005) access to the entire body of work, entitled *Curriculum in a New Key*.

Aoki's leadership in the effort to understand curriculum phenomenologically is legendary. After having read everything now, I conclude that it is only part of the story. Aoki's scholarly work cannot adequately be described as "phenomenological," despite the strong and enduring influence that philosophical tradition exhibits in these collected essays. Ted is enormously erudite; he is not only well-read in phenomenology, but in poststructuralism, critical theory and cultural criticism as well. Even these four complex intellectual traditions fail to depict the range and depth of his study and his intellectual achievement.

In my introduction to the collected essays of the man who taught us to "hear" curriculum in a "new key," I emphasize the range and depth of the work. I focus too on the deft pedagogical moves Aoki makes in these essays, most of which were speeches. I know of no other scholar who took as seriously as Aoki did the scholarly conference as an educational event. Often working from conference themes, Aoki takes these opportunities to teach, and with great savvy and subtlety. Of someone we might say that s/he is a fine scholar *and* a superb teacher. Of Aoki we must say that his brilliance as a pedagogue is inextricably interwoven with his brilliance as scholar and theoretician. It is the unique and powerful combination of the three that makes Aoki's work absolutely distinctive.

In taking seriously the conference and, thereby, construing our coming together as an educational event, Aoki acknowledges the centrality of the social in intellectual – and academic – life. In a time in which careerist self-interest and self-promotion animate and, for many, define professional practice, Aoki's generosity in acknowledging the presence of others is exceptional. It discloses not only his utter intellectual honesty, but his profound sense of the ethical as well. "There are new curriculum researchers," he tells his fellow conference goers in 1973, "with whose ventures I can strike a vibrant and resonant chord. Although not too long ago this chord sounded strange deep inside me, that strangeness is fading. I think it is partly because in being at a conference such as this, I feel a sense of emergent becoming" (2005 [1978], p. 110). Already, in this early essay (the title essay of the collection), we hear the auditory characterization of education as "resonance." The last phrase – and its notion of "emergent becoming" – underscores the dynamic, developmental, and dialectical character of Aoki's intellectual formation.

I intend my introduction to the collected works to function in two ways. First, I hope it inaugurates a series of scholarly studies of Aoki's *oeuvre*. To situate Aoki's achievement within Canadian curriculum studies is a project I trust will be undertaken by several; to those of you listening today, please know there is at least one (but, no doubt, not only one) book series editor committed to supporting such an effort. There should be comparative studies as well, such as of the intersections (and differences) between Aoki's and Huebner's work. As well, there need to be studies of Aoki's influence on generations of younger scholars, and not only in Canada. I would like to see extended studies of Aoki's intellectual life history. And certainly there is room for a biography of this uniquely Canadian intellectual and public pedagogue.

Especially in this time when the academic field of education is under savage attack by politicians (Aoki once described it as "open hunting season for education" (2005 [1993], p. 279)), it is incumbent upon us to maintain our professional dignity by reasserting our commitment to the intellectual life of our field. Such a reassertion of our intellectual commitment includes, perhaps most of all, the study and teaching of curriculum theory and history. Study in neither domain can proceed far without the careful consideration of the work of Ted T. Aoki.

Second, I trust my introduction will function as both teaching aid and study guide. This ambition may seem redundant, given how brilliantly Aoki himself teaches in his essays. While that is the case, it is also true that Aoki's work is complex, nuanced, and profound, and students without backgrounds in phenomenology, poststructuralism and critical theory may well benefit from my sketching of the thematic and pedagogical movements in Aoki's work. I hope that my long and "lingering note" will stimulate students to engage Aoki's essays more actively than they otherwise might.

As students of Aoki's scholarship know, the title of the collection derives from an early essay that was widely read, including in the U.S. But its visibility and familiarity were not the only reasons why Rita Irwin and I proposed it to Ted as the title of the entire collection. The concept of "key" is an auditory rather than visual one, and it is the primacy of the auditory in Aoki's work that constitutes one of his most important and unique contributions to the field. It is Aoki's critique of ocularcentrism in Western epistemology and his honoring of the auditory, and specifically the musical, that enable us to hear curriculum in a new key. Almost alone among curriculum theorists, Aoki appreciated that after the "linguistic turn" comes an auditory one.

In the foreword to *Voices of Teaching*, published by the British Columbia Teachers' Federation, Aoki appreciates teaching as a calling (he notes that "vocation" derives from the Latin *vocare*/to call), and he characterizes the "voices of teaching" (Aoki 2005 [1996], p. 253) in this collection as having "sought ways of attunement that will allow them to hear, even faintly, the call of the calling." Speaking of those who contributed to the collection, Aoki is also, it seems to me, speaking about himself when he writes: "[t]he authors of *Voices of Teaching* offer us narrative of some moments in their experiences of teaching, thereby opening themselves to the lived meanings of teaching." Aoki's theorizing is always profoundly pedagogical, deeply grounded in concrete and specific educational events, occasions for experiencing the lived meanings of teaching.

Disengaging himself from teaching as a bureaucratized profession, Aoki opened himself to his own lived experience of teaching, at first in the Hutterite school east of Calgary (his first teaching job after "relocation" during World War II), then in the public schools of southern Alberta, nineteen years in all as teacher and assistant principal. After accepting a professorship at the University of Alberta, Aoki understood immediately (as we learn in chapter 13: Aoki 2005 [1996], pp. 247-261) that his "job" was not narrowly vocational, but profoundly theoretical, and that there was no unbridgeable divide between theory and practice.

In characterizing these "voices of teaching," Aoki (2005 [1996], p. 253) describes the work of finding themes in others' work as "theming," disclosing his fondness for gerunds rather than nouns, emphasizing the *live* in lived experience. "Theming," he writes, "is understood as a lingering intimately in embedded thoughtfulness in the story – as thoughtful listening in the nearness of the calling. Such theming is, as some would say, reflective thoughtfulness." The labor of "theming," Aoki (n.d.; quoted in Pinar 2005, p. 77) concludes, involves

> what we might call a hermeneutic returning to the lived ground of human experience within the story – a place wherein inhabits a tensionality of both distance and nearing. It understands such a place as a resonant place where emerging from the silence may be heard the movement of melody and rhythm – polyphonic voices of teaching. Where might such a place be? Paradoxically, the place is where we already are – a place so near yet so far

that we have forgotten its whereabouts. Reflecting theming may allow us to come to know how sufficiently as humans we inhabit where we already are as teachers.

This paragraph expresses several of the major themes of Aoki's remarkable career, among them the primacy of "lived experience," a distant but near "place" of "resonance," sounding in unmistakable if silent rhythms the "polyphonic voices of teaching" (Aoki n.d.; quoted in Pinar 2005, p. 77). Where is this "lived experience," this "place" where we can hear the call of teaching? It is where we are "already."

These are deeply evocative themes, recalling phenomenology's critique of contemporary life in the West as estranged from its ground, lost in the chimera of the mundane everyday world. Nowhere is that inauthentic social world more "suffocating" (to use another gerund of Aoki's) than in those classrooms regulated by proliferating bureaucratic protocols, institutionalizations of Western (mis)conceptions of "individualism" and "competence." It is Aoki's voice – no unitary sound, indeed, polyphonic – that sounds the call of our vocation, that calls us back to its lived ground where we are already, if muffled by the distractions and obsessions of the maelstrom that structures inauthenticity. There, where we are already, we can dwell in a conjunctive space, not one splintered by binaries, a lived space marked by generative tensions which we can incorporate, embody, and personify in our dialogical encounters with students and colleagues.

This "third space" space within which we can dwell both incorporates and leads us to the world outside. It is the space between political and bureaucratic stipulation and the classroom re-enactment of those contractual obligations, the space between what Aoki so usefully characterizes as "curriculum-as-plan" and "curriculum-as-lived." It is the space where we work (and play) to understand the educational meaning of our being together, in classrooms, at conferences, in seminars, engaged in improvisation, that disciplined and creative reconstitution of the past in anticipation of a future waiting to be heard in the present. "It is," Aoki explains, "a space of doubling, where we slip into the language of 'both this and that, but neither this nor that.' … The space moves and is alive" (n.d.; quoted in Pinar 2005, p. 78).

It is to this profoundly spatial, temporal and vibrant character of curriculum to which Aoki's work testifies. Significantly, it is not temporality severed from history. Aoki's narratives of his own schooling (the story of Mr. NcNab in chapter 8: Aoki 2005 [1992], pp. 193-195), the family's "evacuation" and "relocation" during World War II and his encounters with ignorance and prejudice, his mention of specific events (such as the Challenger disaster and the Columbine murders) all keep "time" grounded in "history," but never collapsing the two. There is always in Aoki's work an attunement to time that exceeds historicity, an attunement that renders Aoki not only a philosopher, but a historian, an autobiographer, always the sophisticated theoretician, in each instance answering the call of pedagogy, speaking in the voice(s) of teaching.

Aoki is *always* teaching. Nearly all of these essays are speeches; they are, in a profound sense of the word, "lessons." And even though the lessons he teaches are complex, never does he seem distracted by that complexity. Indeed, he is always attentive to the concreteness and singularity of the situation at hand. Invariably he acknowledges (respectfully) the occasion on which he is speaking, often referring to the conference title or theme, and organizing his "lesson" around those "signifiers." He proceeds with the sophistication and savvy of the veteran classroom teacher he is, sometimes disarming his listeners with a folksy story, sometimes taking on their own incomprehension as his own, embodying in himself their struggles to understand the lesson he is presenting, to bridge the distance between where they are and where he invites them to visit. Aoki's pedagogical movements from the concrete to the abstract and back again, and into the spaces among and between them, dazzles me, enables me to linger longer, listening to this master "musician" play.

In that "music" we hear echoes of pieces he has played before, but there is never simple repetition. As in jazz (in chapter 23 a visiting trumpeter makes this point explicit), the narratives Aoki reiterates sound differently each time he speaks them, each time in new context, serving a different purpose, while reconceptualizing an enduring theme. There is in Aoki's *oeuvre* a robust recursive movement, as Aoki returns to lessons past in making points present, anticipating ideas yet to come. It is this temporal enactment of his pedagogy – organizing these speeches into "moments" and "echoes" – that enables listeners to understand the lessons he has to teach.

I had suggested to Ted that he organize these essays chronologically so students could see how his thought evolved over time. Too linear, I could hear him say in that familiar twinkling of his eye. After rereading the foreword to the *Voices of Teaching* I know why; he was "theming," reflecting the gatherings that stimulated his thought, the clustering of concepts, the reconfiguring of melodies, creating new sounds of dissonance and difference out of juxtapositions a simple chronology would have silenced. I am grateful Aoki declined my suggestions and stayed his course, a course, like the one he taught in Montreal, without foundations, in this instance, temporal foundations.

"Foundations" would be too reductionistic, too binary. Aoki is, by his own admission, a "bridge," both a noun and a verb. This theme shows up in the chapters on conversation, on the Pacific Rim, "a person," as he puts it, who is "both self and other" (2005 [1993], p. 288). "It is my wish," he offers in 1988, "to serve as a bridge over the Pacific Ocean" (2005 [1991d], p. 437). Aoki lives on the Pacific Rim, he is Japanese and Canadian (as he remarks on one occasion, a slippery set of signifiers), he is well aware of Western individualism (the limitations of which he has insistently pointed out), well aware of the Eastern side of the Rim. At some point Aoki quotes Roshin, a Taoist teacher, to make his point: "Humanity's greatest delusion is that I am here and you are there" (p. 445). There is no American-style narcissism here, in which the "other" disappears into my "self." Aoki invokes Levinas to ensure that his Western listeners and readers do not mistake the profoundly ethical, relational, indeed, ecological character of "self *and* other" (2005 [1993], p. 212).

It is this enduring sense of the ethical that enables Aoki to occupy a space between history and time, between continents, between the public school classroom and the university seminar room, between a field in collapse in the 1960s and a field experiencing rejuvenation today. Aoki's career started in the Tylerian past, but he never seems to have been seduced by the apparently commonsensical purposes to which Tyler's work was put, namely the conversion of the school into a factory. Over and over again he points out that education is not a business, that a school principal is not an administrative manager (but, rather, a principal teacher). Somehow Aoki knew that we needed not to see a new curriculum model, but to hear curriculum in a new key. And the new key he has composed is breathtakingly beautiful in its sonorous poeticity, powerfully and provocatively multiplying in its concepts.

Because the concept communicates the significance of the auditory in Aoki's theory and teaching (and is a central concept in contemporary curriculum studies in the U.S.), I would like to close by focusing on the notion of "conversation." In the collection it shows up first in Chapter 4, where Aoki revisits his experience during the 1970s evaluating the British Columbia Social Studies curriculum. In what he characterizes as the "Situational Interpretative Evaluation Orientation" (2005 [1986], p. 137), the primary interests are those meanings ascribed to the situation by those engaged in teaching and studying the curriculum. In order to represent those meanings, Aoki and his B.C. Social Studies Assessment team employed "conversational analysis."

Disclosing the primacy of phenomenology in his thinking even at this early stage, Aoki notes that the conversation he has in mind is not "chit-chat," nor is it the simple exchange of messages or only the communication of information. None of these, he suggests, requires "true human presence" (2005 [1991a], p. 180). Nor is language only a tool by means of which thoughts are recoded into words. Curriculum as conversation, in this formulation, is no conveyor belt of "representational knowledge" (2005 [1991a], p. 181). It is a matter of attunement, an auditory rather than visual conception.

Aoki brings this phenomenological critique of "conversation" to bear on issues of intercultural education, specifically as these surfaced in the internationally-attended graduate program in curriculum studies at the University of Alberta. Revealing his characteristic pedagogical movement from the abstract to the concrete, from the theoretical to the anecdotal, here from the local to the global, Aoki conceives of graduate study as "a conversation of mankind" (2005 [1981], p. 220) in a "trans-national situation" (2005 [1981], p. 221).

Speaking with students who have come to Alberta from beyond North America, Aoki is reminded of the instrumentality of his assignment as an administrator and of the centrality of conversation in the process of education. In this intercultural educational experience, Aoki worries about the erasure of originary identities. "[T]o remind ourselves of who we are in conversation," he suggests to these students, "I ask that we turn the conversation to ourselves" (2005 [1981], p. 222).

He poses to students what might be the central curriculum question in an era of globalization: "How will you know that what we consider 'good' here is 'good' in your homeland'?" (2005 [1981], p. 222).

In this same essay, Aoki employs "conversation" to think about what might comprise an "authentic dialogue" among scholars worldwide. "If East-West conversation in curriculum is to be authentically East-West dialogue, if North-South conversation is to be authentically North-South dialogue," he suggests, then "such conversation must be guided by an interest in understanding more fully what is not said by going beyond what is said" (2005 [1981], p. 227). Here he is using a phenomenology of language – and specifically its depth imagery – to remind us that the social surface of speech is precisely that. Authentic conversation requires "going beyond" the surface to take into account "unspoken" and "taken-for-granted" assumptions, including "ideology," what Aoki characterizes as "the cultural crucible and context that make possible what is said by each in the conversational situation" (2005 [1981], p. 227). With the inclusion of the concept of "ideology," Aoki is disclosing a complication of his initial phenomenological formulation, here by critical theory, specifically the work of Habermas.

Aoki reminds us that "authentic conversation is open conversation," never "empty," always one in which the participants engage in a "reciprocity of perspectives" (2005 [1981], p. 228). Invoking one of his favorite metaphors, he tells us: "I understand conversation as a bridging of two worlds by a bridge, which is not a bridge" (2005 [1981], p. 228). Conversation is a passage from here to there and elsewhere, but it is not "here" or "there" or "elsewhere," but in the conjunctive spaces in-between.

Aoki employs "bridge" in both literal and metaphoric senses; the idea seems to foreshadow the bridging movements in his own work. That movement is evident in chapter 9, a 1992 speech to the Association for Supervision and Curriculum Development (ASCD). It is, in my judgement, a most remarkable paper in which Aoki moves deftly between high abstraction and amusing anecdote. Among the abstractions he introduces to this audience of school personnel is interdisciplinarity, specifically, the teaching of science as one of the humanities.

Lest he run off his audience of administrators by such talk, Aoki creates a scenario on Bourbon Street. (Given that this conference was being held in New Orleans, he is enabling his audience to "run off" while remaining seated.) In this scenario, a scientist and a novelist are engaged in conversation, yes, about science taught as one of the humanities. Here he seems to be using "conversation" commonsensically, but this seems to me strategic, and it doesn't last long. Quickly this concrete sense of conversation becomes abstract under the influence, not of drink (as one might suspect, being on Bourbon Street), but of the philosophy of Gilles Deleuze.

For in this encounter between scientist and novelist, Aoki imagines, as he puts it, "improvised lines of movement growing from the middle of their conversation" (2005 [1993], p. 214). Such improvisation in conversation requires, he tells us, "a new language" (2005 [1993], p. 215), still a phenomenological theme, but now emitting a decidedly post-structuralist sound. The language Aoki hears in this

45

interdisciplinary conversation on Bourbon Street has, he tells us, "a grammar in which a noun is not always a noun, in which conjoining words like *between* and *and* are no mere joining words, a new language that might allow a transformative resonance of the words *paradigms*, *practices*, and *possibilities*" (a reference to the subtitle of Bill Schubert's widely-read 1986 study) (2005 [1993], 215). "If that be so," he concludes, returning us from the abstract to the concrete with humor, "we should all move to the French Quarter, so that we can not only listen, but also join them right in the middle of their conversation" (2005 [1993], p. 215).

Conversation understood as authentic attunement to "true human presence" (2005 [1991a], p. 180) was, let us remember, a radical idea in the 1970s; for many trapped in the school-as-a-business it remains so today. By characterizing the exchange of "information" as "chit-chat," Aoki was, in the 1973 essay, calling to us to rethink not only what we mean by "evaluation," but, as we reflect on his later (in chapter 5) questionings of technology, to rethink the so-called Age of Information in which we presumably live. In 1992, not blocks from Bourbon Street, he is employing poststructuralism to disperse disciplinary identities and to create interdisciplinary spaces between the humanities and the sciences, spaces that include both sets of disciplines.

Twenty years after his initial and important formulation of the concept of "conversation" as evocative of and attuned to "true human presence," Aoki (presumably retired) is speaking of conversation in less somber tones. By the early 1990s Aoki is speaking of conversation as a version of jazz, a notion which first shows up in the 1991 Bobby Shew anecdote (see Aoki 2005 [1990], p. 367ff.) and a discussion of improvisation, although the language he employs in the New Orleans speech to ASCD is Deleuzian (see Aoki 2005 [1993]). Rather than returning to something lost or at least in jeopardy ("true human presence"), Aoki now focuses on something futural, something to be created, a "new language," and through improvisation.

There is no question for Aoki of working from *either* phenomenology *or* from poststructuralism. The interest in language and, more specifically, the analysis of the conjunctions of apparently mutually exclusive binaries through deconstruction is present in Heidegger (if in the service of retrieving "true human presence"), as John Caputo (1987) and others have made clear (see Pinar et al. 1995, chapter 8). Aoki never abandons phenomenology, but he follows it to its edge where conversation as hermeneutics becomes conversation as "improvisation."

This is, I submit, a powerful notion that allows us to emphasize not only the creativity of teaching, but enables us to "hear" the relation between theory and practice. As Aoki notes in the title essay (if in visual terms): "Rather than seeing theory as leading into practice, we need now more than ever to see it as a reflective moment in praxis" (2005 [1983, p. 120). In the sounds of our conversation we honor the past by self-reflectively reformulating it in the present, animated by our own and others' "true human presence." That is the jazz of praxis.

If we focus on the auditory character of Aoki's metaphors, we see continuity as well as change in the essays. From the beginning, Aoki is critical of scientistic observation (and its privileging of the visual), emphasizing instead the sound of conversation (and its privileging of the auditory). He makes this critique explicit in a 1991 speech to the British Columbia Music Educators' Association, where he points out that conversation is primarily an auditory experience. In this important paper, Aoki quotes Derrida, Kierkegaard, and Heidegger to emphasize the significance of the ear and of listening in educational experience. He writes:

> I pause [a musical term as well] to reflect. Lingering in the reflection, I confess that, over the years of schooling and teaching, I have become beholden to the metaphor of the I/eye – the I that sees.... For myself, I too had become enamored of the metaphor of *videre* (to see, thinking and speaking of what eyes can see). (2005 [1990], p. 373)

This formulation represents a major theoretical advance in our understanding of curriculum as conversation. In creating a "new language" in which *sonare* becomes as least as important as *videre*, Aoki has changed everything. Gone are decades of behaviorism and its residues in observational analysis. Questioned is the very subject-object binary in Western epistemology, imprinted as that is throughout the school curriculum and mainstream educational research. Questioned is the relegation of classroom teaching to "implementation," a bureaucratic bridge between objectives and assessment.

Present are the sounds of complicated conversation in which teachers are bridges between curriculum-as-plan and curriculum-as-lived, between the state and the multitude, between history and culture. "[C]onversation," Aoki explains, "is a bridging of two worlds by a bridge, which is not a bridge" (2005 [1981], p. 228). "Bridge" here is both noun and verb; it is both literal and metaphoric. It is both spatial and temporal. As Webster's points out, "bridge" is defined as "time, place, or means of connection or transition." Aoki himself performs, indeed personifies, such temporal and spatial connections and transitions: between the traditional and reconceptualized fields, between phenomenology and poststructuralism, between theory and pedagogy, between the West coast and the prairies, between Canada and the United States, between East and West.

To bridge East and West, Aoki moves away from a focus on the separate identities of the binary and into the spaces between them. As he puts it, he is "trying to undo the instrumental sense of 'bridge'" (2005 [1996], p. 316). Such a nuanced sense of "bridge" is implied by the conjunction "and" in the binary. By focusing on the conjunctive space *between* "East and West," and by understanding "and" as "both 'and' and 'not-and'," Aoki proposes a bridging space of "both conjunction and disjunction" (2005 [1996], p. 318). This is, Aoki explains, a space of tension, both "and/not-and," a space "of conjoining and disrupting, indeed, a generative space of possibilities, a space wherein in tensioned ambiguity newness emerges" (2005 [1996], p. 318).

That last phrase describes, I think, the space Aoki has created in his work, wherein we can now listen as if with new ears to conversation across terrains of difference, a complicated conversation in which both separation and belonging together exist in generative tension. The latter phrase is explicated in a 1990 paper, beautifully entitled "The Sound of Pedagogy in the Silence of the Morning Calm"

47

(Aoki 2005 [1991c], p. 389), in which Aoki privileges the gerund "belonging" over the noun "together." "[B]elonging" takes precedence over "together," he explains, thereby revealing the "being" of "belonging." In Aoki's subtle and sophisticated conceptualization, "being" vibrates like a violin string, and in its sound, honors the structural complexity and phenomenological integrity of individual identity and social relationality.

"Bridge" is a musical term as well, defined by Webster's as "an arch serving to raise the strings of a musical instrument." Aoki has raised us, the individual strings of the curriculum field, attuning us to our calling as educators. He has ennobled us by his pedagogical labor, enabled us to "be" in our belonging together, engaged in creative and disciplined "improvisation" as we traverse the terrain of our lived differences as educators and students.

"There are other bridges," Aoki notes, such as those found in Japanese gardens, including Nitobe's Garden on the University of British Columbia campus. In his bridging movements from the abstract to the concrete, from the metaphoric to the literal, from history to culture, he has advanced, as he has complicated, our understanding of our pedagogical and scholarly calling. Aoki's work is a bridge, and like the bridge he describes in chapter 18, "we are in no hurry to cross over; in fact, such bridges lure us to linger" (2005 [1996], p. 316). This metaphoric bridge is "a site or clearing in which earth, sky, mortals and divine, long to be together, belong together" (2005 [1996], p. 316). Aoki's work has created that clearing, wherein we can hear curriculum in a new key.

A/R/T AS LIVING INQUIRY (2004)

In A/R/T, as Rita L. Irwin conceptualizes it, knowing, doing, and making merge. They merge and disperse, creating métissage, a language, Irwin suggests, of the "borderlands," of English and French, of autobiography and ethnography, of man and woman. "Metissage is usually recognized in hyphenated relationships" (Irwin and de Cosson 2004, 30), Irwin explains; "it is an act of interdisciplinarity" (Irwin and de Cosson 2004, 30). A/R/T is a "metaphor" for artist-researcher-teachers who integrate these roles in their personal/professional lives; it creates, Irwin suggests, a "third space between theory and metissage, while opening up the spaces between artist-researcher-teacher" p. 31).

After Ted Aoki (2005 [2000], p. 323), artist-researcher-teachers dwell "in-between" or "third" spaces, spaces that are neither this nor that, but this "and" that. Such in-dwelling expresses and animates, Irwin explains, "a desire to explore new territory, a borderland of reformation and transformation, a geographical, spiritual, social, pedagogical, psychological and physical site intersubjectively and intrasubjectively situated in and through dialogue" (Irwin and de Cosson 2004, p. 30). In such complicated conversation, aesthetic experience integrates knowing, doing, and making.

"Thought and action are inextricably linked" (Irwin and de Cosson 2004, p. 33), Irwin continues, reminiscent of Clermont Gauthier's (1992) dissolution of the binary embedded in the notion of "action research." Contesting the bifurcated logic that imagines "action research" occurs only in schools, Gauthier (1992, p. 193) insisted that "[action research] can take place anywhere: in one's office, in one's mind." Like the creations of artist-researcher-teachers, it seems to me, Gauthier's analysis integrates thought and action.

There are phenomenological as well as poststructuralist elements in Irwin's conceptualization of A/R/T. Not only bifurcated logic is a casualty in A/R/T, so is segmented time. The work of A/R/T is about "deep meaning," a phenomenological phrase and preoccupation. Irwin explains that:

> Theory as a/r/tography as metissage is a way for those of us living in the borderlands to creatively engage with self and others as we reimagine our life histories in and through time. A/r/tography is a form of representation that privileges both text and image as they meet within moments of metissage. But most of all, a/r/tography is about each of us living a life of deep meaning through perceptual practices that reveal what was once hidden, create what has never been known, and imagine what we hope to achieve (Irwin and de Cosson 2004, pp. 35-36).

Forms of aesthetic representation that are movable, momentary, and express deep meaning are evident in Sylvia Wilson's quilt making. "The only way I can make a quilt right now is just start," Wilson tells us, "then see what happens" (2004, 41). Text and image meet in Wilson's visual essay. She describes her work as involving "movable pieces, interchangeable, nothing fixed, maybe there are even some pieces missing, placed elsewhere, lost, and I haven't found others to fill the gaps yet" (2004, p. 41). Creating her quilts, Wilson finds herself "looking into the emptiness, living in the loss, and finding my way to being content and at peace with emptiness and absence" (2004, p. 41).

Quilts are, she suggests, metaphors of women's experience. They are, after Ted Aoki (whom Wilson quotes), places of "generative possibilities" (2004, 47), opportunities (again, after Aoki) for "face to face living" (2004, 44). She faces her child, born with multiple disabilities, and her own experience of "mothering, loss, and of hope" (2004, p. 42) In so doing, she discovers that "both the process of research and the 'story fabric' evolved as both written and visual, an interplay of image and text. I wrote and stitched, and the story of my experience of mothering a child born with multiple disabilities began to unfold" (2004, p. 42).

Wilson's maternal experience of loss is also one of psychological fullness: "I choose to believe instead his life is a gift given, wrapped in unusual packaging perhaps but full of rich and wonderful things, a rare and treasured gift" (2004, p. 43). And the gift who is her son (and her mothering of him) became like "first signs of life pushing up through the ground again (2004, p. 54).... I've seen it in Nathaniel. This life that flows through him, that drives him, that won't let him let go .... Still, I watched him die twice" (2004, p. 56). Quilting and mothering and theorizing, Wilson appreciates that art *is* research, the unique beauty of which derives from its "artistic intent and process" (2004, p. 47) Wilson concludes:

> Throughout my inquiry, and as I've reflected on my quilt-making, I began to think of art not just as an investigative process and research but as spiritual practice as well. I began to see art making as contemplative practice and as a prayerful act (2004, p. 57).

This echo of James B. Macdonald (1995) in Wilson's second sentence signals creation, devotion and hope.

The artwork and research presented in Stephanie Springgay's chapter examines the body in relation to history, culture, and nature. Springgay juxtaposed fractured painted body parts alongside panels of sewn rose petals. In these composites she explored and expressed both "the ephemerality of the body" and the "desire to leave a mark: to create, organize, and understand." The works locate the body "between artifact and archive, as a region of uncertainty" (2004, p. 62).

"The art itself," Springgay testifies, "becomes an art of boundary" (2004, p. 63). The twelve painted body parts are, she suggests, "mimicked" (2004, p. 63) by twelve rose petal panels. In the artwork there were five dresses, hanging suspended in the exhibition space, "both static metaphors and breathing representations of self and other" (2004, p. 66). Additionally, there were a series of five large oil paintings: "Repetition. Duplication" (2004, p. 63).

Abjection, as Springgay understands it, is a violent response to the body's boundaries, which, I suspect, her work stimulates. It is as if she wants to enter the space before and/or after abjection, to locate the viewer in his/her own response to the body's boundaries, inviting him/her to move beyond abjection by moving through it. In these juxtapositions Springgay focuses on the in-between, the seams:

> Boundaries need to be recoganized as shifting; we cannot and should not remove the *seam*, but observe and honor the sewn, sutured space of existence. Bringing multiple roles together, artist, researcher, teacher, suggests partiality and fragmentation (2004, p. 68).

She employs red threads, "disrupting our dwelling in language, disrupting ourselves, our self-understanding" (2004, p. 69).

"My own identity is leaky," Springgay tells us, "porous, performed, and partial" (2004, p. 71). She struggles with labels such as artist, research, and teacher. They are not different roles for her, "split identities," but one: "I am always artist" (2004, p. 71). Dwelling among seams and boundaries, Springgay embraces the complexity, the otherness, of aesthetic creation:

> I paint and sew, collage and create as an act of violence, as a form of resistance.... [A]rt allows us to have the direct experience of being in multiple places at once, feeling multiple emotions, and holding contradictory opinions (2004, p. 73).

Julie Lymburner, too, seems to live along the seams, in-between spaces where "urgent questions surface and resurface" (2004, p. 75). She has accumulated, she tells us, twenty years of questions: "Who am I? How have I evolved as a teacher? What matters most to me? How can I make a difference to others" (2004, p. 75)? These are not separate questions for her; they have become snarled, as if in a knot:

> To unravel the snarl of questions that surround my practice, to examine the interconnection between the roles I inhabit as teacher, researcher, artist, mother, mentor, and to negotiate a path of meaningful inquiry that shifts both inward and outward is no simple task (2004, pp. 75-76).

Not simple, but Lymburner has a strategy: focus on details, both in the world and in herself. "I soon discovered," she writes, "the importance of gazing inward if I was to make substantive gains as an art educator" (2004, p. 78). Lymburger spent four years studying the details of her personal-professional life, situating herself as artist/teacher/researcher, "in-between" and in liminal spaces, "uniquely placed to explore and express the inner complexity of these overlapping roles" (2004, p. 76).

Returning to the university, Lymburger felt the "urgent need within to immerse" herself in art making, "without compromising my teaching practice or my self-study" (2004, p. 81). She achieved this hyphenated-integrated experience by becoming engaged in daily "visual journalling." Arts-based journaling provided her the opportunity to reflect "aesthetically, intellectually, and introspectively" (2004, p. 87).

Lymburger's journal became a "point of departure" for "deeply meaningful images" (2004, p. 82) that she consequently created. The "quick and fragile seeds of ideas" (2004, p. 82) recorded in her visual journal became expressed in a series of mixed-media collages, collages she understood as hypertextual:

> My work emerged as a complex hypertext that subsumed my multifaceted life; it teemed with observations, images, anecdotes, recollections, metaphorical interpretations and dreams. It was, and continues to be, a wonderfully rich and evocative teaching and learning too. Through visual journaling I have the opportunity to think comprehensively and creatively about my teaching, my art, and my research (2004, p. 81).

The snarl becomes smooth and intelligible.

The dual roles of artist and teacher, Patti Pente tells us, moved her from the studio to the classroom and back again. Pente expressed this movement in a piece entitled, "*Shuffle the Cards, Deal a Hand*" (2004, p. 93),composed specifically, she reports, to address of the simultaneity of being artist-researcher-teacher. The piece consisted of a deck of collaged cards, selected for their association with play. Pente understands "play" as a "way of being" that includes "curiosity, enthusiasm and creativity. The player is engaged" (2004, p. 95). Additional elements of this artwork included an instruction page printed on an overhead transparency, a school desk, and a chair.

The desktop had etched in it years of students' engravings. Pente wonders if the viewer understands the well-worn desktop as a "record of vandals, bored and silently rebelling against their teachers by carving their importance into the polished surface" (2004, p. 99), or, perhaps, a "wealth of visual curiosities and beautiful marks, statements of another time and place? Who was "Alex" or "Joe"?" (2004, pp. 99-100) she asks, studying the names etched in the top. "Are they mark-gouging" (2004, p. 100)? Or, playfully, are they "only testimonials of students who were off task?" (2004, p. 100) She writes:

> The graffiti also represent rich histories, and it stirs memories for those of us who sat in desks like this one. It is important to recognize the multiple meanings situated on this surface. Values identified against such inquiries into context, and often, conflicting values are held simultaneously. It is at the edges where these conflicts meet, in that third space, that the interesting conversations about teaching, about art and about inquiry can take place (2004, p. 100).

Each element of the artwork, Pente suggests, constitutes a point of departure for examining relationships between theory and practice. She regards the piece as both educational theory and art. "Theory, for the researcher/teacher/artist," Pente writes, "is located in the classroom/studio and here the card metaphor is especially appropriate. The traditional dichotomy of theory and practice disappears when viewed from this perspective as each theory is *shuffled* around" (2004, p. 98).

From her experience, Pente concludes that "art making is an important part of inquiry for educators who are also artists" (2004, p. 94). By engaging in artistic creation, it was possible to explore aspects of herself difficult to describe in words, but which could be represented artistically. This process – A/R/T – she characterizes as "deep inquiry," which is simultaneously very serious and rather playful: "I shuffle the cards and deal another hand" (2004, p. 101).

"My research has been lived," Nicole Porter (2004, p. 114) reports. Probably *because* the research was lived, it did not come automatically. Like several other participants in A/R/T, Porter had "fears about trying this experiment: bringing my studio work into my own classroom" (2004, p. 103). Like several others, it was a fear associated with the self-disclosure implicit in exhibiting her art: "I was exposing my art, my creativity and part of my private life to my students. I wasn't sure how they were going to react" (2004, p. 103).

Also like the other participants, fear did not dissuade her. Porter proceeded, structuring her inquiry with several questions: How would the atmosphere develop as she did work? How would her teaching and the students' educational experience evolve in the classroom? How would making art at school be different from making art in the privacy and safety of her home? Her final concern re-expressed the fear: what if students didn't like her work? Animating her inquiry was a commitment to reexamine and reconstruct her, and her students', ideas of "what a classroom could, should and might be" (2004, p. 105). In that phrase the echo of Maxine Greene is loud.

Nicole Porter began work. "I don't think anyone noticed what I was doing for a while" (2004, 105), she reports. Her materials included large sheets of plywood, drywall compound, acrylic paint and a variety of *materiel* that could be embedded in the wet plaster. Porter characterizes the work as "loosely figurative" (2004, p. 105). It is part of a series of "Women with Eggs" (2004, 105). The series explores womanhood and femininity through the figuration of several women, each posing, each holding an egg.

Porter recorded in her journal that she sometimes felt guilty about painting in her art classroom, worrying that she should be "marking, prepping or something" (2004, p. 106). Several students didn't seem to understand why she was painting. "What's it for?" asked one student, after asking her who was doing the painting. "I was so struck by this" (2004, p. 106), Porter reports. "What is it for anyway? Students make art because they are in class and the teacher marks it. WHY would a teacher make something" (2004, p. 106)? The logic of the conventional classroom would seem to exclude teacher creativity.

This question of "why" animated her explorations and readings. During the course of her readings, Porter found a term employed by Ted Aoki that intrigued her. Aoki had described teaching and living as happening in "spaces." This became a central metaphor; she dwelled on (as well as in) the physical spaces of the classroom, and in those "attitudinal spaces in the mind and most importantly human spaces between my students and myself" (2004, p. 108). Through her inquiry, Porter was able to create a "space" for students to talk directly, personally. What was the result? Students began to "linger," including those who had never stayed after school unless detention required them to do so. Both students and teacher were "amazed." A welcomed result, and Porter understood that:

> Students are now more likely to see themselves as artists because the space has changed. It is no longer just a classroom but a studio. This is no longer just a school space but their space. And as such I am no longer just a teacher, but a teacher artist. Together we ask hard questions and delve deeply into our explorations for greater understanding (2004, pp. 109-110).

Porter's enthusiasm prompts her to suggest that not only art teachers can benefit. She believes that every "teacher *wants* to be active in their field – that it is a worthy endeavor to learn and grown as a reward in and of itself" (2004, p. 111). From this point of view, the concept of "knowing" is a "living one." Moreover, "this teacher model gives students reasons to learn *beyond marks*" (2004, p. 111). Student learned by watching, and becoming engaged in, the process of aesthetic creation:

> The students also learned something of honoring the *process* of making art. By having the piece in the classroom from the time it was merely a plank of plywood to the finished product, students saw the steps and became curious about the technical processes. It also encouraged students to reflect on *how* they created pieces – not to be too focused on the end result (2004, p. 112).

Anticipating readers who worry that this degree of engagement might make for "discipline" problems, Porter volunteers that the shift in her "status" did not effect classroom management negatively. "There may have been a change of roles," she reports, "but no loss of respect. I was seen as more human and approachable, and couched in the right conditions, my 'weakness' became my strength" (2004, p. 112). Porter concludes: "My research regarding bringing my art into the classroom was a wonderful learning experience for my students and me (2004, p. 114)…. Even now they pester me to start another piece, and I have to agree that it is time" (2004, p. 115).

Anami Naths writes to us from Mexico. It is, she reports, "a warm Tuesday morning in March. I am drinking coffee in the Zocalo, the market-square in Oaxaca" (2004, p. 116). The square is filled with weavings, art made from cotton, wool, rope, baskets, hair, leather. "Everything, it seems" Naths exclaims, "is woven with specific and unique colors and patterns of the diverse local cultures" (2004, p. 116). In the Zocalo, she notes, she is illiterate, unable to read the "cotton-embroidered blouses, the vendors' woven reed belts, the black and white finely woven cotton head piece, the embroidered birds and flowers that dance on skirt edges" (2004, p. 116).

Perhaps it is this of estrangement that prompts Naths to ask a series of questions: "Why am I here? Why am I looking at piles of stone and ropes, peering into the past of a people I am not the least connected to? Why did the ancients of long ago, go to the trouble of inlaying pebbles in temples, walls and pyramids? How much of what I am seeing and experiencing here in Oaxaca is available to me in my limited literacy" (2004, p. 118)? While these questions hover around her like ghosts, partial answers become audible in her text. Echoing the voices and footsteps of a people long absent, the art and ancient graffiti in the tombs of Monte Alban bring her the experience of presence: "Yesterday, I walked in the tombs, leaving behind my footsteps and my stories. Recorded in my journal, those events take form in pen and ink drawings, watercolor and collage. I was there!" (2004, pp. 119-120).

As it was for other participants, the journal was for her both the site and the process of A/R/T. Naths notes that her visual journaling was both "the tool and the filament that runs through my being" (2004, p. 120). In it, she can "re-cord." Playing with the word, she sees that "this pulling back and forth of the cord, the thread that runs through weaves my yarn into artifacts that claim – here I am, I matter" (2004, p. 120). Being self-consciously present in the world enables her to know: "With reflection comes knowledge about self and of the world. Is it true that conscience and the world take place at the same time" (2004, p. 120)?

"What I have come to know from the discipline of weaving and recording" (2004, p. 121)? By "looking deeply and with purpose" (2004, 121), Naths feels she has found and lived a philosophy congruent with what she does in the classroom, in the studio and in the Zocalo, itself a metaphor for the collaged experience that is A/R/T. Acknowledging that she knows more than she can tell, Naths' knowledge is like a cord that stitches together her art, her teaching, her research:

By thinking about what I do, by looking at what others of the world made and do, by examining my practice and making public my search and re-search I feel that I come to have a better hold on the cord, the rope that runs through self as artist, teacher, researcher. Thus, I re-cord (2004, p. 122).

"This is my story," Naths continues, "but it is also connected to the larger of human culture" (2004, p. 122). In the weaving of cloths and rugs, the decoration of eggs and masks or the spraying of paint under the city bridges, questions are being posed, experiences recorded:

Why is this being done? Where do these images and colors come from? Who will be empowered or frightened by this mark making? I have faith that students can be encouraged and supported to go past being mere objects that meddle.... I am committed to an education of connections and questions (2004, p. 123).

Connections and questions seem to be exactly where Alex de Cosson works, among boundaries and ruptures and raptures. "I want to write *in* the aporia that my research places itself" (2004, p. 128), he tells us. It is in "the point of disjuncture" (2004, p. 128) – a nodal point embedded in and on the edge of his making/teaching sculpture – where he makes meaning. In this process, this progression on an aesthetic journey, de Cosson makes "meaning out of the curriculum of being that finds itself doing what it is called to do" (2004, p. 128).

By inhabiting the moment of creation in the studio as an embodied creature, de Cosson makes art, both as objects to be shared in the public world and as lived aesthetic experiences in his body. His aspiration, he tells us, is:

55

To present an embodied moment in the studio process of art making, that
validates my embodied understandings, through the pedagogy of being
becoming (2004, p. 128).

Like Derrida, de Cosson seeks windows opening outside from his embodied cell,
open spaces where he might create passages over and under and through his aporia,
his felt knot, his self-otherness now so familiar to him it no longer feels alien. His
otherness he knows and doesn't, but it is where he performs A/R/T:

Word-windows that Derrida seeks out, to work over and under, to find new
ways around a (the) problem of aporia. Can I retreat from the mission? or am
I driven on to find ways through the border land that is inherent in this space
of not knowing/knowing (simultaneously)(2004, p. 131)?

Driven, that is, if he does not dissolve into the otherness that is his aporia: "The
hard part is to actually get over to the gallery and <u>do</u> the work before the entire day
has slipped away in otherness" (2004, p. 144). As Claudia Eppert (1999, p. 132)
notes in a different context, I think that de Cosson's performance of A/R/T "does
not gesture toward a paralytic aporia, but rather encompasses a positive pedagogy."

In this phenomenological space de Cosson explores, creates, recoils. He tells us,
disarmingly, that:

I am

(*researching*)

the process

of my own doing.

(2004, p. 150)

"Twenty years of sculpting has taught me my process" (2004, p. 144), he tells us.
"Cling to the pedagogical ecology!" (2004, p. 149) he advises.

"Pedagogical ecology" seems to characterize Wendy Stephenson's work, asking
questions, as she does, concerning the role of visual representation in art education
history research. "Can art making encourage understanding and perhaps reveal
shifting historical practices and perspectives?" (2004, p. 155). To answer,
Stephenson engages in art-making, creating a collage/assemblage entitled "The
Archeology of My Parents' Lives, 1943-1949" (2004, 156). "Since then," she
reports, "I have come to consider the near integration of the processes of doing
research, art making, and representing history. For me, history provides
information and introduces new points of view which in turn has the capacity to
teach with a view to changing attitudes" (2004, p. 155).

These conclusions emerged from Stephenson's research on pedagogical
practices in secondary art classes in British Columbia to 1950. "Drawings of
simple objects, design limited to geometric forms, and restricted materials gave
way to a wider variety of subjects and a wider range of media" (2004, p. 161),
Stephenson reports, underlining the "difference between merely providing data and

achieving the visual presentation of history" (2004, p. 164). She hopes to understand changes in art classes, especially in the context of an emerging post-colonial city: Vancouver. Art exhibitions, she asserts, are sites of teaching and learning.

Stephenson terms her mixed media presentations "historical combines," in that they that "allow for the inclusion of objects, fragments of material culture, along with collaged work," all of which "have the potential to represent aspects of educational history" (2004, p. 170). "Like an archeological dig unearthing objects through layers of soil and debris" (2004, pp. 170-171), Stephenson concludes,

> researching involves digging through masses of material and trying to make sense out of it, to see patterns in the layers of facts and artifacts, and to project where the personal or the singular might indicate trends in a culture, including the culture of classroom, of education.... I believe visual representation of education history research, as in the painting collages described or in the historical combines discussed here, could make education history more accessible to and appealing to a larger audience (2004, p. 171).

F. Graeme Chalmers would agree, I think. Chalmers is a professor of art education whose recent research has been "historical." "Those of us who 'do' history often collect and interact with visual images" (2004, p. 173), he notes. "I don't just 'collect,' lately I have also struggled to create new visual images. These found and created images can be both documentary and interpretive" (2004, p. 173). He has come to regard such images not as merely supplemental: "In art education history images are central, crucial, to constructing a thesis" (2004, p. 173).

Chalmers recalls his early career as a painter, a career he abandoned for academic research and writing. "I've always regretted my inability to do both" (2004, p. 174), he acknowledges. "Part of the problem is," he thinks, "that art making is obsessive, compulsive, demanding, totally involving. 'Real' artists don't have time for much else. Art making takes over" (2004, p. 174). Recently he has risked being taken over by art making again, making "paintings/collages" he is not sure are "research" or "history." Like other participants in A/R/T, Chalmers wonders if "research," "art," and "activism" are "mutually exclusive terms." "Arts-based researchers would not see them as such" (2004, p. 178), he knows.

"It has been a long time since I painted on a daily basis" (2004, p. 181), he muses. "But the paintings are big, blatant, and 'in your face'" (2004, p. 181), he notes. "Couldn't this be something that I increasingly bring to my writing?" (2004, p. 181) He concludes:

> As an art educator/multiculturalist who "does" history and who wants to continue making some art, expect to see both papers and paintings, expect to see some cross-over of techniques and concepts, but don't expect them to either be or represent the same things (2004, p. 182).

Harry Pearse tells us he wants to put his money where his *praxis* is. The term, "as I absorbed it from my graduate studies with Ted Aoki and Max van Manen in the late 1970s, ... means the dynamic dialectical relationship between theory and practice" (2004, p. 184). "Like many art educators in the late 1970s and early 1980s," he recalls, "I was attracted to phenomenology.... Phenomenology was attractive because its respect for subjectivity and its encouragement of the use of poetic language made it amenable to studying art making and art teaching processes" (2004, p. 188). That attraction is discernible in his musing on Heidegger's idea of "being in" and "dwelling in" as "an essential research stance that seeks to re-establish the 'primal oneness' of our relationship as human beings with our environment" (2004, p. 185). In that "oneness" Pearse experiences the continuum that is artist (researcher) teacher. "Researcher," he explains, "is bracketed between one's artist self and one's teacher self. Both artist and teacher entities have a researcher component to them. But research can also be seen as a living practice in the space "in between art and teaching" (2004, p. 186). Recalling Rita Irwin's introductory chapter, Pearse theorizes the dialectic shifting into a "multilectic" one.

As did I, Pearse traveled from phenomenology to autobiography. "As a teacher educator," he tells us, "I could see how a life history approach could demonstrate how one's past experiences as a learner might influence the way one thinks and acts during teaching and how one might interpret the experience of teaching" (2004, p. 188). Pearse and his colleagues wrote their own and others' individual life stories as "vehicles for educational insight" (2004, p. 188). At that point they "stopped hedging and called the practice 'autobiography'" (2004, p. 188). Pearse and his colleagues "acted as artists and responded to an intuitive sense of autobiography as art" (2004, p. 188).

It was a "short step" (2004, p. 188) Pearse reports, moving from an interest in writing "life history" to writing about the history of his profession. He is now in the process of researching art education in Canada at the turn of the nineteenth century. Through a series of vignettes he is working to create a portrait of art education in Nova Scotia, Ontario and British Columbia in 1904. This work has shown him that A/R/T can begin with art, research or teaching, illustrating how "each connects with and informs the other. Each contains a component of the other" (2004, p. 195). After all, "one of the roles of research is to reexamine the taken-for-granted, to refute it, to modify it, to re-affirm it" (2004, p. 196). Pearse concludes:

> What can I say that I learned about teaching and about the impact of daily drawing on students' learning and about the influence of the teacher-artist as a model? I can say that I reject the modernist notion that teachers should not show their own work to students. I can say that teaching generates both cultural knowledge and self-knowledge for both teacher and learner (2004, p. 196).

For Pearse, art, research and teaching contain parts of each other and, in *praxis*, form an aesthetic synthesis.

Alison Pryer concludes this remarkable collection by thinking about "living with/in marginal spaces" (2004, p. 198). For Pryer, the phrase that reiterates, in different terms, the praxis of A/R/T is "intellectual nomadism" (2004, 208). "One Sunday morning a few years ago," Pryer reports, "I happened upon a large cream-colored tent itched in the middle of a white, sun-filled art gallery.... The interior of this tent was surprisingly spacious and light, its walls made of felt, and fabric, feathers, hair, fur and skin, an intriguing array of treasured objects lining the interior" (2004, p. 198). The tent turns out to have been a "*ger*," that is, a Mongolian circular communal dwelling, more commonly called a *yurt* in North America.

The metaphor of nomadism was central to the installation, and that metaphor, Pryer reports, "has stayed close to my heart" (2004, p. 200). Upon first learning about A/R/T, she was reminded of the metaphor communicated by the tent installation. How?

> The metaphor of nomadism illuminates certain recurring thematic elements contained within the personal, theoretical, and visual narratives of many of these artists/researchers/teachers, in particular: understandings of identity, belonging, space, place, boundaries, change, temporality, direction, orientation, presence and absence (2004, pp. 200-201).

In their daily work, Pryer points out, artist/researcher/teachers traverse disciplinary, professional, and cultural spaces and boundaries. In so doing, she continues, they often find themselves living with/in marginal spaces. The presence of spaces marked by invisible boundaries is indicated, Pryer postulates, by the small slashes located between each of the words: artists/researchers/teachers. Emphasizing metaphors of movement, she continues:

> These spaces and boundaries are traversable. They are the gullies and gorges that comprise the varied landscapes and the institutional terrains of academic culture, public schooling practices, and the, often hermetic, art world. Rather than concentrating on each of the separate roles of artist, researcher, and teacher, in this paper I linger in the spaces and boundaries between, and the movements with/in these lived practices (2004, p. 201).

In the slashes between A/R and /T, Pryer notes, are the hyphenated identities that comprise the lives of artist-researcher-teachers. In the slash, the hyphen, the space between one role and the others, are spaces of possibility, sites of radical openness. Pryer attributes these ideas to Ted Aoki, whose conception of curriculum and pedagogy as dwelling in "the third space" invites movement. Pryer notes:

> The political, cultural and social positioning of all these artists/researchers/teachers, their consciously chosen non-fixity of identity, and the heightened awareness and simultaneous disregard of institutional frameworks and boundaries, marks them as marginal to mainstream artistic, academic and pedagogical practice (2004, p. 203).... As intellectual liminars, artists/researchers/teachers might learn much from the ways that other luminary peoples have prospered and flourished in the midst of their marginality (2004, p. 204).

Like the nomad, the artist-researcher-teacher does not wander aimlessly, Pryer notes. "Her movements are not romantic excursions, but grueling treks, often across inhospitable terrain.... At times, the nomad may seem to behave in ways that appear contradictory, aberrant, or even mad and absurd to the outside observer" (2004, p. 205). But the nomad is not homeless, Pryer asserts. She enjoys the ability to create "home" everywhere.

While "nominally" a part of the Academy, Pryer continues, artist/researcher/teachers challenge the norms and customs of an Academy organized around more sedentary metaphors. While invited to join and participate in officialdom, "the true liminar will continue to abandon the center, choosing instead to speak from the margins, regularly shifting locations, roles and voices, continuing always to challenge the dominant culture all around them" (2004, 208). As for herself, "I purposely seek out the margins of my field – curriculum theory – and explore the many moods and meanings of intellectual border areas" (2004, p. 209). Moreover,

> I deliberately dwell in the hyphenated space between "non" and "dual," a space that is dual and non-dual, neither dual nor non-dual, a space of liminality and hence great possibility. This marginal space touches upon areas that many curriculum theorists and educators consider impure, taboo even – including, the erotics of teaching and learning, and the interrelationships between pedagogy, violence and desire. Such topics are currently "ob-scene," literally meaning off stage in the theater of education (2004, p. 209).

Like the *Yurtopia* artists Chen and Von Michalofski, Pryer and the artist-researcher-teachers (on whose work her essay perceptively comments) choose "to gather 'data' on their long journey by foot, and who then set up camp in an art gallery" (2004, p. 211).

INSIGHT, INNER STRENGTH AND PUBLIC PRACTICE

"Aesthetic experiences ... involve us as existing beings in pursuit of meanings," Maxine Greene (1988, p. 293) once pointed out. The presentations of A/R/T in this collection underscore that point in all its complexity, excitement, and promise. Foreshadowing the sophisticated poststructuralism evident in this collection, Greene (1988, p. 295) offered: "if the uniqueness of the artistic-aesthetic can be reaffirmed ... old either/ors may disappear. We may make possible a pluralism of visions, a multiplicity of realities. We may enable those we teach to rebel." For me, Greene's notion of the rebel – borrowed, perhaps, from Camus (1971 [1956]) – resonates with Pryer's notion of the nomad. Both Greene and the artist/researcher/teachers present in this volume appreciate the political/pedagogical potential of art, not only for restructuring the public sphere, but the private one as well. In fact, the two seem inextricably linked.

From the performative pieces in this collection, it is clear that A/R/T permits students and teachers creative and disjunctive distantiation from and intense engagement with their everyday functional existence. Such distantiation and engagement permit, indeed, invite aesthetic-intellectual transformations that bracket (and hyphenate) taken-for-granted, naturalized understandings of knowledge, teaching and the school. While, as Greene (1978) has observed, encounters with the arts do not in themselves guarantee what she has called "wide-awakeness," they can open spaces – "third spaces" as Ted Aoki and several of his former students in the collection point out - which stimulate reflection, creativity, and self-knowledge. A/R/T provokes questioning, wondering and wandering that brackets the everyday and the conventional as artist-researcher-teachers study and perform knowledge, teaching, and learning from multiple perspectives, enabling students to emerge from submerged realities and to see themselves, and art, as if for the first time.

The work published in this collection represents a significant advance in that sector of scholarship and research William Reynolds, Patrick Slattery, and Peter Taubman and I characterized as understanding curriculum as aesthetic text (1995, chapter 11). While informed, no doubt, by scholarship that preceded it, including that of Maxine Greene (2001), Dwayne Huebner (1999), Elliot Eisner (1979), Madeleine Grumet (1988), and especially Ted Aoki (Pinar and Irwin 2005), and by more recent work (jagodzinski 1997a, b; Barone 2000; Jackson 2002; Bagley, Cancienne, and Babst 2002; Mirochnik and Sherman 2002; Dunlop 1999; Slattery 2001, 2006), the contemporary arts-based research featured here is performative, experimental, and, in a progressive political and pedagogical sense, avant-garde. Such a significant step for the field holds, unsurprisingly, great value for the participants. On that point, Julie Lymburner summarized what seemed to be the sentiments of all:

> In an era fraught with difficulties in education and low teacher morale, my experiences as teacher-researcher have been most uplifting. This period of intense self-examination invited me to perceive my world more closely, re-search the details of my practice, develop inner strength, and eventually, expand my repertoire of skills and sphere of influence (2004, p. 79).

A/R/T points the way out of the "fraught" present, into a creative and vibrant future we can, thanks to this collection, now imagine.

TEACHING AGAINST OPPRESSION (2004)

Kevin Kumashiro began his teaching career as did many others; he wanted to "help." He joined the Peace Corps and was assigned to Nepal where he realized that the Peace Corps relied on a commonsensical definition of good teaching, a culturally-specific definition, namely one informed by how teaching was practiced in the United States. Kumashiro is critical of the Peace Corps' failure to critique its unspoken assumptions about U.S. superiority. "Good teaching" is not, he observes, a neutral concept (2004, p. xx).

His experience in the Peace Corps underscored for Kumashiro the limits of common sense. "Oppression is masked by or couched in concepts that make us think that this is the way things are supposed to be," (2004, xxiv) he observes, a point made by Michael Moriarty (1991, p. 36) in a different context: *"Coercion is camouflaged as the statement of the obvious."* "Common sense," Kumashiro concurs, "does not often tell us that the status quo is quite oppressive.... And it rarely tells us that schools need to place a priority on challenging oppression" (2004, p. xxiv). Oppression is a plural noun, he points out; it is multiple in nature. And anti-oppressive education draws upon multiple traditions, among them feminist, critical, multicultural, queer, postcolonial traditions, as well as other movements toward social justice.

Working toward social justice requires anti-oppressive teaching. No teacher education program, Kumashiro reports, requires significant coursework in critical perspectives, such as multicultural critiques of mathematics, feminist histories of the natural sciences, postcolonial perspectives on English literature, and queer re-readings of history. Moreover, no programs make central the study of anti-oppressive methods that focused on differences, equity, power and oppression. Kumashiro comments:

> It is certainly important that teacher try to know their students, know their subjects, and know how to teach, and programs should continue to ensure that teachers are learned in these ways. However, it is equally important that teachers know the limits of their knowledge. (2004, p. 7)

Kumashiro appreciates that the hegemony of academic psychology in many schools and departments of education limit the ways prospective and practicing teachers can understand themselves and their students. This point – made compellingly by Dwayne Huebner (1999 [1966]) almost forty years ago – is reiterated by Kumashiro: "Psychological models are not the only ways to know our students and different models or lenses can lead to different insights. It is problematic, then, to privilege only certain (psychological) ways of knowing students" (2004, p. 8). The reification of psychological constructs – such as "skills" – has done much to damage our capacity to think creatively about education.

The obnoxious demand for "standards" (as if teachers had not had them before) is, among other things (such as the erasure of academic, i.e. intellectual, freedom), a suppression of creativity. As Kumashiro observes, "Learning to standards in the disciplines is a practice of repetition, of repeating or perpetuating only certain ways of knowing or doing the disciplines" (2004, p. 8). In this regard, "standards" tend to obscure the dynamism of the disciplines, including their own interdisciplinary tendencies, and their profoundly historical and political character. Kumashiro does not fail to make this last point, noting that "since any perspective or practice is partial, learning to standards is a practice that reinforces the privilege of only certain perspectives and groups in society" (2004, p. 8).

When teacher education attends to "standards," then, it betrays the very disciplines the idea presumably honors. And by their bureaucratization, "standards" standardize and bureaucratize the school subjects as they impoverish, intellectually, academic education courses. Certainly they denude many university-based courses of any "critical" content. As Kumashiro reports, "Almost no [teacher education] program made central use of readings and assignments on anti-oppressive methods that focused on differences, equity, power, and oppression" (2004, p. 7). What would attention to these subjects require?

"TROUBLING KNOWLEDGE"

First and foremost, attention to these subjects would require "troubling knowledge," by which Kumashiro means "to complicate knowledge, to make knowledge problematic" (2004, p. 8). The emphasis here is on the gerund. "Troubling" means

> to work paradoxically with knowledge, to simultaneously to see what different insights, identities, practices, and changes it makes possible while critically examining that knowledge (and how it came to be known) to see what insights, etc., it closes off. (2004, pp. 8-9)

Second, by "troubling knowledge" Kumashiro means knowledge that is "disruptive, discomforting, problematizing" (2004, p. 9). Focusing on the noun, he asks for curriculum that is unfamiliar, does not coincide with commonsensical understandings, that disrupts taken-for-granted conceptions of what is. Becoming a practitioner of troubling knowledge, then, can never be about "mastery or full knowledge; the goal can never be to fill that partiality and erase the politics" (2004, p. 10). Nor can we assume that troubling knowledge is "better" body of knowledge, since, as he points out, "any body of knowledge is partial" (2004, p. 10). "Rather," he continues (and here is the core of his conception), "the goal is to examine the different uses and effects of different bodies of knowledge, and explore the anti-oppressive changes made possible from them" (2004, p. 10). This means that "learning to teach in anti-oppressive ways also needs to involve examining how 'good' teaching can be problematic" (2004, p. 13).

"An anti-oppressive teacher is not something that someone is," (2004, p. 15) Kumashiro asserts. "Rather, it is something that someone is always becoming" (2004, p. 15). Why? First, the practices of anti-oppressive teaching require constant problematization: "No practice, in and of itself, is anti-oppressive" (2004, p. 15). Second, mainstream conceptions of what it means to be a teacher do not often include anti-oppressive roles and responsibilities. The identity of "anti-oppressive" teacher is "paradoxical," Kumashiro concludes, as an "anti-oppressive teacher is always trying to change what it means to be a teacher. The teacher is always becoming anti-oppressive but never fully is" (2004, pp. 15-16). The point is not fix the identity of "teacher." That identity is always situated, in flux, ever-changing, always critical.

Teachers and students often resist such "paradoxical" understandings of their roles and responsibilities, desiring fixed, authoritative positions. Resistance and desire are, Kumashiro asserts, "central to the process of learning," (2004, p. 24) even in learning to challenge oppression. "The reason we are not doing more to challenge oppression," he suggests, "is not merely that we do not know enough about oppression, but also that we often do not *want* to know more about oppression" (2004, p. 25). As a consequence, resistance and desire ought not disdained or denied as "hindrances," and thereby suppressed or ignored or overpowered. Rather, resistance and desire should become part of what students study: "Students' desire for and resistances to learning need to become part of what they are learning" (2004, p. 24). In terms of challenging oppression," he suggests, "it would also be important to address the political, social, *emotional* reasons why oppression so often plays out invisibly and unchallenged in our lives" (2004, pp. 25-26).

There is smart discussion of "learning through crisis," (2004, 29) wherein Kumashiro notes, with the voice of experience perhaps, that "crisis can lead a student to desire change, but it can lead a student to resist change even more strongly than before" (2004, p. 29). Consequently, "when students are in a state of crisis, teachers need to structure experiences that can help students to work through it" (2004, p. 29). Moreover: "Learning through crisis not a process that can be standardized for all students" (2004, p. 29).

In order to prepare teachers for uncertainty, "maybe we need to start feeling very uncomfortable about the processes of teaching and learning" (2004, p. 30). Gender is a case in point, as he recognizes that "the intentional lessons on gender stand little chance in countering the unintentional ones" (2004, p. 33). In this sense, teaching is "impossible." Kumashiro continues:

> Yes, teaching is impossible, but only if we believe that teaching is successful when student learn exactly what we said beforehand that they were supposed to learn. Were we to define teaching as a process that not only gives students the knowledge and skills that matter in society, then we should expect that there will always be more to our teaching than what we intended (2004, p. 37).

The point, he suggests, "is to conscientiously make visible these hidden lessons and the various lenses being used by students to make sense of them" (2004, p. 37).

Kumashiro expresses his "profound discomfort at the idea that there are 'foundations' to teacher education and that through the required set of courses, all student teachers will learn these foundations," (2004, p. 40) a discomfort I have also felt, if directed toward a different end (see Pinar 2006b, p. 191, n. 26). Like other fields, Kumashiro suggests, "teacher education ... does not seem to acknowledge the partial nature of what it requires students to learn, and in doing so, often remains disconnected from the everyday lived realities of students" (2004, p. 40). To explore the possibility of connection, he asks: "What might socially engaged Buddhism tell us about teaching and learning against oppression?" (2004, p. 40). To answer, he draws upon Nhat Hanh, for whom learning is not equivalent to the acquisition of more knowledge. "Learning," Kumashiro tells us,

 is about releasing our dependence on knowledge that has, until now, framed the ways we live in this world. In other words, central to the processes of teaching and learning is addressing the imitations of how we teach and learn and what we know and are coming to know. (2004, p. 42)

Such a process is not primarily psychological nor expressed in self-reflection; it is a matter of activism.

Kumashiro asks us to think about preparing teachers for activism. To do so, he offers "a reflection on things queer" (2004, p. 43). Just as his discussion of Buddhism is no argument to teach students to be Buddhist, so too his discussion of queer activism is no argument that we should be teaching students to be sexually queer. Rather, reflecting on queer activism enables him to ask: "What would happen if we explored approaches to social justice that were premised on being uncomfortable?" (2004, p. 44) While "not the answer to our problems," Kumashiro suggests, "queer activism can suggest ways of thinking that go beyond common sense" (2004, p. 44). It requires us to ask: "What is problematic with the norm?" (2004, p. 45). He concludes: "Like queer activism, queer teaching always works *through* crisis" (2004, p. 47).

To illustrate how such teaching might work in the current curriculum, Kumashiro focuses on one topic within several of the school subjects. He has no intention of presenting "*the* anti-oppressive way to think about and teach these discipline," or how "to revise the entire curriculum within a discipline" (2004, p. 49). "Rarely," he confides, "have these reflections on my lessons left me content with my teaching" (2004, p. 59).

While endorsing curriculum change in literature courses – "more and more educators are recognizing that teaching and learning English literature in ways that challenge oppression requires changing what we read" (2004, p. 61) – he does not assume that reading multicultural literature is unproblematic: "Some writings can merely repeat stereotypes or create new ones by glossing over complexities, contradictions, and diversity, thereby suggesting that an entire culture or a group is *like this*" (2004, p. 61).

Moreover, exploring issues of identification and dis-identification with characters in multicultural literature does not necessarily change how students think about themselves. He notes that the "classics" are not necessarily oppressive. Much would seem to depend on how they are taught, and Kumashiro asks that teachers critique their own "lenses" for reading and teaching texts, requiring of them, he suggests, "a level of vulnerability that we do not often expect in the classroom" (2004, p. 68). "[P]erhaps," he offers, "this modeling of self-critique can be exactly what helps students to look beyond the lesson" (2004, p. 68). He continues:

In fact, sometimes when teachers raise questions about their own cultural assumptions, they can model the kind of self-critique and vulnerability that they invite their students to experience. Teachers could show that even teachers have work to do when challenging the norms that govern our lives. (2004, pp. 85-86)

Kumashiro began this book critiquing the Peace Corps' cultural imperialism, a critique he was able to make, in part, due his experiences growing up in Hawai'i. He points out that "Christian missionaries worked to help 'them' be more like 'us,' and in this case, to educate Hawaiians in the ways that 'Americans' are educated and to get Hawaiians to worship in the ways that Protestant Americans worship" (2004, pp. 72-73). He reports that it was not until "well beyond my elementary school years that I noticed that the lyrics of my favorite Hawaiian song centered on a Christian theme" (2004, pp. 72-73). To help students to "look beyond" the lesson and learn in "anti-oppressive ways," teachers might, for instance, point out that Hawai'i is not only a tropical paradise, but a site "of domination and racism against which people have long struggled and continue to struggle" (2004, p. 73).

Such a lesson provides little comfort for the teacher working against oppression, as there is the danger, Kumashiro points out, that "teaching about differences can further objectify the Other" (2004, p. 83). He seems to suggest that this danger is moderated when lessons focus on both "self and other." "Fortunately," he writes, "lessons about other cultures do not have to teach only about the Other. It can also teach about ourselves" (2004, p. 84). In the chapter on teaching "foreign" languages in anti-oppressive ways, he notes that our aspiration involves "changing our ideas about and relationships with others. But it also involves changing our ideas and feelings about ourselves" (2004, p. 85).

Contesting the academic vocationalism currently structuring curricula in the natural sciences, Kumashiro advocates becoming literate and savvy regarding the social, political, and cultural consequences of those fields. In sync with the work of poststructuralist theoreticians such as Michel Serres and Bruno Latour, Kumashiro suggests that it is important that students learn that "we are using different stories to understand the world, that different stories have different political implications, and that the stories currently framing the natural science do indeed have oppressive implications for U.S. society" (2004, p. 88).

To illustrate, Kumashiro focuses on gender, specifically on the ideology of "opposite sexes." "Of course, this binary, hierarchical story is not the only way to understand gender," he notes, and "throughout history, other cultures in this world have indeed understood gender in different ways" (2004, p. 91). But in the contemporary science curriculum, this ideology often passes for science. Acknowledging that there is a continuum of possible genders, that "gender" can be ambiguous conception (he cites intersexed births), makes less likely naïve assertions of gender and sexuality. Acknowledging that there are more than two genders, he continues, "makes it difficult to assert that we are supposed to be sexually attracted only to members of the 'opposite gender'" (2004, p. 90).

Not only science is presented as apolitical and beyond culture in the current school curriculum. Kumashiro reminds: "Math is often treated as a neutral tool that, once mastered, can be used to objectively understand our world" (2004, p. 101). The educational point is that "students need to be examining the underlying stories of the curriculum and the ways that the stories can both reinforce and challenge oppression" (2004, p. 92). This "never-ending and ever-contradictory nature of anti-oppressive education," (2004, p. 105) Kumashiro allows, can seem discouraging. Anti-oppressive education faces many barriers, "both practical and political" (2004, p. 105).

To illustrate the "practical," Kumashiro focuses on classroom management. For many teachers, "good classroom management precede[s] real teaching" (2004, p. 106). Kumashiro reminds that anti-oppressive education does not occur "only when all the complexities are known, when all the contradictions are prevented, and when all the weaknesses are addressed" (2004, p. 106). Anti-oppressive education, it is clear, occurs as we articulate complexities, work the contradictions, and acknowledge weaknesses. "As educators look to the future," (2004, p. 107) Kumashiro, with a hopefulness I think few feel but which all will welcome,

> I urge engaging in anti-oppressive education in this step-by-step, lesson-by-lesson manner. Such a process may seem tedious. But to me, such a process is what helps to make teaching exciting, and challenging, and liberating. Such a process is what gives me hope that anti-oppressive education is possible in my own classroom. (2004, p. 107)

While the academic – intellectual – freedom educators enjoy in their own classrooms contracts in standardized examination-driven curricula, that freedom can only be claimed but those who can work the complexities, the contradictions and weaknesses of those ever-changing spaces of the classroom. "Plain talk" to teachers is more urgent than ever, and I thank Kevin Kumashiro for contributing significantly to such conversation.

There has been an ongoing debate over whether or not such "plain talk" is possible. Some have argued that "theory" is necessarily removed from the conditions of the classroom; others have insisted that such remove is "elitist" and that those of us located in the academy must abandon theory in order to address questions of practice. It seems to me that Kumashiro has settled this debate. His book is a sophisticated, nuanced work of "theory" that clearly and accessibly addresses the practical problems of the classroom teacher.

The conditions of public education today are oppressive. The hour is late and the sense of emergency acute. Amidst the maelstrom of the present, the calm, clear, and unwavering voice of Kevin Kumashiro is very much needed. It is incumbent upon us teacher educators to offer this voice to our students. Kumashiro appreciates that we are key; he says so simply, humbly, but with confidence:

> I hope many educators will find these ideas useful as we prepare more teachers for anti-oppressive education. And I look forward to the changes in our schools and society that result. (2004, p. 107)

So do I.

CURRICULUM

A River Runs Through It (2003)

William Reynolds began writing about curriculum in 1981. As he points out, his essays derive from seven years as a classroom teacher, and some twenty years as a professor-intellectual very much concerned "for the future of the curriculum and the world our children will inhabit" (2003, p. xxii). In 1981, such concern was understandably focused on the tidal "wave of coercion" (Noddings, 1999, p. x) that accompanied the political earthquake that was the election of Ronald Reagan. Bill's first essay, published in 1982 and entitled "Freedom from Control," employs the then new notion of resistance (see Pinar, Reynolds, Slattery, Taubman 1995, p. 252 ff.) to fashion professional practice in an age when "teachers ... are literally forced to teach what they are told" (2003, p. 12), a state of subjugation that has only worsened in the twenty years since Bill first wrote about it. "Alternative education should be conceived in the mind of the individual teacher" (2003, p. 12), and to help teachers so conceive, he taught the theoretical scholarship in the reconceived field of curriculum.

Teaching at that time at a campus of the University of Wisconsin known for its technological education, Bill reports on his experience in "Critical Pedagogy within the Walls of a Technological Institution." His students find the texts he assigns difficult; he understands he must work with this "difficulty," in fact he must make it "the basis for the dialogue" (2003, p. 15). To speak together, the students and he must cultivate "a common language" (2003, p. 15), that is, speak with each other about the texts in "the language in which students perceive and discuss their everyday lives" (2003, p. 15). Reynolds' progressive pedagogy helped form "a community of readers" (2003, p. 15).

Bill worked similarly with public-school teachers in Sugar Creek, a small and rural town in northwestern Wisconsin. Teachers there had been "asked" to compose a mission statement, and Reynolds was determined that the process be educational, not just another meaningless bureaucratic procedure. He notes that "the term 'mission,' replete with all of its religious connotations, is defined in one sense as giving a person a mission to perform" (2003, p. 21), probably a different emphasis in definition than the bureaucrats intended. Indeed, Reynolds asks Sugarcreek teachers questions inspired by James B. Macdonald (1995): "What is the good person? What is a just society? How to relate to others? And how to best live together?" (2003, p. 22). Bill helps the teachers to focus on 1) developing new liberating and democratic perspectives, 2) clarifying values, 3) stimulating and developing educational thought, and 4) communicating significant ideas and values in these statements (2003, p. 22).

This is not work teachers can do in isolation; Reynolds appreciates that "the community should participate in major decisions such as a school mission statement" (2003, p. 22), recalling the heyday of progressive education in the United States, a time brought to an authoritarian end by right-wing politicians during the 1950s (see, for instance, Butche, 2000, for the right-wing dismantling of the progressive Ohio State University School). In the chapter that follows, Reynolds reminds us of the importance of historical scholarship in contemporary curriculum studies.

In part due to the ahistorical character of many teacher preparation programs, few teachers today know about the great progressive experiments of the 1930s, submerged, as many are, in the bureaucratic present. With understatement Reynolds notes that: "It is within this non-participatory tradition that I and others have been working on a school improvement plan which included the construction of a mission statement" (2003, p. 24). He starts by asking teachers to read and discuss curriculum theory, anticipating the work that William Schubert would later perform with Chicago teachers and administrators (see Thomas and Schubert 1997, pp. 281-282). Performing this contemplative and reflective labor, teachers at Sugar Creek took on the project of writing a mission statement "with utmost seriousness and power" (p. 30). Moreover, Reynolds reports, teachers "became strong advocates of the positions described in the mission statement" (2003, p. 30). From this heartening experience it is clear to Bill that "in this time of increasing standardization," we in the university must worker harder "to develop in schools and communities participatory democracies" (2003, p. 30). He closes by reminding us, quoting Dewey, that "democracy is more than a form of government; it is primarily a mode of associated living, of conjointed communicated experience" (2003, 30).

Bill's sense of humor – mixed as it is with serious critique - becomes visible when he discusses "an educational wolf in sheep's clothing," (2003, p. 37) i.e. Outcomes Based Education. He links it with William Bagley's 1905 and Franklin Bobbitt's 1918 curriculum formulations: "[t]he words have been changed (ah, the sheep's clothing) … but social efficiency remains alive in American public education" (p. 38). Like the overhead projector, transformational grammar, and "other such bandwagons" (2003, p. 40), Reynolds continues, Outcomes Based Education too "eventually will disappear in a cloud of dust. I worry, though, that the dust will remain for a time" (2003, p. 40). Those of us working in the university "should be like the guard dog, [and] let out a loud, ornery bark of warning" (2003, p. 40), warning teachers of the approaching wolf in sheep's clothing.

In "The Curriculum of Curiosity or a Curriculum of Compassion," Bill laments that programs designed to increase teacher "effectiveness" such as Outcomes Based Education and the infamous Madeline Hunter Model remain the basis of school operations and goals. "These present day notions of curriculum," he observes, recalling the opening essay of this collection, "have never flowed away from the control theory that James Macdonald elaborated in 1975, and have been the controlling paradigm in education from the turn of the twentieth century" (2003, p. 43). Invoking Macdonald's (1995) notion of "technological rationality," Reynolds situates it within the present historical moment, dominated, as it is, by obsessing over the "global economy." Despite these rhetorical shifts, Bill notes, "students ... leave school will full heads and empty hearts" (2003, p. 43).

Bill's heart is, in contrast, full: that is clear in his elaboration of a curriculum of compassion, a curriculum, he writes, that would allow "the passion for knowledge" (2003, 44) – in contrast to "the prescribed paths of a compassionless and disabling school system with its preordained curriculum" (2003, p. 44) – and allow us "to support our children, believe in our children, endure for the sake of the children, and hope for the children" (2003, p. 44). There can be no such hope, he notes, in predominant modernist curriculum designs, "for children will live in a different world than you and I may have experienced. The world our children will face and be responsible for, will be, in so many ways, different than what we have known" (2003, p. 45).

Employing a Heideggeran conception of curiosity – "[i]t seeks restlessness ... [and] is concerned with the constant possibilities of distraction" (2003, p. 46) – Reynolds appreciates that the contemporary school curriculum "is silent on issues of the heart.... Schools see the excitement of continual curriculum novelty" (2003, p. 46). He continues: "In the curriculum of curiosity, we are about what other people think" (2003, p. 47). Recalling the conditions Jonathan Kozol exposed, Bill entreats us: "We must take compassionate responsibility" (2003, p. 50).

Bill acknowledges that, as educators, we are lost, "but [that] being lost is not a bad place to be," (2003, p. 54) a point Alan Block (1998a) has made as well. The phenomenological theme evident in the previous chapter is here asserted in relational terms, as he emphasizes "our interconnectedness to each other and our planet" (2003, p. 55). [Recall that Bill has worked phenomenologically for over a decade; see, for instance, Reynolds (1989) and Pinar and Reynolds (1992). Indeed, at one point in this collection Bill quips: "I am a recovering phenomenologist."]

In the realization of our interconnectedness with each other and the planet, Bill suggests, "there is hope." There is hope because "interconnectedness and compassion are linked. And interconnectedness demonstrates the interdependence of compassion, spirituality, science, [and] hermeneutics" (2003, p. 55). In this notion of "connected knowing" we hear echoes of Dwayne Huebner (1999) and Florence Krall (1994). "Spirituality is a manner of dwelling in the flux" (2003, p. 58), Bill suggests, pointing out that "this notion of a spirit-filled, life-centered education ... is another way of discussing education as a critical, compassionate, passionate conversation" (2003, p. 60).

In "Curriculum Theory in the Age of Dole and Clinton," Reynolds laments the degradation of political debate, and specifically the simplistic state of the candidates' understanding of education. "On the table were the books that I had been reading. They are such good books, these curriculum theory texts. What prevents these candidates from knowing about these ideas? Why do they keep discussing education in terms of schools of choice, literacy, standards, national testing?" (2003, p. 62) To answer his question he ponders (not for first time – see his chapter 2) issues of language and the role of the intellectual. To frame the former, he quotes Camus: "[I]'d come to realize that all our troubles spring from our failure to use plain, clear cut language. So I resolved always to speak – and to act – quite clearly as this was the only way of setting myself on the right track" (2003, p. 62). To frame the latter, he quotes Christopher Lasch's (1995, 178) *The Revolt of the Elites and the Betrayal of Democracy*: "Left-wing academics cannot be bothered to argue with opponents or to enter into their point of view.... They defend their incomprehensible jargon as the language of 'subversion,' plain speech having been dismissed as an instrument of oppression" (2003, p. 63). He is reminded of Tom Barone's (2000) suggestion that we turn "away from a posture of scholarly detachment toward one of passionate commitment to the redistribution of social resources; away from texts aimed exclusively at our academic colleagues toward direct communications with additional constituencies" (2003, p. 63).

"Passionate commitment" and "communication with larger constituencies rather than disembodied scholarship and detachment" preoccupy Bill in this essay. He wonders if "the commitment to social change is but a dream and a lost cause?" (2003, p. 63). If so, it is, I think, not only a function of the complexity of scholarly language and because academicians have "given up" (in Lasch's view) the attempt to communicate with the "public." It is because the "public" – as a civic space in which debate matters – has disappeared. In its place is the shopping mall in which our public identities are not "citizens" but "consumers." This aspect of our dilemma Bill seems to suggest when he asks: "Is passionate engagement with the daily lived experience of those involved with education (parents, teachers, children) still possible?" (2003, p. 63). Given this conundrum, he is left focused, most appropriately in my view, on his own practice with students: "I guess I remember that work to change begins with working from within. I do not wish to prescribe any new directions for the field as a whole, but only to elaborate on the individual struggle to understand one academics' place in the broader social context.... I am focusing on two questions. Whose interest does my scholarship serve? And what am I going to do about it?" (2003, pp. 63-64)

Such questions function to keep him "wide-awake" (after Maxine Greene), still pondering the possibility of writing Barone-style articles for general magazines, magazines that "teachers, parents, administrators, legislators discuss on their coffee break or at lunch in local hangouts" (2003, p. 67). It is, I think, a good fantasy, one worth performing, but Bill is clear we do not live in a time when "citizens" tend to spend coffee breaks "improving" themselves. That Bill knows what time it is becomes evident when he quotes Sophie Scholl, the young woman, who along with her brother Hans and his friends formed the White Rose, a resistance group to the Nazis: "We have to do something. There is an enormous stone wall of impossibility, and our job is to discover the minute possibilities that we can chip or blast out the wall" (2003, p. 71). "As curriculum theorists," Bill comments, "let us be about chipping away" (2003, p. 71).

This stark assessment of the present historical moment continues in the chapter that follows, "The Perpetual Pedagogy of Surveillance." Here Reynolds appreciates that the present discourse on "standards" amounts to another form of control. The situation of teachers today reminds him of Deborah Britzman's discussion of the AIDS campaign, a campaign that declared "No One Is Safe." Reynolds suggests a parallel with the standards and ethics-hotline movement, the latter "yet another instance of surveillance" (2003, p. 81) where no one is safe. The "ethics hotline" called PhoneMaster – with an internet address – invites parents and students to report anonymously the activities of their children and fellow students. What is there to do? "Understood poststructurally," Bill writes, referring to *Understanding Curriculum*, the text he wrote with Patrick Slattery, Peter Taubman and me (1995, p. 84), "political struggle is discursive; it involves destabilizing patterns of thought, which cannot, finally, be separated dualistically from physical behavior or action." "Let us avoid being terrorists or nihilists," he continues, sounding like Jacques Daignault (1992). "We do not need to continue creating an indecent curriculum machine or a terroristic fascist surveillance monster.... The middle spaces are the hope for multiplicity in the phantasmagoric postmodern" (2003, p. 84).

Bill demonstrates this poststructuralist position in the final chapter, "Uncommon Ground: A Continual Conversation." Despite the eruptions of terrorism within the academic field of curriculum studies, despite the temptations to rejoin in kind, Bill counsels a "middle space," reminding his listeners that "[N]o one voice can capture the richness [of the field]" (2003, p. 86). Instead of counter-decreeing "what is," he suggests four points for discussion: "First, that complexity and diversity of thought is a strength of the curriculum field. Second, that we stop bickering. Third, that we focus on working from within. Fourth, that we concern ourselves with children" (2003, p. 86). He emphasizes that "it is complexity and abundance that is the health and richness of the field. I do not believe that the field needs more order or that diversity is a problem. The proliferation is what should be encouraged, not uniformity or conformity. The conversations that ensue from this complexity are evidence of the intricacy, richness and health of the field" (2003, p. 86). Yes.

The subtitle of this collection suggested to me images of inspiration, movement, continuity, integration. While composing this foreword, I emailed Bill about the image, asking him if our views of the image coincided. He replied:

On the simple level it does speak, as MacLean's novel demonstrates, to the notion of integration and wholeness, and that is certainly part of the concept I am using, as you can see from a couple of the essays, particularly the "Compassion" essay and the "Rough Edges" piece. Also the idea that thread(s) or theme(s) run through my work is another way I was looking at it. But, as I have been reading Deleuze and others, the notion of lines of flight has intrigued me, and lines of flight and rivers seem to merge.

Lines of flight or rivers open up the possibility to confront the fascism of our time. It seems like I had been dealing with this for a long time and this notion of lines of flight caught my attention, and though I would use different words, rivers instead of lines; the point would be consistent, as Deleuze says this about lines of flight: "We set against this fascism of power, active, positive lines of flight, because these lines (rivers) open up desire, desire's machines, and the organization, of a social field of desire: it is not a matter of escaping 'personally' from oneself, but of allowing something to escape, like bursting a pipe. Opening up flows beneath the social codes that seek to channel and block them" (Deleuze 1995, p. 18).

And, these lines of flight or rivers that run through the work are really "us" engaging in being philosophers. Deleuze says you become one "by engaging in a very special form of creation in the realm of concepts" (Deleuze 1995, p. 26). As control societies take over from Foucault's notion of disciplinary societies: "It is not a question of worrying or hoping for the best, but of finding new weapons." So, these rivers one looks for and travels down are lines of flight, creation in the realm of concepts, the search "for new weapons" (although I don't like the weapon metaphor) to deal with the "tracking down of all varieties of fascism, from the enormous ones that surround and crush us to the petty ones constitute the tyrannical bitterness of our everyday lives" (Foucault in Deleuze and Guattari 1989, p. xiv). This suggests the notion of performative acts, although I don't think the only answer is dressing in drag (Butler), but it is this notion of lines of flight, but if one river is blocked or line of flight halted one seeks another and so on. One is constantly creating notions, concepts. So the river runs through it is two-fold: a) wholeness integration from which I am moving down the river b) to the notion of the lines of flight. (Reynolds 2000)

Indeed, we can, in this collection, discern a set of integrated themes with which many have struggled, few more honestly than has Bill: there is the pain and indignation over the schools and their imprisonment in politicians' rhetoric, in business thinking, in seemingly ever-intensifying forms of control; there is the struggle to teach students – prospective and practicing teachers – about the history and politics of their situation; there is the movement, at once phenomenological and political, to articulate a conception of curriculum beyond present institutional constraints, a curriculum of compassion, and the search for pathways to an "uncommon ground," a ground of integrity, inclusion, and caring.

These "lines of flight" take him through critical theory, autobiography, phenomenology, and post-structuralism, and in this intellectual journey Bill personifies the pedagogical labor of many of us over these past twenty years; indeed, he exemplifies the best of professional practice in his engagement, his honesty, his erudition. He has faced the primary issues of our time and he has reported faithfully his efforts to grapple with them. Who among us can claim more than this? At one point in these essays Bill ruminates that "I need to make a statement, a lasting contribution to the curriculum field" (2003, p. 54). You have done that, Bill, as this collection testifies.

For those of us who have also been struggling with these issues – among them control, resistance, compassion – there is always the danger of discouragement, a danger heightened by the difficulty of our circumstances, both in the schools and within the field, with its balkanization and in-fighting. Almost twenty years ago I pondered this danger in a short piece entitled "Death in a Tenured Position" (in

Pinar 1994). With that danger in mind, I am struck in these essays by the dogged determination of William Reynolds, his refusal to succumb to discouragement and to what (in the above quoted passage) Foucault (1989) termed "the tyrannical bitterness of our everyday lives," the "fascism of our times," both in the schools and in the academic field of curriculum studies. I admire you, Bill, for that, for your stubborn insistence on looking for "lines of flight," for creative, affirmative intellectual forms that support flowing and movement, not arrest and death.

In the introduction to this collection Bill remembers walking for the first time into my office at the University of Rochester: "The face of Virginia Woolf looked down on me from the wall.... That was the start.... So, the words write me as I write the words. And, the river flows" (pp. xxi-xxii). I am struck by your associations of your "river," your "flight," with the photograph of Virginia Woolf in my office over twenty years ago. I have that photograph still; it hangs at home now. It was taken not long before she succumbed to the voices, hallucinatory voices yes, but also the voices of fascism that threatened her husband, a Jew, herself, an avant-garde artist, that threatened everyone she loved and cared for.

It was, we are told, a "bright, clear, cold day" in England the morning of Friday, March 28, 1941. As usual, Virginia Woolf went to her studio room in the garden. There she wrote two letters, one to her husband Leonard, the other for her sister Vanessa. In each she explained that she was hearing voices again, that this time she would not recover. Returning to the house, she wrote a second letter to Leonard, putting it on the sitting-room mantel-piece (Bell 1972). Then, we are told, about 11:30 a.m., she

> slipped out, taking her walking-stick with her and making her way across the water-meadows to the river.... Leaving her stick on the bank she forced a large stone into the pocket of her coat. Then she went to her death, "the one experience," as she had said to Vita [Sackville-West], "I shall never describe." (quoted in Bell 1972, p. 226)

It was the River Ouse that welcomed Virginia Woolf that day, that provided her a "line of flight" from this world. I have that photograph in front of me now as I write. Her head is slightly bowed in weariness it would seem, but she holds herself upright, her cigarette holder in the fingers of one hand, her book open in the other, her eyes staring forward, gazing, perhaps at her approaching death. Perhaps she was thinking of those she loved, her mother Julia, whom she portrayed as Mrs. Ramsay in *To the Lighthouse*. Perhaps she was remembering the dinner-party scene in that novel. I am. I am remembering when she writes: "Some change went through them all, as if this had really happened, and they were all conscious of making a party together in a hollow, on an island; had their common cause against that fluidity out there" (Woolf 1955 [1927], p. 147).

We who work in the field of curriculum studies have also made a common cause, although we often refuse to acknowledge that, so often so that Bill must use the phrase "uncommon ground" to refer to community, to the party we have made together, our conversation sometimes inspiring and enlivening, at other times only angry and distressed, but often animated by the progressive dream of curriculum as conversation, as "lines of flight." As those of us who have lived through the past twenty years face our final phase, may we, like William Reynolds, continue to listen to those voices outside and within us. Before we slip into the river that allows us to take final flight, let us continue to make honest and vigorous conversation through the last course, the curriculum of our time. As Bill would say, a river runs through it.

CHAPTER 7

THE TIME OF SELF-DIFFERENCE AND SELF-RESISTANCE (2003)

"The time of *Nachtraglichkeit*, then, is the time of self-difference and self-resistance."

Alice J. Pitt (2003, p. 101)

"What do we use the personal to do?" Alice Pitt (2003, p. 87) asks. One use is narrative, she answers; we employ stories that are our own in order "to make good our lives" (2003, p. 87). Stories enable us to make sense of ourselves, so that our lives become meaningful. In doing so, we are performing more than a literary operation. "We might," Pitt (2003, p. 68) suggests, "understand our interpretative narratives as psychic events." They are about "the world," but, as we learn in this profoundly provocative book, they are about ourselves as well.

A second use of the personal occurs, Pitt points out, when we – teachers and students – face demands that we include the details of our private lives as curriculum content. While personal stories can help us to forge relationships with others, Pitt allows, the *demand* that we "share" can sometimes "feel creepy." Why? If Winnicott's postulation of a "secret self" has merit (as Pitt implies it does), it can be ontologically awkward to be faced with a pedagogical demand to disclose ourselves. Such a demand can feel like a violation. Given the hide-and-seek character of communication, we cannot be surprised, as Pitt so nicely puts it, that "ambivalence marks the use of the personal itself" (2003, p. 88).

THE SECRET SELF

Near the end of his life, Pitt tells us, D. W. Winnicott explored "the right not to communicate" (2003, p. 83), a right tantamount to "a protest from the core of me to the frightening fantasy of being infinitely exploited" (2003, p. 83). Winnicott associated this "frightening fantasy" with dependence in two orders of relationships: mother/child and analyst/analysand. We might add a third: teacher/student.

Not unlike the phenomenologist Langeveld's (1983a, 1983b) notion of the "secret place," Winnicott postulated, at the individual's very core, the existence of a separate and secret self. The existence of such a "self," Pitt suggests, "opens the underside of object-relations theory" (2003, p. 83). While acknowledging the social and specifically collaborative character of self-formation, the "secret" self signals

79

"a protest" to the pleasures of communication. Our profound need to communicate and our need to use the communications of others to constitute individuality is mediated by an equally pressing need to defend against intrusion into the sphere of our most inner and secret selves. Consequently, Pitt concludes, "communication itself is experienced as an urgent game of hide and seek" (2003, p. 83). Moreover, she continues,

> The idea that communication with the secret self is experienced as profoundly exploitative poses new challenges to psychoanalysts for whom the analysand's refusal of analytic interpretations continues to be construed primarily as resistance to be worked through. It is also a challenge to educators who value the personal as the grounds of teaching and learning. (2003, p. 83)

Winnicott's metaphoric use of the popular children's pastime of "hide-and-seek" underscores, Pitt suggests, the ambivalent labor of communication, including its corresponding states of illusion and disillusionment. "Our capacity to think begins without tolerance of disillusionment," Pitt (2003, p. 91) asserts. The three moments of the personal that so preoccupied Winnicott – illusionment, disillusion, and re-illusionment – caution, Pitt counsels, against demanding too much of the personal.

Pitt is surely right we she asserts that "the personal is something a great deal more complicated than either the developers of the French lesson or some educational researchers might be willing to admit" (2003, p. 88). She elaborates:

> The personal is not merely a set of attributes that can be pointed or named, nor is it a bank of experiences to be drawn upon unproblematically to render the world visible. Rather, the personal is constituted within a web of relations that includes relations of time (how the past works on the present) and relations with others, knowledge and authority. The hide and seek of the personal is played out on this terrain, but its movements may exceed the force of the ideological and the institutional. (2003, p. 89)

Does such "excess" constitute transitional space, and, concomitantly, the sphere of the personal? Or, as Pitt asks, "How does the personal become, well, personal?" (2003, 89). To answer, she turns to Winnicott's exposition of cultural experience as a transitional space. Such a conception suggests that the personal is located not in content that reflects the world. Rather, Pitt offers, the personal is "a method for observing how we experience ourselves in the world" (2003, p. 89).

"AN INTERMINABLE UNDULATING FORCE" (2003, p. 96)

If a method, the play of the personal would appear to be temporal in its structure. After Freud, Pitt points out that traumatic events can only be approached by means of deferred revision, what he termed *Nachtraglichkeit*. It is "the interminable undulating force of *Nachtraglichkeit*" (2003, p. 96) that intrigues Pitt, its movement in psychoanalytic life-history making, movement enabling us to notice "how we find and lose sight of our capacity to apprehend what matters most to us:

the surprise of intersection between our movements onward and our detours back" (2003, p. 96).

The notion of "detour" implies that we cannot proceed straight on. Rather, we are forced (lured?) to leave our path, required us to work on ourselves indirectly, and in the time apparently lost – *Nachtraglichkeit* – we revise our direction, relocate our path, reassemble our selves. Does "detour" in fact name our path, specifically its divergence from the official route, in excess of the ideological and the institutional? Is this transitional space between interiority (as Winnicott's secret self) and exteriority (as the public sphere), a gap that, for Pitt, is the site of pedagogy? If the curriculum is comprised of cultural representations, to teach we must dwell in the gap between the institutional and the ideological, the space in excess of them. Perhaps, then, in the transitional spaces – the gaps – between interiority and exteriority we can discern "the play of the personal."

In my intellectual life history, the "personal" became compelling before my engagement with feminist theory and gender studies, before the phase of "coming out" during which time "the play of the personal" became, for me, revolutionary. For many women, the two events occurred simultaneously (see Pinar et al. 1995, chapter 10, section III). As Pitt notes, Jane Gallup attributes the scholarly interest in the personal to feminism. Insofar as the private spaces and public sites of gender have been traumatizing, gender has animated both men's and women's efforts to occupy and articulate "the personal," that (pedagogical) gap between interiority and exteriority.

After Shoshana Felman, Pitt asks what it means to read and write autobiographically from traumatic sites of subjectivity, and, specifically, from the trauma of being a woman living in a patriarchal culture. She quotes Felman's dramatic assertion that "that *none of us, as woman, has as yet, precisely, an autobiography*," (2003, p. 97) noting how counterintuitive the claim seems, given the power of women's autobiographies, the extensive feminist scholarship on autobiography, not to mention "the tremendous pleasure many of us experience when we read women's autobiographies" (2003, p. 97).

Pitt finds Felman's approach to women's autobiography resonant with Sarah Kofman's observation that philosophical and theoretical studies have often functioned as detours that point the way to women's autobiography. Felman argued that women's autobiography "must pass through the detours of literature and theory," and, "moreover, [that] literature and theory must pass through the detours of autobiography" (2003, p. 97). But Felman's essays are not autobiographical in any traditional sense, Pitt notes; they do not narrate a life history. Rather, they narrate the autobiography of a reading practice, a distinctive reading practice characterized by "the reconstitutive tracing of self-implication," (2003, p. 97) a tracing reminiscent, in Deborah Britzman's (1995) memorable phrase, of not reading straight. Such a reading practice, such tracing, Pitt suggests, discloses "the force, the significance, and the surprise of *Nachtraglichkeit*" (2003, p. 97).

"[I]t becomes clear that we cannot think of the 'personal' as something we possess," (2003, p. 117) Pitt points out. "Rather," she continues, "the personal emerges as a dynamic that is made in performance and remade within the work of interpretation" (2003, p. 117). Sometimes such "performance" represents "resistance." To illustrate (calling on Keyssar and Gallup), Pitt notes that a male student who refuses to behave properly might well perceive the role of student as gendered, as feminized. For such a student, to "behave" requires a transgendering performance. There is nothing wrong with that.

For Chodorow, "individuation is itself gendered male" (2003, p. 117). In this view, the mother/daughter symbiosis is judged as pre-social and then restructured by the masculinist world of the social. If the pre-oedipal phase is feminized, what is the gender of the "secret self" that Winnicott imagines? What is the gender and sexuality of the communicational play of "hide-and-seek"? Is it heterosexual? Is autobiographical confession by definition a feminized activity, positioning one as the feminized patient, animated by one's suffering to seek recognition from the (male) Master? Or, given the apparent impossibility of this communicational aspiration, does the therapeutic encounter provide an opportunity for hiding as well as seeking, for protecting the "secret self" safe in (mis)recognition? Is the feminized patient triumphant in the dissolution of the Master's position that his failure to alleviate feminized suffering precipitates?

If autobiographical confession is a feminized and feminizing project, is that why when many "men" practiced autobiography, they were compelled to deny their libidinal relational currents of dependency by fabricating an "individuated" identity separate from and independent of others? Is this the genesis, then, of the fantasy of the "self-made man," that compensatory model of nineteenth century (white) manhood that lingers still today? Do such split-off (and self-divided) male egos guarantee the multiplication of "others," repudiated contents of the white male mind politically subjugated in concrete lives of disavowed alterity?

IDEALIZATION AND ALTERITY

After Kaja Silverman, Pitt asks us "to imagine a subject whose capacity to idealize can combine with a specificity of culture to work against the logic of incorporation and, at the same time, toward the idealization of socially repudiated bodies" (2003, p. 75). Pitt points out that "idealization, if it is to become a tool for political cinema, must take the form of enhancing, not self-love, but rather loving relations with others" (2003, p. 78).

Combining Lacan's notion of "self" as structured from within and the Wallon-Silverman view that it is structured "at-a-distance" allows us, Pitt notes, to understand now the ego recognizes another subject as separate from itself. This potential of intersubjective recognition, she continues, is crucial, for it allows Silverman to imagine "a politically productive relation to bodily otherness," built upon processes of identification that are "exteriorizing rather than interiorizing" (2003, p. 76). Pitt points out:

This other subject, apprehended as both near and at-a-distance, can be idealized as "good" or "beautiful" even if it does not possess the features that would make it a good candidate for affirming and elaborating the ideal ego. Moreover, when the logic of identification proceeds along a trajectory of exteriorization, the image that is reflected back to the viewer is not assimilated to the self and thus retains the features of its own corporal singularity. (2003, pp. 76-77)

This is what late nineteenth-century southern white men were unable – and unwilling – to do, and so they misrecognized black men as the sexual predators they themselves were (Pinar 2001).

Processes of exteriorized identification cannot proceed apart from interior psychic contents and processes; Pitt observes that Silverman does not overlook the dangers of idealizing forms of love that exalt the object. In my example, nineteenth-century southern white men exalted southern white women; their positioning of white women on pedestals of the "saintly mother" and the "gracious wife" left them imprisoned within domestic cells fashioned by white men's imagination, enforced by white men's laws.

Pitt points to Silverman's description of the ways in which ideal images play a role in facilitating relations to all love objects, as these "create a space for theorizing love as a gift that can be bestowed on identities who are idealized from afar and, hence, in relations that locate the desires of wanting to be or wanting to have the other within a broader range of social markers of idealization and de-idealization" (2003, 77). Those nineteenth-century "ladies" who became "women" – for instance, suffragists – were indeed de-idealized, scorned by men who were unable to perceive women apart from their "place" in men's self-split imagination.

"If identity is to be conferred at-a-distance," Pitt writes, "students need opportunities to engage with materials that call attention to – even as they disrupt – identificatory practices that are aligned with normative practices" (2003, p. 80). After Silverman (and Maxine Greene, I might add), Pitt suggests that imaginative works may prove to be more influential than we assume "in creating the conditions for learning about social hatreds and discriminations" (2003, p. 80). Art, she seems to be suggesting, works at the level of fantasy, and thereby encourages the elaboration and expansion of the ego's libidinal attachments. Indeed, the political potential of art may reside more in its structures of fantasy than in its verisimilitude with "the truth."

It may be, Pitt theorizes, that we require the aesthetic experience of the world-not-yet (a beautiful, futural world wherein social difference animates rather than disturbs human intersubjectivity), before we can conduct ourselves ethically with others. "The psychoanalytic subject," Pitt underscores, "is an effect of its libidinal ties to others" (2003, p. 69). "Simply put," she concludes (beautifully), "the surface of the self is not there, waiting to be fully experienced by the developing individual; it is, rather, more like a work of art that comes into being as the effects of touching and being touched, seeing and being seen" (2003, p. 72).

But, Pitt notes, "we seem to be less clear about the complicated ways in which people attach or do not attach to knowledge and how these attachments turn into actions" (2003, p. 73). Nor, may I add, do we seem very interested in providing public-school students with many opportunities to explore these attachments, as the predetermined curriculum with its standardized results obliterates any possibility of personal attachment. Presumably that is reserved for graduate school, an experience relatively few public-school students (and not all graduate students) experience. For the rest, knowledge remains unattached, split-off from lived experience, free-floating like the anxiety Freud's female patients sometimes suffered.

UNSPEAKABLE SUFFERING, MASTERY AND DESTITUTION

Because the female patient (Pitt discusses the case of Irma) gave Freud her resistance, the patient/doctor relationship was radically altered. Resisted, stymied, Freud was no longer the *master*, not of the cure, not of the patient, not of the illness. After Felman, Pitt suggests that the "fecundity" of the psychoanalytic relationship proceeds, in fact, from the destruction of the doctor's (Freud's) mastery, from what Felman terms "the *destitution*, in effect, of mastery as such" (1993, p. 109; quoted in Pitt 2003, p. 109). Is this destitution a version of Silverman's (1992) "male subjectivity at the margins" or Bersani's (1987, 1995) ecstatic "self-shattering" that he associates with anal sex, with being penetrated by the Other, thereby becoming Other to oneself? Does the fecundity of the analytic – and pedagogical? - relationship follow from the (male) doctor's (teacher's) structural performance of the "crisis of masculinity," a crisis that enables the (feminized) patient to experience her own (masculinized?) unconscious, surfacing as resistance, sinking the "ship" that is the doctor's self-sealed sense of mastery?

This reading of what constitutes a psychic event within the psychoanalytic session – that it follows from "transformed power relations between (male) doctors and their (female) patients" (2003, p. 109) – is congruent, Pitt suggests, with Lacan's own understanding of the psychoanalytic dialogue. The altered power relations between doctor and patient transformed the psychoanalytic dialogue into an exchange between two individuals who are both self-divided, and whose communication – through hide-and-seek? - occurs through their self-division. Such a structure of communication inaugurates psychoanalysis as a theory and as a method of self-analysis. Such a structure, for Felman, originates in Freud's identification with his female patient and her "unspeakable suffering."

Felman seems to be suggesting, Pitt postulates, that as long as such suffering remains a "nodal point" of psychoanalysis, fundamental questions of gender (what does a woman want?) and understanding (itself gendered in psychoanalysis as what Freud, or the [male] doctor, wants) remains unresolved, knotted or conflated in "femininity," both the site and expression of resistance and desire. It is to Lacan's work that Pitt turns to underscore that the "desire" for understanding becomes a trap of the ego, an inviting trap both for psychoanalytic theory and for its participants.

Pitt notes that it is this desire to be understood, as a woman, by her male analyst that prompted Felman to write her essay on Freud. While Felman found her listener "caring, compassionate and astute," she also found him lacking, unable to understand her as a woman. "Felman's wish to be understood as woman by a man is structured," Pitt writes, "like the plea of the hysteric who addresses her question about what it means to be a woman precisely to the one who cannot give her what she wants and then lets him know that she is not, will not, be satisfied" 2003, 110). Addressed to an imagined Master – the teacher? – the analyst (Freud?) declined (failed in) the position, unable meet the expectation of understanding the very position (structured by the plea, animated by suffering) demands. Does the "destitution" of "mastery" enable the patient to retrieve the Otherness of the analyst as her own lived "nodal point"? In the destitution of his mastery – the "crisis" of masculinity now played out - does the castrated analyst now claim his self-difference, his identification as "woman" as well as a "man"?

Pitt juxtaposes Freud's famous question "What does woman want?" with Lacan's famous pronouncement "*La femme n'existe pas.*" Are these two questions not related? (Pitt allows that Lacan's assertion does not "exceed the structure of Freud's question" (2003, p. 111)). Is not the question Freud posed (also) self-addressed? In addition to his desire to address and to relieve the suffering of the gendered Other, is he not (also), like the feminized patient, trying to reclaim his (Adam's) "rib" (a myth that cannot conceive of "woman" apart from His relation to Himself: see Pinar 2006a, p. 64), inaugurating self-difference and internalized otherness? Because the mode of address – hysteria and unspeakable suffering – requires the fantasy of the Master (a fantasy that obliterates the gendered formation of "woman"), does it also castrate, make destitute, render Him now hysterical and outside the patriarchal structure in which he might imagine himself capable of satisfying feminized desire?

Is this mode of address embedded in historical forms of autobiographical practice, as feminist theorists such as Leigh Gilmore (1994) have suggested? Pitt seems to say so, noting, in response to the Lacanian assertion (that *la femme n'existe pas*) that "perhaps she [woman] has not [existed], at least not quite in the way much feminist writing has wished" (2003, p. 111). Pitt notes that Felman did not know how her project was also a testimony to her own autobiography as missing: missing because, she writes, "I still could not essentially address it to myself – truly address it, that is, to a woman" (2003, p. 111).

AN UNYIELDING KNOT

Not only does "woman" not "exist," it appears neither does the "child." Pitt examines Winnicott's claim that there is no such thing as a baby (or a child: see Pinar 2006b, p. 42). For Winnicott, "There is no such thing as an 'infant,' meaning that whenever one finds a infant, one finds maternal care, and without maternal care there would be no infant" (1965, p. 39; quoted in Pitt 2003, p. 115). As in childhood as in psychoanalysis as in education: Pitt asserts that "the breakdowns of meaning that occur between two subjects are necessary for the development of the individual" (2003, p. 115).

Pitt reminds us that Lacan's account of the mirror stage theorizes the infant's apprehension of "self" as installed at the moment of self-recognition in the image reflected by the mirror. This is, Pitt underlines, also a misrecognition, and she notes that, for Lacan, this structure of self-(mis)recognition effects the split subject. Drawing too on Wallon's work, Pitt points out that this process is not "instantaneous." Rather, "self-recognition is a culminating rather than inaugurating event" (2003, p. 76).

"The knot of the unknown that resists interpretation" (2003, p. 104), Pitt acknowledges, is what Freud termed the "navel" of the dream? Is the "secret self" the knot of the self-system that guarantees self- (mis)recognition and self-difference? Are the meanings of the dream and the meaning of the "self" both beyond interpretation, or only resistant to it? If "hide-and-seek" accurately describes the movements of interiority and exteriority, does the former hide while the latter seeks? Is Winnicott's "secret self" also Lacan's Real, in which case one's very capacity for interpretation, even for resistance, must necessarily, inevitably, break down? Is our seeking a hiding from the incoherence and unintelligibility of the Real? This would seem to be implied in Pitt's observation that "It is this failure of the ego to maintain its coherence that Lacan links to the subject's quest for signification set into motion by a terrifying encounter with the real" (2003, p. 105).

In this scenario, the journey toward communication – intersubjective intelligibility and recognition – is animated by hysteria, a terror of the unspeakable and unknowable. Pitt relies on Colette Soler to situate Lacan's distinction between the ego – that is, the sum of identifications – and the speaking subject, the "self" who comes into being and indeed must be made to appear through speech. Is this process, in part, an instance of Althusserian appellation, in which the subject is hailed into existence by the "other," (mis)recognizing itself in its identification with the Other's signification?

Self-formation involves learning how to position oneself in the place of the cause of one's own desire, Pitt tells us. If so, such learning, precisely because it involves learning, dissolves narcissism, unselfconscious as that state is. Such learning engages one in "the interminable struggle to symbolize the cause of desire" (2003, p. 106), a primal force whose tip may not break the water's surface. There can be no fantasy of avoiding the "iceberg" – is that psychic fact one cause of the enduring fascination with the Titanic? – and not because there is insufficient time. It is because there is no time in advance; the project of learning occurs afterward, and through peering through the opaque depths of the unconscious up toward a surface refracted unevenly, free-associatively. In this interpretive sense time is always past, even when it appears before us. We cannot avoid the "iceberg" because we are already "sunk." It is already after the tragedy that we find ourselves suffering, traumatized, asking for recognition from Him who cannot see us apart from himself, by whom we could not bear being seen anyway. Still, we demand to know, to understand: was our demise avoidable? Is it decipherable? Perhaps if it had not been our maiden voyage, we rue. Surely we can raise ourselves from the ocean floor. Is this the fantasy of free-association, a technique that takes us back before the "collision" with the Real, before demise?

Effort at such learning – "this autobiography of learning" as Pitt puts it – "takes place in the strange time of *Nachtraglichkeit*" (2003, p. 6). It is "a time," she suggests," that is neither representation nor identity but difference and self-difference" (2003, p. 108). "What Freud seems to be circling around," Pitt concludes, "is the notion that, at the very center of relations between education and psychoanalysis, lies an unyielding knot" (2003 p. 13). It is no doubt true, as Pitt asserts, that "the productivity of this version of subjectivity and its implications for theorizing all manner of relations within teaching and learning have yet to be realized" (2003, p. 106). It is Pitt's work here that helps us believe in such productivity by so significantly contributing to it.

I have only circled around the knotted complexity of Alice Pitt's remarkable accomplishment. As this provocative and important work underscores, there is no tradition of systematic inquiry into the sphere of the subjective, into the processes of self-formation – and their complex and ever-changing relations to the social and historical – that offers us as many conceptual tools as do the various strands of psychoanalytic theory. In the broad field of education - in which curriculum theory is situated - there is a long if attenuated tradition of interest in psychoanalysis. During the Progressive Era in the U.S., efforts to theorize a psychoanalysis of education were initiated (see, for instance, Cremin 1961, p. 209ff.), but these disappeared as, in the U.S. at least, "business thinking" and the "national interest" dominated school curriculum and the scholarship surrounding it.

In our time there is a renaissance of scholarly interest in psychoanalysis in education, led by Deborah Britzman (1998), Stephen Appel (1999), Doug Aoki (2002), Wendy Atwell-Vasey (1998a, 1999b), jagodzinski (2002) and Alice Pitt. It is also evident in a number of important studies not exclusively or even primarily psychoanalytic in orientation, among them Madeleine Grumet's (1988) study of women and teaching, Alan Block's (1997) theorization of the school's psychological violence against the child, in Marla Morris' (2001) research on curriculum and the Holocaust, and in Julie Webber's (2003) exposition of school violence.

I have employed psychoanalytic theory – a version of object relations theory (see Chodorow 1978) – in my effort to understand the gender of racial politics and violence in America (2001). It was psychoanalytic theory that enabled me to appreciate – however incipiently - the "queer" dimensions of racial subjugation. It is psychoanalytic theory – and, specifically, Alice Pitt's sophisticated and subtle performance of it – that enables us to appreciate the play of the personal in the complicated conversation that is the curriculum.

"HIGH VOLUME TRAFFIC IN THE INTERTEXT"
(2003)

What is an "afterword"? Is it a space "after words"? It is, of course, "after" the "words" in this collection, and I will try, collage-style, to perform the echoes I hear as I dwell in the space "after" these "words." The words the contributors have written reverberate through me, rewriting my space, my lived space, into another … middle space, not here, nor there, but somewhere else. I remember: it was a space where I lived long ago. It was one summer in upstate New York, when I was probably 25 years old, before I became a father, before I became gay, before I became "Bill Pinar," a place-time of infinite if unnerving possibility, "lines of flight" (Deleuze and Guattari 1987, p. 35) amidst cool sunny summer breezes off Lake Ontario. I was reading – it was not a cliché then, she will never be for me a cliché – Virginia Woolf, Quentin Bell's biography, and *To the Lighthouse*. I was rewriting the story, so that Professor Ramsey didn't blame his family for failing to reach R, so that Mrs. Ramsay didn't aggress against herself by selfless devotion to others, so that she and Lily Briscoe became lovers and the War never happened and the summer house – a middle place neither home nor away – wasn't left abandoned to the rain and the wind and the pounding sea. I was rewriting the boat-ride to the lighthouse.

That was a long time ago, but it is also a time now in the present, as I look out the window of my study this foggy, early summer morning in Louisiana in late April 2002. This book has transported me to my own "Lynch's Lane," returned to me a remote past into my intimate present, a present now restructured as an intertext, a space in-between "the tough old stars" which hover over me, tasks to do, tasks I want to do, but which, in their number and urgency, twinkle at times too brightly. This intertext is foggy and moist; it's where I can pay attention and not know, listen to whispers of a bright cool summer morning long ago, as the words in this collection echo through me and onto this page. This intertext is - might Ted Aoki agree? - a site of living pedagogy.

Where, Ted Aoki asks, are sites of living pedagogy? Where are they located? Ted suggests that we look at the spaces between representational and non-representational discourses (after words?), what Homi Bhabha calls the "third space" of ambivalent construction, what Trinh Minh-ha calls "a hybrid place," what David Jardine calls "the site of original difficulty (quoted phrases in Aoki 2003, p. 5). It is this site, Ted tells us, of "ambiguity, ambivalence, and uncertainty, but simultaneously a site of general possibilities and hope" (2003, pp. 5-6). After Ted, alongside Ted, in honor of Ted, the contributors to this collection articulate this site, what the editors – Erika Hasebe-Ludt and Wanda Hurren – term *intertext*. There is here "high volume traffic in the intertext" (Palulis 2003, p. 273).

What is intertext? Sannie Yuet-San Tang quotes Erika Hasebe-Ludt who tells us that the concept "implies a multiplicity of meaning present in any text.... [A]ny text is the absorption and transformation of another" (Tang 2003, p. 25). In this collection, these processes of absorption and transformation are everywhere evident, for me most vividly in the regular referencing of the teaching and writing of (the legendary) Ted Aoki. Contributors' absorption in Aoki's work and pedagogical presence clearly effected multiple and various transformations of "possibility" and "hope."

"High traffic volume in the intertext"? Not automobile traffic, but, as Patricia Palulis (2003, p. 273) notes, "trafficking in counterfeit exchanges, trafficking as/in *trans*lation – trafficking as/in sur-vival." Traffic, then, as "movement," an "import and export trade," maybe even "illegal or disreputable commercial activity," but definitely "communication ... between individuals" (Webster's New Collegiate Dictionary, p. 1238). These are "archaic" meanings, the Dictionary suggests. "Movement" was one of them, "messages" another. In a bottle from the sea, from an in-between space, somewhere in inner/outer space? Is that the meaning of "high" in the phrase? Lofty, as in transcendental ego, as in distantiation and bracketing? Yes, a quiet meditative space, but "intertext" would seem to be a place of loud, high-volume silence, behind and between and after the words. For some, words are the passages to, from, and among intertext(s); Renee Norman (2003, 257) tells us "[i]t is enough to play/the words." For Patrick Verriour (2003, 73), the intertext is the healing/sick body. "Each morning," he tells us, "I take the same walk starting out from one seacoast and not returning home until I have glimpsed the sea again at the other end of the road."

Carl Leggo (2003, p. 139) glimpses the sea, in his memory: "[a]lways going back in my poems, knowing I have left and never left, knowing I can/always go back and never go back, the world written in the geography of our growing up." A counselor told him: "Your first year is written in your body; your life is a series of revision" (Leggo 2003, p. 135). That first year was inside his mother's body, then nearby it: "I once lived in my mother's house: perhaps I have grown bigger, perhaps I have grown smaller" (2003, p. 138). Why are you so large in your absence, Mrs. Ramsay, in your presence in me?

Patricia Palulus thinks of the building that houses the Faculty of Education where she teaches, remembering a comment about it being a very *scary* place. "Are we not speaking of a haunted house?" (2003, p. 265) she asks. Are we the living haunted by those who loved us, who taught us? Do we become, as Palulus quips about the Faculty of Education structure, "A building that houses hauntology?" (2003, p. 265). Let's inaugurate *that* discipline. Recalling Zizek, she asks: does a spectrality fill the ontological gap? Is this also a gap between past and present, future and past?

"SEDUCTION BY THE SUPERFICIAL"

David Blades (2003) paints a picture of the gap. Humanity has finally died, sometime in the future. Humanity died sometime in the twentieth century, according to Pier Paulo Pasolini, who attributed our extinction not to the desire for immortality, as does Blades, but to consumer capitalism (see Greene 1990). Maybe these are two phrases but the same thing? In Blades' reverie, "Humans simply evolved into their machines" (2003, p. 206). In the margins of the historical narrative the caretaker finds, the last living human being, an Historian, has scribbled two comments: *seduced* and *Heidegger was right*. The final pages begin with the comment: *It's OK to die*. In this comment, Blades tells us, the Historian was reacting to a comment made at the start of the twenty-first century in a keynote address at a teachers' convention: "We are in danger as a species of inventing ourselves to death" (Blades 2003, p. 213).

The warning not heard, our future fate was cast; the Historian knew that "every school should have embraced a curriculum of questioning since through questions children could more deeply understand their situation and Being (2003, pp. 219-220)...Questions are thus crucial to the survival of humanness" (2003, p. 219). But "in their seduction by the superficial," Blades continues, "schools silenced the provocative questions that following from asking why" (2003, 220). Instead, he notes, schools sanctioned a cult of the right answer, policed by standardized examination. "As the twenty-first century began to unfold," Blades (2003, pp. 222-223) concludes,

> teachers increasingly complained about the side effects of individualization of instruction through computer integration in schools, but no teacher association went on strike over this issue.... Schools could have been the agency to develop the public collectivist ethics to determine what is morally right in the evolution of a technology.... But the potential was never realized. Humans, far too comfortable with their inventions, slid into the twenty-first century in almost comatose state, missing the opportunity to discover with children the humanizing potential of asking the important questions. The final words of the Historian served as an epitaph for humankind: "Seeking immortality, we neglected to ask why."

Karen Meyer (2003) has not neglected to ask why. As Director of the University of British Columbia's Centre for Study of Curriculum and Instruction, Meyer's labor has been the co-creation of a "third space" wherein an educational community can become self-reflexively engaged in own educational process. Members of the community became mobilized when budget cuts (made by administrators "seduced by the superficial"?) threatened this space; they wrote letters and arranged meetings with Faculty of Education and University administrators to appeal the cuts. Community members articulated the distinctive character of their student-centered academic unit, namely that it is a site where "individual students began to (re)consider how they want *to be* in an academic environment" (Meyer 2003, p.

15). How to *be*? This is - is it not? - a question of ontology and ethics, precisely the question Blades' reverie on the future invokes.

Neither are David Jardine, Sharon Friesen and Patricia Clifford seduced by the superficial. They are interested in ontology, specifically, an ontology of mathematics and mathematics education. "What if," they ask, "instead of production and consumption, the *world* of mathematics (as a *living, breathing, contested human discipline* that has been handed down to us) needs our memory, our care, our intelligence, our work … and understanding if it is to remain hale and healthy and whole" (2003b, p. 41)? This is a question, they note, "posed not *by us* but *to us*" (2003b, p. 42). Are we haunted? Because "[t]hings are their interdependencies with all things," Jardine, Friesen and Clifford observe, "to deeply understand any thing, we must understand it as *being itself* only in the midst of all its relations" (2003b, p. 43). This ontological meditation reveals mathematics to be "all the actual, human, bodily work which is required if it is to remain hale and healthy, if it is to continue as a living practice which we desire to pass on, in some form, to our children" (2003b, p. 47). After Gadamer, David, Sharon, and Patricia assert that mathematics education, i.e. the experience of mathematics, "is not something we *possess* (like some commodifiable object) but something we *endure*, something we *undergo*" (2003b, p. 47). Bodily and on the earth, the ontological and ethical ground.

Jeannette Scott MacArthur is not seduced by the superficial, as her meditation on ethical research makes clear. MacArthur understands that the "the system tempts us to uncomplicate the world" (2003, p. 52), and that this not only an intellectual problem, but an ethical one. She rose to the occasion: "[I] chose Obligation instead of Ethics, radical hermeneutics instead of idealistic essentialism, foolishness instead of sensibility" (2003, p. 53). Following John Caputo's lead she found herself "[s]tanding, not on moral *terra firma* as expected, but, like Caputo, on ground which tended to shift" (2003, p. 54). Is this the "Response-ability/Metonomy/Bridge" drawn in "In-Between Piece #4, wherein Patricia Sorensen (2003, p. 277) asserts that: "Response-ability requires dwelling in the third space, on the bridge between the dichotomies, with equally clear views of both sides"?

"[L]ANGUAGING IN SUBJECTIVITIES OF PERFORMED RELATIONS"

Sannie Yuet-San Tang knows that translation is shifting ground. Inspired by Ted Aoki, Tang asks: "What is translation? Where are translation and the translator located" (2003, p. 24)? She answers that they are located intertextually. "Translation takes place," she suggests, "in what I would call the 'diasporic space' between cultures" (2003, p. 28). Patricia Palulis (pp. 260-261, 262) knows this space:

> In exile, we enter a diaspora of words. Diaspora is a postponement of homecoming – the gap – the void – the interval – the space of home/not home – a place of occupant and the ghost … within the same text. Uncanny.

Also inspired by "scholar and sensei, Ted Aoki," Marylin Low (2003, p. 57) can appreciate Tang's sense of translation. Her Japanese student has asked her: "Can we meet? ... I want us to read me together." Low reflects on the student's remarkable invitation:

> An invitation to respond to a mark is returned and, in its return, I am marked. The performative words of this student, dwelling in a global(ized) site, disrupt a comfortable certainty of how I had come to *mark* her English. In life complicated by intertexts of *différance*, cries from the margins of a pedagogical place called English as a second language (ESL) could be heard – a location the student continued to agitate and contest. And she is not the only one. (2003, pp. 57-58)

Erika Hasebe-Ludt is thinking of location, about "the where" of knowing, where she, in relation to her students, colleagues, friends, and family, situates herself "in the face of other knowledge, other traditions, and other communities, and whose knowledge we draw on, whose we challenge, in order to become wiser, more informed, more inclusive, more able to effect change" (2003, p. 149). Questions of where are important for her at this time due, in part, to her own "geographical re- and dis-location" (2003, p. 149). She writes:

> Traveling and living away from home, moving from Europe to Canada, moving to a different place of work, living in the tensioned space of cultural and geographical displacement, my interest is to investigate how this positioning of self in relation to other cultures and locations can be/come a generative place (Hasebe-Ludt 2003, p. 149).

Is teacher education such a generative place? Hasebe-Ludt worries (as do I), that in becoming a teacher and a teacher of teachers, "I have become part of a relentless busyness to implement a rigidly structured and disembodied curriculum that has left few openings for creative expression for both adults and children, for us to draw, paint, sing, dance, and write together differently" (2003, p. 154). But her worrying, I suspect, suggests she has managed to remain apart from such "busyness" (ed. biz), living and teaching the light(ness) she thanks Carl Leggo for offering. The "gift" of Leggo's writing is that it enables explorations of "the alchemic possibilities in the spaces of the heart" (2003, p. 156).

Cynthia Chambers writes from the heart, from where she remembers "ugly conversations" she wishes she could forget, but which "keep surfacing in my memory like stones on my trail down to the river" (2003b, p. 107). She remembers a parting exchange with a lover of four years, a memory juxtaposed with the news of his sudden and accidental death, robbing her of the opportunity to speak with him again, to speak healing words, to him, to herself. "Death," Chambers notes, "alters the landscape of memory drastically like a volcano or an avalanche" (2003b, p. 107). "The landscape of memory," she continues, "is filled with these bits and pieces torn from their original circumstance, now bleached and tattered" (2003b, p. 107). Is the heart, then, an intertext? Chambers seems to suggest as much when she suggests: "Memory is the homeland from which you are always in exile" (2003b, p. 109).

It is in the spaces of his heart where Patrick Verriour struggles for his life, walking each morning to glimpse healing. "When I first started this road nearly two years ago," he confides, "I was still in the early stages of inoperative and incurable cancer. I could barely reach the top of the first hill before turning back. In spite of my frequent protests, my wife, physicians, and nurses told me to keep on walking" (2003, p. 73). In his life and career as a drama educator, Verriour worked to teach his students "to story their lives, to be playful, to be prepared for the unpredictable and unexpected, to value their intuition and to be always shifting their perspectives of themselves and others" (2003, p. 74). It was a lesson, it seems, he learned as well as he taught.

"PAYING ATTENTION AND NOT KNOWING"

Verrriour's acknowledgement of his dependency upon his caregivers and his wife underlines human (and non/human) interdependency, made stark during times of crisis, such as Verriour's, but quietly still the fact even in times during which struggle or "tension" or "difficulty" are not obvious. In the classroom, perhaps, where Renee Norman (2003, p. 244) remembers Ted Aoki saying: "the tension is in teaching, in living, at home. If you're alive, there's tension. If you're dead, no tension." There are numerous acknowledgements of Ted's teaching in this collection, acknowledgements of relationality, generosity, of "living pedagogy."

With gratitude Renee Norman recalls the first day of class, 1994. When she enters, Aoki is already there, a physical fact yes, but metaphoric one as well:

[I] am eager to hear him speak after reading some of his writings. What draws me to Ted's work is hope and goodness and vision. He asks us, students in a narrative/curriculum course, to introduce ourselves. I speak about the profound effect his words have had on me philosophically, about the crossroads I feel I have reached in my work, and how I intuitively sense that I am in need of Ted's wisdom and poetry in order to proceed.... I feel immediate relief that this eminent scholar openly admits to movement and change, and admiration that Ted seems constantly in motion: reading, rereading, relearning, reconsidering. The re at work, Ted would say. (Norman 2003, p. 248, emphasis in original)

In Ted's course Norman dwelled in what Aoki characterized as "a middle place for culture, a place where people of varying backgrounds and opinions, Eastern and Western, could meet, study, discuss, share, and laugh" (2003, p. 249). She attributes the creation of this middle place to Aoki's "living pedagogy":

Ted created an atmosphere that evoked difference and supported it. He envisions a cultural space that is open, inclusive, and in the middle.... How does one put such a philosophy into practice? Ted did by honoring the respecting in the diversity with/in the class, pulling out the varied backgrounds that people arrived with. He did it by insisting not only that we examine the new ideas of scholars from varying backgrounds, but also that we should continually question ourselves.... There was no invisibility in this class (Norman 2003, p. 251, emphasis in original).

Also in that 1994 class Norman remembers "the moment that remains for me most potent and memorable," the moment

when Ted told the story of being asked years ago where his allegiance lay when war with Japan put Canadians of Japanese descent under scrutiny. I am Canadian, Ted told us he had replied, and his quiet voice rang with dignity as he related this story.... When Ted spoke these words, the very last day of the course, there was a palpable listening silence in the room: a silence permeated with past mistakes, present hopes, and future visions. A silence that laid open a new kind of cultural Canada.... Here was Ted's middle place for culture.... I still feel the imprint of Ted Aoki... I still hear the memory singing. (Norman 2003, pp. 255-256, emphasis in original)

Renee Norman honors Aoki, not only with this memory, but with a poem, five lines of which sing here.

Middle Place

(for Ted Aoki)

Dwelling with Ted
in the and
where the teacher disappears
the I's dissolve
and in their place.

(Norman 2003, p. 254)

What happens when the "I's" dissolve? Antoinette Oberg knows. One is released to teach in a middle place, a place between "paying attention and not knowing" (Oberg 2003, p. 123). The intertextual spaces in which Oberg is interested (from the Latin *inter esse*, she points out, already in the midst of) are encounters with graduate students in which they "unfold their inquiries" (2003, p. 123). "There I find that paying attention and not knowing (which I have characterized as suspending expectations and delaying the desire to conceptualize) invites another layer of a student's inquiry to unfold itself" (2003, pp. 123-124). Oberg is interested in the moment when she glimpses a "congruence" between topic and method of inquiry. "At some point during my meeting with each of these students," Oberg (2003, p. 126) reports, "I perceived a patterning in what had up until that moment appeared to be formless."

Not only Antoinette is "already in the midst of" (2003, p. 123) an intertextual space when she encounters her graduate students. It seems they are as well. Her pedagogy of "paying attention and not knowing" (p. 123) enables students to appreciate that they already know how to proceed; they know how to remove obstacles and to allow "the patterning [that] already existed in their professional work to become the patterning of their inquiries" (2003, p. 127). This is self-reflexive pedagogy as well, as Antoinette "seek[s] to discern the patterning of my own inquiry into my practice of paying attention and not knowing" (2003, p. 127).

"SILENT SCARS"

There are congruences in Ingrid Johnston's account as well, if ironic and, perhaps, uncanny. She recalls her initiation into teaching in apartheid South Africa, where she taught in an all-white segregated high school. "As their teacher," she acknowledges, "I was complicit in such framing. Nothing in my own life experience had prepared me to challenge my own or my students' assumptions about whiteness as the cultural and racial norm" (Johnston 2003, p. 227). Now, many years later, she finds herself a teacher educator in a faculty of education where more than 90% of the student teachers are of European descent, but many of whom are preparing to teach in urban schools whose students are not of European descent. Confronting her past and engaging the present, Johnston (2003, p. 237) challenges racialization: "As a white, middle-class woman who teaches student teachers, the majority of whom are also white, I feel I should be addressing and challenging the perceived norms of whiteness" (p. 229). And that she does, foregrounding in her curriculum classes "the historically privileged positions of power conferred by 'whiteness'."

Aristides Gazetas, too, is interested in the pedagogical politics of cultural identities, especially as these are represented in popular culture, specifically film. In his discussion of Margaretha von Trotta's film *Marianne and Julianne* (1981), "a modernized translation of the Antigone-Creon confrontation," Gazetas emphasizes "that cultural identities are locally and historically specific, and that they become available for human understanding only within certain 'language games,' 'paradigms,' and 'discursive formations'" (2003, p. 189). Gazetas argues that "Von Trotta's film serves as a cultural text, as part of a postmodern society, to show (quoting Derrida) that the 'condition of possibility of deconstruction is a call for justice'" (2003, p. 201).

Lynn Fels performs such "a call for justice" when she demands: "Stop! Don't destroy our forests! Who are you to reap profits from our mountains" (2003, p. 180)? This demand, this question, Fels (2003, p. 183) asserts under "an empty sky and in the silent scars that map our presence."

The earth grounds Fels' calls for justice: "*At the edge of the sea, in the shelter of the mountains*, issues of environmentalism, native rights, ownership, birth, and community are spelled in the embodied interactions that are our momentary presence" (2003, p. 184). It is, she reminds, "within performance we are performed" (2003, p. 184). Moreover: "Our performative intertext(s) invite a reimagining of curriculum. These new interstandings lead to changes in our practices of schooling" (2003, p. 185). Indeed, as Bruce Russell's essay testifies.

Bruce Russell is concerned with the earth as well. His hope is to "widen the curricular space" (Russell 2003, p. 93) in which we have historically conceived "nature" through a pedagogy of haiku. Such a pedagogy involves "an intercultural consideration of the poetic, historical, and spiritual values that lie at the heart of a Japanese aesthetic sensibility" (2003, p. 93). To illustrate, he points to the use of various devices in haiku – among them, assonance, alliteration, and internal rhyme – which, coupled with a "Zen-inspired simplicity" (2003, 94), creates a poetry aware that being "extravagant with words may risk putting an over-played description between the reader and the lived experience the poet hopes to capture and convey" (2003, p. 94). For Russell, "the essence of haiku" is "immediate life experience" (2003, p. 94), experience which provides a living basis for "intergenerational dialogue" (2003, p. 96) – such as Aoki's pedagogical conversation with his students – and "intersecting temporalities" (2003, p. 97).

Russell is thinking of "our inability to take the time to reflect upon moments of personal significance" (2003, p. 97). It is important, he suggests, to guide students in the expression of emotion, but he is not thinking of reporting "the latest experience that has moved us" (2003, p. 97). Rather, he refers to a "different kind of rationality involved when one attempts to interpret the importance of the understatement" (2003, p. 97) reminiscent of haiku. Also referring to Aoki, Russell suggests this sensibility might mean the "opening of many middle spaces in the curriculum" (2003, p. 99), in which we can explore "the influence of events in our lives" (2003, p. 101).

"A GOOD PLACE TO LINGER"

The lingering influence of events, especially intellectual events, is evident in Leah Fowler's remembrance of "a life-altering master class with Dr. Aoki in 1985" (2003, p. 159). Fifteen years later, after several years on the Pacific coast, Leah finds herself back in Lethbridge, where, she notes, "Aoki once taught as a disenfranchised Japanese Canadian schoolteacher" (Fowler 2003, p. 159). So layered, these "narrative plains in these Alberta spaces, where I am at home and not at home" (Fowler 2003, p. 159) provide the palimpsest for questions that traverse the "private" and "public," for instance: "How can narrative research lead to an aesthetic and ethical inner government of a teaching self" (2003, p. 159)? As a schoolteacher Leah found herself no longer able to traverse the space between the private and the public, as "the inconsistencies and paradoxes began to erode my (teaching) self" (2003, p. 164). As she notes, with understatement: "Our entire education system is in deep difficulty" (2003, p. 166). Through her "working from within" (2003, p. 165), Leah "come[s] now to teaching with more attunement, humility, and care" (2003, p. 170).

Wanda Hurren recalls Cynthia Chambers' invitation to begin at home in curricular theorizing as she formulates her notion of "auto-geo-carto-graphia" (2003, p. 111), a curricular collage. In this structuration of self and place, Hurren (2003, p. 111) explores "ways in which curriculum might enhance what we know of our places and our selves and I am interested in exploring how what we know of our places and selves might enhance curriculum theory and research." "Home" would seem to be the "ground level," from where she can compose "stories of place and self within the lines of my everyday maps of teaching, learning, living, and researching" (2003, p. 112). Why collage?

> I have chosen to use collage as a textual strategy in order to indicate how these elements, self, place, and curriculum, happen in mingling ways.... Collage works requires a deliberate overlapping arrangement of bits and pieces. Within collage there are no clean edges or borderlines between the bits and pieces. In my arrangement of bits and pieces of teaching and living and learning and self and place and theory and research, my desire is to create a collage that catches up the constitutive role of the mingling dance of signification. (Hurren 2003, p. 113)

It is a dance "under the tough old stars" (2003, p. 114), as Hurren "interrupts" her "prairie winter" to read David Jardine's collection of eco-pedagogical essays by the same title. She "emerge[s] from the readings glistening with river spray. Such a moist, scholarly text. His writing is a performance of how place and self mingle in curricular theorizing" (2003, p. 114). Still under the stars, perhaps, Hurren (2003, p. 116) writes:

> I turn back toward town
>
> welcoming the same breeze
>
> that has blown
>
> over my body
>
> all these years.

The "ground level" where Hurren works is, yes, phenomenological; it is also the ground of the earth: "Becoming aware of where our bodies touch the earth is part of this practice and it is this same awareness – being mindful of where our bodies touch the earth and noting the sensations that arise – that I want to bring to the practice of curriculum" (Hurren 2003, p. 120). In this essay, may I say, you have.

I have myself employed collage as a curricular figuration, in the book on lynching and prison rape (Pinar 2001). There I tried to perform the self-shattering I imagine hegemonic white masculinity must undergo to restructure itself as "moist," to borrow Hurren's adjectival characterization of Jardine's book. Now I understand more about collage, thanks to Hurren, and about performance, thanks to Lynn Fels. Fels' work "investigates curricular places of possibility, absence, and disruption realized through performance. *Performance not as a process nor as product, but as breath, intermingling, unexpected journey landscapes reeling against the sky in a sudden moment of recognition*" (Fels 2003, p. 173, emphasis in original). Recognition and misrecognition played structuring roles in the queer politics of "race" in nineteenth-century America.

Fels notes that, etymologically, "*performance* brings us to *form* as structure and *ance* as action, as in (d)ance. Performance is, then, both form and action" (2003, p.

175). Together, as in synthesis? It is performed, she continues, on "the edge of chaos, a space where possibilities seduce and life dances into being" (2003, p. 175). Fels, too, has been inspired by Ted Aoki, recalling a conversation in which Aoki "inquires about the 'impossible,' that which is not yet possible to imagine into being, that which remains beyond our grasp like the force that moves the tides, unseen yet present in all our innocence and ignorance of movement" (2003, 175). Are racial and gender justice already present, unforeseen, in our movements? Education, Fels tells us, involves *"surprise – freefalling through moments of crisis and recognition of possibility"* (2003, 180, emphasis in original).

Surprise, freefalling, crisis and recognition of possibility: do these occur as well on Lynch's Lane in Corner Brook, Newfoundland, where the young Carl Leggo is cycling "all the way to Old Man Downey's house" (2003, p. 132)? Surprise and astonishment, cycling toward the sea, the same sea that draws and repels as it gives Patrick Verriour a glimpse of healing. "[A]stonishment," Leggo (2003, p. 133) tells us, "is a good place to begin and a good place to linger." "I seek to disclose and know again," Carl (2003, p. 134) continues,

the location of my backyard,

and how this specific geographical space

represents a location for locution in the bigger world.

These are, as he notes, "alchemic transformations" (2003, p. 134).

Like Carl Leggo, Renee Norman (2003, p. 243) knows that "place is not necessarily a physical place, but a mental and emotional and intellectual state of being that resides in the head." She too remembers Ted Aoki; on this occasion he was speaking of place, and in so doing, "he dis/placed us in many different spaces and locations and inbetweenesses of curriculum" (2003, p. 256). For Norman, "curriculum is a dream." In this place:

days pass

filled with plans

filled helping others

see their dreams

like a fiddler

I play on

wanting them

to hear the music

not the pied piper

I want them dancing

to their dreams

want the caves

that imprison them

empty

(Norman 2003, pp. 243-244)

...

when at last i enter the right room

i see wariness in my students' eyes

they are searching too

it's then i know

where i am

(Norman 2003, p. 246)

...

"[I]f curriculum is a dream," Norman (2003, p. 244) notes, "I am the dreamer."

"SUBLIME OPENNESS"

Dreams can be messy, as Marylin Low appreciates. "Reading out of education as a way of reading in," Low (2003, p. 58) thinks of Ted Aoki, whose "living pedagogy began as a psychoanalytic curiosity that invited an inter-disciplinary re-reading of education and its 'difficulties' as vibrant sites of tensional anxieties – sites that are not clean and controlled as I had been taught they should be, but as sites always already complete, complex, and ambiguous." Like dreams, perhaps? Low (2003, p. 59) continues:

> Opening to these difficulties creates the conditions for a happenstance of radical contingencies in the classroom – what Ted Aoki inscribes as metonymic moments of living pedagogy – a living pedagogy that brings under suspicion the traditional distinctive binary of teacher/learner and rewrites teaching as a messy text.

Messy is not simple or plain. "Resisting the desire for plain language," Low continues, "I ... was at once both startled and affirmed by Doug Aoki's claim that this 'translation of complex material into plain language is actually a refusal to teach'" (2003, p. 61). The father taught the son well, did he not?

Is appreciation of complexity also openness? Patricia Palulis recalls Zizek's characterization of the hole in the flag as a moment of sublime openness. In such a moment, what Palulis (2003, p. 259, emphasis in original) terms "*an Aokian moment,*" we might remain "*mindful of our location in the language of pedagogy – for just as language course through us, we are located in discourse – a doubling movement.*" Is this this "doubling movement" possible when we enter the gap, dwelling in the intertext? "Drawing from the Aokian notion of Metonymy as a chiasmatic "in-between" space of metaphor/metonymy," Palulis (2003, p. 266) writes, "the place of the slash – the place of the gap – is the space of generative possibilities in a drifting, uncertain habitation – in moments of persistent in/stability." Is this the "drifting" and "uncertain habitation" of the boat-ride, as the Ramsays make their way through the bright blue sea toward the lighthouse? "What happens as we begin to ask questions in a 'third' discourse?" Palulis asks (2003, p. 271), "Could this be an Aokian Metonymic moment?" Are these the moments made parenthetical, intertextual, in this collection in the "In-Between" pieces (4 of them, including two by Constance Blomgren and Tasha Henry) punctuating this collection?

"*Aoki re-writes a trope for pedagogy,*" Palulis (2003, p. 272, emphasis in original) acknowledges, "*a trope that dwells with/in a third discourse – a trope that trembles even as it is spoken.*" She continues:

As I read in search of Aokian Metonymies in pedagogy – textualities as doubled gestures – I find my "self" trafficking through intertexts – trafficking through a polysemy of signature and countersignatures – through the readers reading-the-writings – writing-the-readings – high volume traffic in the intertext – trafficking in counterfeit exchanges trafficking as/in *trans*lation – trafficking as/in sur-vival – *entamer* – biting into as/in para-site to host – ec-static moments. (Palulis 2003, p. 273)

Ecstatic moments of "*sublime openness*" (Palulus 2003, p. 259, emphasis in original). These are the locations of living pedagogy, are they not?

In my rewriting of the boat-ride to the lighthouse, Mrs. Ramsay is there, umbrella open to protect her face from the bright crisp sun on the sea. Professor Ramsay, Cam, and James, yes they are still there, but Andrew is too (not killed in the Great War), and Prue as well. There are sandwiches and drink, blue brightness all round. Father and son are reconciled. But Mrs. Ramsay doesn't notice; her eyes are fastened onto the hill below the summerhouse where her beloved Lily Briscoe sits, looking intently at her canvas: "it was blurred." "With a sudden intensity," we are told, "as if she saw it clear for a second, she drew a line there, in the center. It was done; it was finished. Yes, she thought, laying down her brush in extreme fatigue, I have had my vision" (Woolf 1955 [1927], p. 310). Thanks to Erika Hasebe-Ludt and Warren Hurren and those you brought to this intertext, now, thanks, too, to our "line in the center" – the living pedagogy of Ted T. Aoki – we too have had our visions. May they reverberate – "after-words" – in ourselves and our students.

DIFFICULT MEMORIES (2002)

As Marla Morris observes in her introduction, this collection is "many voices sounding difficulties" (2002a, p. 1). It is a sounding that reverberates through the reader, into one's past, into one's future, shaking the present with its dissonance, its irresolvability, its cacophony of cries, screams and howls as we "children of the damned" (Anijar and Mascali 2002, p. 254) face our fate "after" the Holocaust. It is not "after" or "post," as Marla notes; to suggest so is to "commit the sin of historization" (2002a, p. 1). There are other "sins," not the least among them the pedagogical attempt to "apply" "techniques" of "good teaching" to deliver a Holocaust unit more "effectively." Morris (2002a, p. 2) warns:

> Professors will always already fail in an attempt to teach the Holocaust if it serves as a lesson to be learned, a lesson with a plan, a pedagogy with clever strategies. We must avoid becoming clever.... If teaching leads students to believe that we can learn lessons from horrific suffering that suggest that god has a plan for us all and that hope and light are at the end of the tunnel of darkness, we have betrayed our commitment to social justice and the memory of the dead.

There is no betrayal in this collection. It is, as Morris so perceptively and lyrically describes it, "a slippery, fragile, wounded spark" (2002a, p. 3). She has another "spark" in mind as well, the Holocaust survivors who are dying now. "The spark," she writes, "is flickering in the wake of the twenty-first century because many Holocaust survivors are dying. The urgency of this collection, thus, weighs on me" (2002a, p. 3).

This urgency also weighs upon all who open themselves to this momentous collection, a collection that is, not incidentally, excitingly interdisciplinary, informed by, as Marla points out, "as many different kinds of Holocaust memory ... as space will allow" (2002a, p. 7). "Fiction, autobiography, politics, historiography, philosophy, pedagogy and curriculum are all concerns to us" (2002a, p. 7), she notes. That becomes evident in the very first chapter, as Grace Feuerverger, a child of Holocaust survivors, dwells on the fate of the Yiddish language, "a haunting and constant reminder of the devastation of the Jewish people – as well as members of my own immediate family" (2002, p. 13). It is a fact that leaves her "forever wounded." "Yiddish is," Feuerverger (2002, p. 14) writes, "my destiny and my tragedy." Alan Block (2002, p. 25) has tragedy and destiny in mind as well, acknowledging "I am what I remember, even as I am what I forget. What I remember sometimes helps me forget. What I forget sometimes helps me remember. The uncertainty of memory unsettles the certainty of my self."

But while it unsettles, memory is, he suggests, the very prerequisite for selfhood: "Memories create selves. Without memory we do not exist" (Block 2002, p. 36).

The trauma of remembering the Holocaust may shatter the self, but one must not remain dispersed and immoblized. One must gather up the pieces and – this is a key concept, for Claudia Eppert as well as for Marla Morris – take responsibility. One must embody and personify responsibility. "[R]esponsibility," Eppert (2002, p. 60) tells us, "makes no claims for truth, as such. Rather, it foregrounds an unceasing search for truth.... The labor of mourning thus is at once the taking on and learning of responsibility." Like Morris, Eppert (2002, p. 60) warns us that: "Learning cannot be secure or consolatory.... Educational theory and practice, it seems, needs to reorient itself to such an 'insecure' learning."

Such learning is not only arduous, it is itself self-shattering, and it comes as no surprise, as Jutta Schamp (2002, p. 71) reports, that in Germany "there has been very little discussion about the construction of a non-Jewish German 'post-memory,' i.e. the memory of non-Jewish Germans who did not grow up in the Third Reich." Instead of discussion, there "exists a museumalization and a philosemitism that is the flip side of antisemitism among non-Jewish Germans" (Schamp 2002, 75). She quotes journalist Richard Chaim Schneider: "Germany loves its dead Jews, living Jews are repellant" (quoted in 2002, p. 75). "[M]ost Germans," Schamp (2002, pp. 90-91) reports, "repressed the pain that would accompany the enormous grief of accepting perpetratorship, by emotionally repudiating the past, identifying with the victors, and the fast building of a new state."

The flight from the "insecure" and non-consolatory character of learning is evident in Schamp's observation that when the history of Third Reich is taught in Germany:

> Non-Jewish Germans often discuss the crimes and genocide committed by their ancestors in a very rational manner, sometimes losing themselves in figures or dates instead of connecting to their feelings and sharing their family histories for example. Due to this rationalizing and lack of mourning labor, grief is kept at bay, which implies that no real healing can occur. (Schamp 2002, pp. 91-92)

Such an observation seems in sync with those of William C. Doll, who reports that: "I learned a lot about not shouldering responsibility while I was in Germany. I've visited many times and with each return I see more of the dark underside so few Germans want to acknowledge, much less deal with" (Doll 2002, p. 126). For Will, Germany is best expressed by David Lynch's film *Blue Velvet*, in which a patina of normalcy covers violence and perversion. It is this "underside," Doll is suggesting, that must be examined. "But the longer one puts it off," he notes, "the harder it is to reconcile; currently, Germany hasn't begun to reconcile with itself. I know Germans need to; I even bet they want to" (Doll 2002, p. 130).

So should we Americans, with our multiple identities, illustrated by Judy Goldsmith's (2002, p. 117) acknowledgement that: "I am Jewish, American, German." Goldsmith knows three Germanies: "the one of my grandmother's stories, the one from the histories of the world wars, and the one I visit now" (2002, p. 123). The three complicate her identity. There is testimony of lived complexity from Canadians as well, as in David Blades' (2002) moving tale of identification and conversion, and Dennis Sumara's (2002) reflection on his German-born mother. As Dennis points out, "Every moment is two moments. Each speech act, each event (whether remarked upon or not) is the confluence of history and memory" (2002, p. 142).

In the former category is the anti-Semitism of Christianity, which was, as Mary Aswell Doll points out, to be understood by what it was not. It was not Jewish. The complicity of the Church – Protestant and Catholic – during the war is well known. Mary notes that the Church's antisemitism surfaced recently in the present Pope's, John Paul II, advancement of Pius IX to the state of beautification, the last formal step before sainthood. Pope Pius IX, who reigned from 1846 to 1878, was called "The Last King Pope," given that he was of noble birth. But, Mary notes, Pope Pius IX "was anything but noble in his attitude toward Jews," declaring that "of these dogs, there are too many of them present in Rome" (2002, p. 206). The Pope confined them to ghettoes. In fact, Doll continues, the Jewish Roman ghetto was Europe's last enforced ghetto until the Nazi era. There was to be no discussion of his decision; in his proclamation in 1864 of the Syllabus of Errors, Pius condemned the idea of freedom of speech as a "modern error".

Freedom of speech did not typify intellectual life during the Third Reich, evident in the status of "science" during the Nazi period. James R. Watson (2002, p. 108) asserts that:

the practices of Nazi racial hygiene – sterilization, euthanasia, and the industrialized, bureaucratic annihilation of Jews and Gypsies [and gays and lesbians[1]] – can and should be understood today in the context of the rapidly increasing portion of the world's population becoming more superfluous each day. Those comprising what the Nazi doctors called *Ballastexistenzen* are today the global "underclass" for whom there is little remaining compassion.

In their essay, Belinda Davis and Peter Appelbaum (2002, p. 172) work to bring "history to science education and science education to memory," and in so doing study science as a "social and cultural enterprise." During the Third Reich science was in the service of murder. The Nazis did not hesitate to use the status of science, as Davis and Appelbaum (2002, p. 176) point out, in an "expansive" conception of "education,"

seeing the most modern media to communicate its teachings, both within and outside the classroom. Radio shows, posters, film strips, and films informed Germans of the scientific validity of Nazi principles, precisely building on the notion of science's impartiality and essential "truth." Scientists helped validate this image.

Scientists who cooperated with the National Socialism were, as Davis and Applebaum notes, "fellow travelers." Other scientists imagined themselves "bystanders." "The point for school science," Davis and Appelbaum (2002, p. 185)

105

explain, "is not to cultivate students as scientists in either position, but to create skepticism about both roles, and make it possible for science to be practiced in ways that acknowledge and attempt to work through the conflicts identified by different publics."

A contentious issue (and not only for curriculum scholars) concerns the status of the philosophy of Martin Heidegger, influential to many in the field, among them Dwayne Huebner, Ted Aoki, and David Jardine. I too have been a student of Heidegger's work. In this collection, David Jardine (2002, p. 210) tries to work through the horrifying question: "How could someone who thought *this* do *that*?" David declines to deal "with the facts of Martin Heidegger's affiliations with National Socialism, not because these facts are not important, but because no amount of factual dwelling ever ends up especially satisfying" (2002, p. 209). Rather, he concentrates on "Heidegger's insinuation of the generative, bloody mess of interpretation into the heart of (what Husserl wished to be a 'pure') phenomenology, [so that] his works ends up oddly more 'Jewish' than the work of his converted-Jew teacher, Edmund Husserl" (2002, p. 210). Husserl was, Jardine informs us, born into a home in which Yiddish was regularly spoken; his father was a Jewish clothing merchant). Jardine (2002, p. 216) suggests that

> Husserl fell, in his phenomenological project, into the casting of ordinary, everyday life, into the role of the riotously unruly and roughly uncivilized (i.e., "the Jew") needing the salvational clarifications of a transcendental phenomenology (images and aspirations and missionary-zeal of which originate in a conversion from Judaism to Christianity). This certainly gives a chilling read to Husserl's incessant invocation of the need for "purity" and "purification."

"[W]ith the gift of his inheritance from his great teacher," David continues, Martin Heidegger "placed the subject of phenomenology back into the contestations, occlusions, blindnesses, choices, inheritances, obligations, insights and aspirations of the very life that is it topic, its topography, its geography, its homeland. The German is placed back admist the Jews" (2002, 220). For this intellectual accomplishment, it seems, David forgives Martin, or, at least, suspends the matter of his Nazi involvement by focusing exclusively upon his intellectual accomplishment, his "gift" to us. Jardine (2002, p. 224) concludes:

> We have to thank God, then, for Martin Heidegger's interruption of his great teacher's project. And, just as Edmund Husserl offered us the gift of the life world but could not himself walk this path, so Martin Heidegger offered us the gift of interpretation but could not, in the early years of National Socialism, understand his own Jewishness.

Marla Morris is not about to forgive Martin Heidegger. In her essay, entitled "Curriculum Theory as Academic Responsibility: The Call for Reading Heidegger Contextually", Marla asserts that "the project of remembering difficult memories such as the Heidegger Affair demands that we do not forget Heidegger was a Nazi; that we remember that his philosophy devoted to the forgetfulness of Being has already forgotten the Jews" (2002b, p. 243). It is a chilling accusation, namely that Heidegger's philosophy cannot be separated from National Socialism, that it is, in fact, a complex expression of National Socialism. Accordingly, a "contextual" reading requires us to repudiate Heidegger's work as Nazism. "Curriculum as memory text," Marla argues,

> demands that educators teach in ways that do not gloss over the paradoxes of Heidegger. I read Heidegger suspiciously. A contextualist approach, at least for me, leads to condemnation. Heidegger was ungodly, guilty, forgetful and without conscience. As a response to David Jardine's more formalist approach, I suggest that students might have a better understanding of Heidegger when contextualizing his work against the backdrop of the Holocaust. (2002b, p. 243)

Morris' argument is compelling. When I think that one of the Heideggerean notions that has been most influential for me – *Dasein*'s being-toward-death – might be a symbolic recoding of Jews' extermination in the Holocaust, I am horrified. Can this notion – which has been so powerful for me in structuring my remaining time, in answering the question "how shall I live?" – be lifted from its anti-Semitic ground and made over in a life-affirmative fashion? Jardine answers yes; Morris answers, emphatically, no.

This question seems to me to express the larger question that this collection raises, i.e. what is the character and curriculum of "difficult memories"? In our struggles to answer, we must acknowledge, with Karen Anijar and Barbara Mascali (2002, p. 250), that "we are direct inheritors to a historical rupture, a fissure, a chasm, so vast that no leap of faith could forge a bridge." As we struggle with status of Heidegger's work, with the status of ourselves as scholars and intellectuals and teachers "after" the Holocaust, are we left only with a deafening silence, a silence many decline to hear? "[N]obody wants to listen to silence," Anijar and Mascali (2002, p. 262) observe, "which invariably is consigned to nothingness." "But," they remind, "it is still there gnawing away – silently" (2002, p. 262).

Certainly the silence of the dead and the living gnaw away at us as we work our way through this important collection. Marla has forewarned us. "The collection is not a happy one" (2002a, p. 4), Morris tells us in her introduction. "If you, dear reader, are looking for consolation and comfort you will be disappointed.... The systematic annihilation of six million Jews does not have a happy ending.... Perhaps it is at the site of the void that thinking begins. Thus, scholars continue to grapple in the realm beyond comprehension, the realm beyond the thinkable" (2002a, p. 4). Marla's co-editor, John Weaver (2002, p. 170), directs us toward our pedagogical labor beyond the thinkable: "Our task is to build from their [survivors'] words some kind of understanding so our humanity can be (re-)buildt from the ashes of humanity." Marla Morris' *Holocaust and Curriculum* inaugurated this project within the field of curriculum studies; this collection importantly advances it. Let us scatter ashes among our students and ourselves: in remembrance, in responsibility, in reconstruction.

NEGOTIATING THE SELF (2002)

At the beginning of her chapter six, Kate Evans tells us about the day "it" finally happened. The incident underlines the key concepts of this remarkable study as well as the keen intelligence with which Evans brings to bear on its execution, and so I'll start there. One day Evans' partner Annie - a middle-school teacher of art - came home and told her that "it had finally happened" (2002, 175). "It" was the long-anticipated moment when a student asked Annie, in class, "are you a lesbian?" (2002, 175). Annie's response, Evans points out, speaks to a central issue in this study: "Do you think school is a place in which someone could answer 'yes' to that question and feel safe?" (2002, 175).

As Annie and Kate discuss the incident further, one point is clarified right away. Annie felt certain that the student's question was asked only "locally." By this Annie - and Evans - mean that she experienced the question as "between them." Indeed, the student seemed to like and respect her. He wasn't trying to "out" her; he was, evidently, only expressing curiosity about his teacher's sexual orientation. But such questions do not, Evans explains, circulate only locally. Especially by asking "it" in class, Evans notes, the student's action ignored the larger (heterosexist) context of the middle school, in which such questions amount to epithets. In the context of the school there are, presumably, only "straight" people, indicated by, for instance, bulletin-board announcements of teachers' weddings and a heteronormative Health Fair. Moreover, the question ignored the more global context in which homosexuality is often fantasized as a danger to children. In a global context, then, a lesbian teacher is an unacceptable presence in middle school.

In such a local/global setting, Annie did not feel safe chatting about her sexual identity, despite the friendly interest of the respectful student. How could she? As Evans points out, Annie's feeling of being "not safe" was hardly a private emotion, even though it expressed itself to her privately. It was a feeling circulating in the classroom, in the school, however unarticulated, and her experience of it, while personal, was a "negotiation of who she was as a lesbian and a teacher" (2002, 175). Such a negotiation is hardly restricted to her, but occurs with "everyone else in the [class]room and [depends] on depictions of Queer and Teacher that preceded her" (2002, 176). Annie's answer functioned to reconceptualize the question from an innocently "local" to a much more complex "global" one, a deft pedagogical move on her part. Evans writes:

> Her [Annie's] response illustrated how her feelings of discomfort around responding to that question were related to larger social structures. The student may have wanted information, but no information is neutrally local.

The global and local work together, and being aware of how the local and global are working in a particular scenario can help address the complexities of negotiating the self. (2002, 176)

This passage underlines two key concepts in the study: *negotiating identities*, and *local/global*. Evans defines identities as "involved in movements, shifts, and surprises.... I am calling these movements *negotiation*.... Identity [is] a process of connection, disjunction, and movement" (2002, 4). Evans understands that "we negotiate our identities in relation to daily lived experiences as individuals - the *local* - and to larger concepts - the *global*" (2002, 4).

Employing performative senses of "self" and "identity," then, Evans is less interested in asking "what *is* identity" than in "what do identities *do?*" If the self is always in motion, always "doing," then why, Evans asks, does it usually appear to stand still, to remain virtually the same? She answers:

The workings of identity produce the illusion of stability or sameness (identical-ness) through identifications, or what Butler calls *citationality*. Citationality refers to the ways in which social norms are cited through body movements, dress, and speech. Identity is also enacted through repudiation: being female is worked through sufficiently enacting not-male. (2002, 26)

The binary upon which Evans focuses in her study is not so much the female-as-not-male as it is the teacher-as-not-queer. She views the discourse of teacher-as-professional as positioning the teacher as "neutral/heterosexual." A queer teacher is, she suggests, "a threat to the profession" (2002, 129). To the heterosexist, homophobic profession, that s/he is.

Evans' analysis situates the self squarely in the social, more specifically in the political, in the flows of power. She writes:

Not only is identity in the strictest sense (in terms of categories of gender, race, and so on) produced by power; being anything, including *being a human being*, is implicated in subjection. Similarly, we become intelligible in roles such as student, teacher, parent, and child through dialogic processes. (2002, 26)

Here we see the imbrication of the local and the global. Implicit here is Althusser's notion of appellation, of being called to subjecthood, an identity in relation to the other, a politicized relation in which the flows and structures of power position one locally and globally (but not necessarily identically). All this becomes clear in Evans' intriguing interviews with four preservice teachers: Clare, Ruth, Dawn, and Jonas.

Especially noteworthy, I think, is Evans' analysis of emotion, which she suggests is a function of relation. This situates emotion not only "in here" but also "out there." In so doing, Evans points to the political structuring of emotion as well as the politics of emotional work. When lesbian and gay students and teachers suffer emotionally in school settings, we understand that that suffering is the political effect of heterosexism and homophobia. But Evans takes us further. She asks us to focus as well upon the ethical and pedagogical responsibilities embedded in such situations. Evans writes:

> While it can be helpful to pay attention to the emotional work that everyone engages in, I argue that it is incumbent upon those who are part of historically privileged groups to consider the qualitatively different emotional work that those on the margins engage in.... Where there is social pressure to be the same, not different - when difference is branded as deviance - I believe the brunt of the emotional work borne from double consciousness rests with insiders. (2002, 32)

This insight is a major breakthrough in our understanding of teachers' professional (i.e. ethical and pedagogical) responsibility to lesbian and gay students and teachers. What Evans is suggesting, it seems to me, is that it is not enough for "straight" students and teachers to "tolerate diversity" in classrooms. In ethical and pedagogical terms they are called to perform whatever emotional work is required so that queer students and teachers feel and are *welcomed* in their midst, so that queer students and teachers feel and are *safe*.

We can expect many "straight" students and teachers to be surprised when they learn that emotions are, in part, political, and that the heteronormativity of the school requires rather constant emotional labor on the part of queer students and teachers. Why? "Because dominant identities are read as natural," Evans (2002, 34) writes,

> those in dominant groups are less likely to be put in situations in which they must engage in the emotional work of positioning themselves in relationship to norms, or others' expectations. Such emotional work for those in privileged groups tends to occur not so much when their own identities are directly challenged or questioned, but when they are in interaction with someone perceived to be an other. The emotional work of negotiating one's sociohistorically imbued self is likely to be qualitatively different, while in some ways similar, for those who live in the sphere of the naturalized norm than for those who live as deviantly marked others.

Evans' point here is that, again in her words, "we all engage in emotional work, but that it is crucial to consider the context of a given scenario, as well as the historical framing of given identities" (2002, 34). Emotions and emotional work vary according to our positioning, and how we called to negotiate our identities. For those of us deemed "deviant," that work sometimes seems like constant craving.

QUEERNESS IN EDUCATION

As significant as these insights are to our understanding of the negotiations (or movements) of the self, and, in particular, how emotions are implicated in these negotiations, it is not all that Kate Evans achieves in this provocative work. She also provides us with portraits of four preservice teachers' first experiences of negotiating concepts of "queer" and "gay" and "lesbian" and "homosexual." Evans looks at how each teacher speaks about her or his conceptions of, and feelings about, queerness before entering teacher education programs.

Beginning with Clare, then moving to Ruth, Dawn, and Jonas, Evans presents key aspects of each of their stories, lacing them with theoretical threads that respect but highlight the theoretical significance of these autobiographical narratives. In doing so, Evans theorizes how these queer preservice students negotiate "Teacher" in a broader "psychic/social/historical context of ongoing, lived experiences with concepts of Queer." Among the questions Evans poses are:

> What discourses about queerness circulate in the participants' lives? How do the participants understand queerness? What has affected their thinking about this aspect of the self? How have their unfolding understandings of what queerness means to them - in relationship to their families, friends, and colleagues - affected their sense of self? What feelings are evoked as the self is in negotiation, particularly in relation to an abjected psycho/social/historical position? (2002, 118)

What Evans discovers is that while these preservice teachers addressed several contexts in which these questions were significant, the family - not school – turned out to be central one in their narratives.

Back at the university, the four teachers recount how membership in a cohort functioned for them. These groupings, presumably structured for collegiality, were problematic for the participants in Evans' study. Rather than providing an opportunity for professional friendship and support, the fact of being compelled to share "personal" information required emotional labor on their part. These teachers-to-be became quite conscious that their queer selves "were potentially disruptive of the ostensibly smooth heteronormative waters" (2002, 177).

In university courses, the four faced apparently well-meaning professors who nonetheless reiterated binaries of us/them in their pedagogical efforts to address queer issues in education. Evans observes:

> The paradoxes of being a queer self in education became especially evident in Ruth's and Jonas' articulations of feeling both fear and pleasure in negotiating the self. This points to the conundrum of the closet - a position in or outside the closest is not what is at stake. Instead, what is stake is how the workings of the glass closet, the open secret, affect lives. (2002, 177)

When Clare, Ruth, Dawn, and Jonas entered the schools, the global and the local intersected, intensifying the discourses of queer-as-abject and queer-as-dangerous-to-children. The (false) professional notion of teacher-as-neutral (i.e. heterosexual) also intensified, as these four teachers-in-training were positioned as guests and professionals in the classroom. Their interactions with cooperating teachers and students continued to underline the hegemony of heteronormativity, as well as the conundrum of the "open secret," especially as the presence of these prospective teachers challenged conventional gender norms. Evans concludes: "These four stories work through the complex negotiations of the self in relationship to other selves, as well as in relation to global discourses. These discourses are particularly pervasive now, at the turn of a new century, as more and more people view queerness as an issue in education" (2002, 177).

Evans' discussion of several anti-gay incidents underscores just how intense an issue queerness in education has become. There is a very smart analysis of the James Merrick case. There is as well a discussion of the case of a Brookfield, Connecticut teacher named Veronica Berrill. Berrill was accused of "homosexual recruiting" when she declared her high school classroom a "safe zone" for gay students. A San Leandro, California, high-school teacher was disciplined for teaching about racism and homophobia after two parents complained about discussions held in his honors English classes about "issues for minorities and about why gay students may feel unsafe" (2002, 178). The district reprimanded Debro, declaring that he "was guilty of 'unprofessional conduct'" (2002, 178). Shortly thereafter, the "school board devised a "controversial issues policy" specifying that "classroom discussion of controversial issues ... must be cleared in advance by the school principal" (2002, 178). In too many American public schools - especially when queer concerns are articulated – the practice of academic freedom amounts to "unprofessional conduct."

How might teacher education help? One way, Evans answers, involves "critiquing heteronormativity and other invisible structures that naturalize dominant identities" (2002, 179). But, as her study has demonstrated, while including materials about queer issues in teacher education courses can support the rhetoric of inclusion, it can at the same time reproduce normal/deviant binaries if taught without questioning heteronormativity. This occurs when everyone in the classroom is assumed to be straight, or when homosexuality is characterized as a disability or, simply, the opposite of "straight." It can occur as well, Evans tells us, "when Teacher is constructed as neutral (in contrast to Student constructed as diverse)" (2002, 180). She asks: "If an education professor shows a film on gay issues with the implication that 'today is gay day,' the fact that heterosexuality structures the remaining class sessions is likely to go unstated" (2002, 180).

What this implies, Evans points out, is that the pedagogical work of questioning heteronormativity and the self-in-relation-to-others cannot proceed on a rational, cognitive level only. On such a level, in fact, "it is possible that addressing issues of heteronormativity might actually fortify resistance and homophobia" (2002, 182). She affirms Deborah Britzman's profound point that all learning involves conflict, risk, and ambiguity: "In psychoanalytic views, learning is a psychic event" (quoted in Evans 2002, 182). For Evans this means that the self cannot be understood as static or solitary, "not as a thing but as a process ... that we take into consideration that we are both connected to and separate from one another" (2002, 184). It means that emotions are political events, events that must be situated locally and globally, and negotiated, within oneself and among others.

Drawing upon and extending the work of theoreticians and scholars as diverse as Boler, Britzman, Butler, Ellsworth, Foucault, Kristeva, Probyn, and Young-Bruehl, and not without humor, Kate Evans has produced a landmark study that makes several highly significant contributions. Evans has advanced significantly our understanding of the pedagogical politics of emotion, especially in schools and in teacher preparation programs. Now we understand that what we feel, while "ours," is also a social and political event. Consequently, those of us deemed "deviant" must work "overtime" to ensure we do not fall victim to the flows of heteronormative power, flows which are visible on school bulletin boards, but are also invisible as they surround and complicate innocent classroom questions such as "are you a lesbian?"

Moreover, it is clear from Evans' study that the reaction of heterosexist and homophobic students and teachers amounts to a reactionary refusal to perform those orders of emotional labor that those in dominant positions cannot imagine they can or should have to perform, but which they are ethically called to perform. It is a major breakthrough to understand what we (as "queers") are asking "straight" students and teachers to do when we enter "straight" spaces, like classrooms, is the performance of emotional as well as intellectual work, work that they, the dominant gender class, are ethically – professionally - obligated to perform.

Kate Evans' notions of "local/global" and of "negotiating the self" are major additions to our conceptual tools. Her smart analysis and discussion of anti-gay incidents in various regions of the nation underscore the "reality" and power of these concepts. Her conversations with Clare, Ruth, Dawn, and Jonas provide analytical as well as autobiographical vividness and urgency to anti-heteronormative initiatives in teacher education. Her discussion of her own positionality and her inclusion of Annie's experience underline her methodological sophistication, performing, as do her conversations with the four teachers-to-be, the notions of "negotiating the self" in the context of the "local/global." We know now the answer to the question Kate Evans herself poses, "What does it feel like to negotiate Teacher and Queer?" It is a complex feeling, not entirely our own, one requiring labor, intellectual and emotional, animated by constant craving for that safety which permits a student's innocent question of curiosity – "are you a lesbian?" – to be precisely that.

AESTHETICS, POLITICS AND CULTURE (2000)

How lucky for us to have Tom Barone's essays between two covers! How easy it is to miss a scholar's intellectual formation when articles appear here and there, when everyone feels (and is) submerged under the tidal wave of scholarly publication. While every serious curriculum scholar has heard of Thomas Barone, not all of us have been able to follow his intellectual career over the last two decades. Now we can. And now we can make available to our students Barone's unique and important contribution.

Thinking about these past twenty years, Tom is clear about the autobiographical character of his writings. He says at the outset that these writings can be recoded as a life story. Five writers have influenced him most, he tells us, have "alter[ed] most the course of my quest" (2000, p. 2), producing "invaluable disruptions and advancements in the flow of my professional and personal identity" (2000, p. 2). One of these happens to be one of my five (if I were to make a list), Jean-Paul Sartre, the early (or in Tom's words) the "optimistic Sartre." By that he means the Sartre before his Marxist conversion -- the author of *Nausea* and *Being and Nothingness*, almost twenty years before the *Critique of Dialectical Reason* appeared -- the Sartre "still infatuated with the possibilities of a socially committed literature as a means for promoting critical awareness" (2000, p. 4). This is a theme that Tom will emphasize throughout his work.

While Sartre may be one of Barone's intellectual heroes, who was present concretely, in a pedagogical relation to him, was his Ph.D. mentor Elliot Eisner, whom Tom terms his "mentor," "friend," "teacher/critic," a "connoisseur of life" (2000, p. 10). The first and distinguishing feature of Eisner's intellectual leadership, he tells us, was "a courage born out of a deep sense of professional responsibility" (2000, p. 18). Second was his civility. Barone must have been an exemplary student, for these two qualities also mark his achievement. We can discern Eisner's influence in Barone's early concern for "the experienced curriculum" (2000, p. 19), the lived reality of those in classrooms, a reality he wants from the start to honor. How? As a curriculum theorist, he wants to honor it by describing it precisely, by which he means "qualitatively," narratively, and specifically, fictionally. Not only empathetic loyalty to the experience of those in schools prompts him to structure his research so: a larger sense of professionalism leads him to argue for writing which inspires and persuades a seemingly indifferent public. Early on he suggests that the point of curriculum inquiry is inspiration.

Characterizing the work of scholars such as Dwayne Huebner (and Pinar) as curriculum "philosophy" (in contrast to "theory"), Tom argues that "curriculum theory can also serve a somewhat more traditional purpose: that is, to be more directly helpful to practitioners in planning and using actual curricula" (2000, p. 51). While both Dwayne and I would insist we are trying to be helpful to teachers too, true enough it is not our, especially my, only motive. Faithful to his mentor, Tom writes (2000, pp. 58-59) that

> The kind of theory envisioned here is for thoughtful practitioners ... portraying curriculum-in-use. And so, a research agenda for interested parties: to insinuate such theory in portraits of curricula-in-use, to provide these critiques to practitioners, and to carefully watch what happens.

Over time, he also wants these portraits to persuade politicians and policymakers to change their perceptions of schools and schoolpeople. But for now, in the early essays, Barone is thinking about a new version of curriculum inquiry, one, like "great literature ... lures he or she who experiences it away from the shores of literal truth and out into uncharted waters where meaning is more ambiguous" (2000, p. 61). With writers such as Truman Capote, Norman Mailer, Tom Wolfe, and Joan Didion in mind, Barone writes: "Ultimately, I erased the boundary between the realm of the text which purports to give only the facts and that of a metaphor-laden story which dares to (as Sartre once put it) lie in order to tell the truth" (2000, p. 62).

For those who may have pigeonholed Barone's scholarship as "aesthetic" or "simply" an extension of Eisner's, think again. Barone demonstrates throughout his work an explicit political commitment, one that he situates generationally and historically:

> For I remain deeply appreciative of the opportunity for coming of age in an irreverent, socially committed era like the 1960s, a time which fostered sensitivity to the imperfections of society, which opened our eyes to the plight of the less fortunate around us, to the groups of disenfranchised -- including (since my eyes are still open) today's public school teachers whose professional autonomy and status have steadily eroded within our increasingly bureaucratized and depersonalized system of schooling. (2000, pp. 64-65)

The obsession with equating education to business, the naive faith in technology (which hardly began with computers; examine the literature on slides, educational radio, TV -- see Pinar et al., 1995, p. 704 ff.), and the epistemological narrowness of mainstream social science research in education are all related, Barone suggests. They have to do with the fact that:

> We Americans are indeed inhabitants of a callow culture, a nation in its adolescence, one lacking the maturity that could provide a strong sense of who we are and where we want to go as a people. This partially explains, I believe, our infatuation with the tools which science gives us. With no clearly defined vision of our own we find it convenient to partake of the half-hidden values implicated in the use of technology. (2000, p. 66)

He adds: "Educators, we too are children of our culture, and have lacked the vision and the voice, the will to question where we are being led by our inventions" (2000, p. 66). Children in an immature culture: we have much to study if we are ever to grow up.

SELF, SOCIETY, AND THE SCHOOL

Given these cultural conditions and such macro-political initiatives such as America 2000, Barone asks: "can schools of education hope to transform schooling from the 'bottom up'?" Discussing that 1991 example of school reform, Tom finds it "hard to argue with the premise that the rigid, omnipresent, traditional organizational structure of the American public schools needs rethinking" (2000, p. 119). But he doubts that the kind of school designs sought in America 2000 would break that mold. Indeed, the promise of most macro-reforms has been a "continuation of pedagogical practices aimed at molding American students into a standardized product" (2000, p. 120). Observing that "it is hardly news to note that the American school is patterned after the industrial workplace" (2000, p. 120), Barone reminds that "standardized schools with standardized visions of success tend to produce standardized human beings" (2000, p. 121). If we're serious about devising truly "New American Schools," ones that would break the mold of standardization, we would support schools that

> offer students and teachers the autonomy of the artist who works toward an end that is emergent, and not yet in view. They would be concerned less with molding students in accordance with "national consensus standards" than with providing the growth of unique, powerful, integrated identities. They would support a process wherein teachers assist each student in the weaving (and reweaving) of profoundly educational, aesthetic experiences into a narrative, or story, of a unique and responsible *self.* (2000, p. 121)

Were we in a political position to pull this off!

Barone then explicates the main points in this vision of school as profoundly autobiographical. Narrating one's life story, he reminds us, represents nothing less than the construction of self. It is in a fundamental sense an aesthetic and interpretative (i.e., hermeneutical) process. Relying on George Herbert Mead, Barone views personal identity as neither a material substance nor a spiritual soul, but a sense of oneself constructed by a conscious human person. So conceived, he conceives of schools as communities of strong poets and storytellers in search of the good life.

But what, you say, is the good life? To answer he invokes the work of Charles Taylor, Richard Rorty, Harold Bloom, and Friedrich Nietzsche. Like Nietzsche, Barone suggests that: "a good life is like a good original story or poem insofar as disparate thoughts and actions are consciously shaped into a narrative unity, an aesthetic form" (2000, p. 125). Such a coherence does not derive from "weakness and imitation, but through will and autonomy" (2000, p. 125); it is what Nietzsche called "style." And style, Barone suggests, is the primary attribute of the "strong poet," by which he means:

> someone who refuses to accept as useful the descriptions of her life written by others. Instead, the strong poet is a strong storyteller, continuously revising her life story in the light of her own experience and imagination. The strong poet constantly redescribes her past interactions with the world around her, constantly reinvents her self, so that she may act in the future with greater integrity and coherence. The strong poet plots her life story toward her own emergent ends and purposes. (2000, p. 125)

These ends and purposes are not formulated "in solitary confinement" (2000, p. 125).

A strong poet is no "disengaged esthete" (2000, p. 125), busily weaving an effete self in rarefied existential isolation. Instead, s/he is very much "a social being and a moral agent, a responsible citizen of a shared community." Barone thinks of Dewey here, who reminded us that the renewal of self and community are interwoven and can occur only within a democratic culture. The more democratic and equitable the distribution of power in any given society, the more likely, Barone suggests, that strong poetry will be composed and communicated broadly. "Now," he asks, "what if the New American Schools adopted the notion of a strong poet as the ideal student" (2000, p. 126)?

Now that *would* be revolutionary. Tom Barone is clear that we'll get no help from "above," that whatever gains we make we will make by ourselves in collaboration with our friends teaching in the schools. So it is "we" who will have to elaborate an agenda based on the notion of "strong poet," and to that end Tom asks: "[w]hat educational moves could we make toward realizing our hopes for students who have style" (2000, p. 126)? He suggests two, "two phases of the educational act, each of which must, to be successful, exhibit certain aesthetic attributes" (2000, p. 126). In the first of these the teacher "reads" those narratives of the life-text of the student that s/he has composed and lived through. In the second the teacher invites the student to explore aesthetic experiences that, the teacher hopes, will provide "wondrous" avenues toward the future.

Autobiographical work is not certain, as Barone is well aware. He points to a sharp sense of "uncertainty that accompanies this process of self-creation" (2000, p. 126), uncertainty that is (after Frank Kermode) the source of considerable human anxiety. There is, then, a certain courage prerequisite to the process of self-fashioning, not only a courage that enables one to dwell in uncertainty over one's self, but a courage that supports one in facing up to others, including those one encounters in the often predatory world of politics. So understood, stories "can be, as Foucault put it, *transgressive*" (2000, p. 128), offering "radical alternatives for thinking about the world and acting within it" (2000, p. 128). Most fundamentally perhaps, "composing stories is an additional mode of sense-making that offers practice for the imposing task of living" (2000, p. 128).

Key to this process is the teacher's presence, and it is a particular modality of being present that Barone pinpoints: "The pedagogue plays important role in making these engagements more likely to occur.... [S/he] must engage in the aesthetic project of empathic understanding" (2000, p. 129). As an "aesthetic project," empathetic understanding is, Barone suggests, "more than mere intuition or feeling because what is striven for is not purely emotional identification but rather an *idea* of a piece of subjective life" (2000, p. 129), one, I would add, that must not collapse one's own critical distance. As I have suggested elsewhere, empathy conceals as it reveals, and I think Tom's distinction between "identification" and an "idea" of another subjective life helps reduce the risk. Risky business even so, empathy can permit one to encounter another's "life expression," a process (referring to Dewey) that "can deepen the teacher's appreciation of the student's *funded biography*, the integral mass of her accumulated life experiences" (2000, p. 130).

"The learning event," understood from this perspective, "may become the kind of aesthetic experience that Dewey called *educational*: a growth-inducing experience that grants the capacity for having even richer experiences in the future" (2000, p. 130). Key to this capacity is storytelling, by means of which "a student may have discovered new options for interpreting the world and new possibilities for living" (2000, p. 130). These possibilities offer greater autonomy, including the possibility of redescribing, refashioning the self. Moreover, "with the guidance of a wise and empathetic teacher, she may have written some mighty strong poetry" (2000, p. 130). That is one point of empathy: educational experience. Barone puts it this way: "[T]he educator comes to understand empathetically the lives of her students in order to arrange the environment intelligently toward the promotion of aesthetic experiences," experiences that lead "toward the continual revision of the poem of who that student, specifically, can be" (2000, p. 131). Yes.

QUALITATIVE INQUIRY

None of this is self-evident or easy. The rigor and discipline of such pedagogical labor requires regular rest, and in one essay Tom thinks of Sunday morning as one occasion for a "sabbatical." Perhaps, as Tom tells he does, one listens to music, reserving "Sunday mornings for engaging in a musical kind of celebration, for listening to the contrapuntal harmonies of a fugue" (2000, p. 137). Barone seems to be thinking of educational research as a kind of fugue, for he writes: "When used for educational purposes, a text of qualitative inquiry is, I propose, better viewed as an occasion than as a tool. It is, more precisely, an occasion for the reader to engage in the activities of textual re-creation and dismantling" (2000, 138). Tom goes on to point out that such activities -- recreation and dismantling -- require a narrative mode of thinking, one that suggests "a reordering of the totem pole of qualitative inquiry genres, a challenging of important premises of the educational research establishment" (2000, p. 138).

He is *not* thinking about "the high priests Campbell and Stanley," who "offered holy communion in strict accordance with paradigmatic canons, and *every day was Sunday*" (2000, p. 150). In this testament, qualitative inquiry is a kind of heresy, a research heresy involving the "steady recovery of the human voice" (2000, p. 150).

119

This trend leaves Barone optimistic about the future of qualitative inquiry, so much so that he imagines a day when "editors of prominent journals of educational inquiry will publish the most accomplished pieces of literary fiction with educational themes" (2000, p. 151), when "the teacher-educator should act as critical-co-investigator ... serving as leader of a discursive community of professionals in which each member shares responsibility for critical reflection and discussion" (2000, p. 153). This form of qualitative inquiry, Barone suggests, transcends distinctions between objectivity and subjectivity, terms that, he suggests (after Richard Rorty), have become "nuisances." Instead, he continues, "I will recommend that as educational inquirers we no longer talk about research texts as being objective or subjective but about texts that are more or less useful or, in varying degrees and ways, persuasive" (2000, p. 162).

To help us think about was such texts would look like, Tom turns to literature, not education. He summons Charles Dickens, Theodore Dreiser, Harriet Beecher Stowe, and Richard Wright, whom he praises for having "offered readers occasions for reconstructing their tired, safe views of social conditions into more radical and utopian one. My hope is for educational inquirers soon to do the same" (2000, p. 172). Barone's emphasis upon social justice leads him to think of another novelist (and playwright and essayist and philosopher): Jean-Paul Sartre. "I explicitly endorse," he tells us, "a Sartrean brand of storytelling that is both popular and socially conscientious" (2000, p. 179). To illustrate, Tom tells us the story of Billy Charles Barnett. It is, I think, the most poignant piece in the collection.

BILLY CHARLES

Eschewing "professional" labels of expert and client, Tom names himself and the 15 year-old boy as "representatives of two subcultures, meeting at McDonald's along an interstate highway in northeastern Tennessee" (2000, p. 181). Across from him is "Billy Charles Barnett, a tall lanky boy with dark hair, green eyes, a pug nose, and an infectious grin. He is a member of the rural 'disadvantaged,' a 15-year-old nominated by the vice-principal as the student least likely to remain in Dusty Hollow Middle School. I am a middle-aged urban academic who, secure in a tenured university position, will never leave schools" (2000, p. 181). There are echoes of Dickens here. And there is Sartre's commitment to classlessness, as Barone positions himself, not the boy, as the one lacking knowledge: "Even more jolting is a sudden realization of my vast ignorance about the ways of people who live within a two-hour drive of my home and about the fundamentals of a world no longer honored in the dominant culture" (2000, p. 181). Stuck in seventh grade for a second year, "Billy Charles ... has expressed on numerous occasions his intentions to drop out of school as soon as he can. And I know that, on occasion, he has entertained fantasies of dropping out of life, as well" (2000, p. 182).

Part of Billy Charles story has to do with class and region, and part of it, as Barone tells us, has to do with his father. There had been a period -- "a glorious time, according to Billy Charles" (2000, p. 183) -- when he and his father were very close, when the older man guided the younger one "into his own Appalachian manhood. Almost daily Billy Charles and his father went out in the wilds, the two of them together, teacher and apprentice. Billy Charles was joyously receiving an education in the real basics, eagerly learning the time-honored skills of survival.... He was absorbed in the fundamentals of the world around him. Almost daily for a year, rain or shine, this wilderness school was in session" (2000, p. 183). But the son is forced from the Garden after the father begins beating him. Barone: "So a father turns viciously on a son, who, in a time of delicate adolescent need, is reluctant to leave -- until the final incident of abuse when the new family decides to vacation in Florida" (2000, p. 183). While there Billy Charles writes his mother for help, to which she responds, and "so, on the verge of manhood, Billy Charles went back to Mama, back to a place strewn with so many obstacles to his escape" (2000, p. 184).

Back with mother, Billy Charles finds himself in the wilderness that is the school, a place from which he is rather completely estranged. But here too Barone refuses to blame the boy, writing that "what use, after all, are passivity and punctuality to denizens of the forest" (2000, p. 187)? I leave the remainder of the tale to Tom, but I do want to underline the conclusion he draws, for it is at the center of the essay and of this book:

> His case revives our fading dreams of a broader sort of empowerment that schools once hoped to provide for *all* American children, regardless of their economic or social backgrounds. This included the power to use the disciplines for penetrating more deeply into one's own past and present world, the power to imagine a wide range of alternative worlds in other times and places, and the power to express these understandings by employing many forms of literacy -- verbal, visual, musical, kinesthetic, and so on. (2000, p. 187)

That is a dream many of us share, however faded the last thirty years have rendered it. For all his determination and hopefulness, Tom Barone has his somber moment. "Empowering teachers (and students) in this way," he admits toward the end, "may require more resources than our society is willing to provide. We will need to reeducate teachers, to reduce their workload, and to purchase material resources to link the local community with the larger one" (2000, p. 188). As unlikely as that is in the short term, we have no choice but to work to make this dream come true, "because Billy Charles Barnett has reminded us that doing anything less is till a very risky business" (2000, p. 189).

SOCIALLY COMMITTED LITERATURE

Risky business indeed, but as Barone realizes, the public sleeps, complicit in the failure of the school to do what it could, must, do. That sleep and complicity call to mind another historical period in which the public denied what was happening around it, Europe in the 1930s, a time during which the young Sartre formulated his concept of a socially committed literature. No doubt that plus his experience as a resistance fighter in Vichy France (he was captured and served time as a prisoner of war) formed in him a strong commitment to participate in the predatory politics of post-war Europe. Sartre was determined to speak to that world, to influence its formation through his writing, to reach not only other intellectuals but literate readers everywhere through his essays, articles (in *Les Temps Modernes*, for instance), plays and, in the 1960s, street politics. In the shadow of this great twentieth-century intellectual, Barone is not asking so very much of us, education professors who might, he hopes, try to influence the public to support the formation of a world that children and teachers might gladly inhabit: the school.

We in the academy, Barone urges, must "strive to reverse the usual pattern of research-follows-funding by going over the heads of government policy-makers to the primary source of our political democracy" (2000, p. 206). Yes, he wants to speak with our neighbors, our friends, with politicians, with anybody who will listen. "We speak to them," he tells us, "not from a distance, not through texts that need translation by intermediaries, but directly and compellingly so that the public ceases to imagine teachers and schoolkids as essentially negligent and malevolent characters in need of externally imposed discipline, and begin to understand the nature of the unfortunate culture and institutional forces that impinge upon their lives" (2000, p. 206).

There have been non-fictional examples of educational writing that, in part, achieve this aim of speaking directly to the larger public on behalf of teachers and children in schools. Barone thinks of Kozol's *Savage Inequalities*, which "exemplifies the kind of writing I call socially committed literature" (2000, p. 230); it is "a latter-day example of the sort of literary endeavor favored by John Paul Sartre" (2000, p. 230). Barone reminds us that Sartre was committed to the "irreducible historicity of the writer" (2000, p. 230), but that "as an inhabitant of a later era, a participant in a postmodern intellectual culture, I cannot endorse every Sartrean assertion about the nature and purpose of committed writing" (2000, p. 230). What Barone does draw from Sartre is the primacy of the researcher/author's commitment to social justice, a sharp sense of her/his intended audiences, and her/his conscious choice of rhetorical tools for engaging those audiences in the issues in which one is engaged. Sartre was not satisfied with mere description, for description is "pure contemplative enjoyment" (2000, p. 231). Nor was he content to explain it, for, again in Sartre's words, "explanation is acceptance, it excuses everything" (2000, p. 231). Why did he write? Tom answers: "Sartre wrote to transform the world" (2000, p. 231). As Sartre put it: "The world and man reveal themselves by *undertakings*. And all the undertakings we might speak of, reduce themselves to a single one, *making history*" (quoted in Barone 2000, p. 231). In this respect, like Sartre, we must become committed to the elaboration of "particular historical contingencies [i.e. schools] at the expense of academic abstractions" (2000, p. 236).

This capacity and commitment to speak to the public in the name of making history is not limited to exceptional individuals like Sartre. "I believe," Barone (2000, p. 238) asserts, "that many of today's educational researchers (especially qualitative researchers) also possess, to a much greater extent than they can imagine, the 'very special talents' needed for making history." "What has prevented us from trying?" he asks (2000, p. 238). The answer, he suggests, has to do in part with our conception of what our work is. We must, he urges us, move

> away from a posture of scholarly detachment toward one of passionate commitment to a redistribution of social resources; away from texts aimed exclusively at our academic colleagues toward direct communication with additional constituencies (such as educational practitioners, policymakers, and the public-at-large) who must join in the enactment of such a redistribution; away from the detached, arcane, technical languages of philosophical and scientific theory, toward modes of discourse feared by powermongers throughout history, the vernacular languages of literature.... I believe that we can transform, not only the field of educational research, but also the landscape of American schooling. (2000, pp. 238-239)

As the title of his book suggests, Thomas Barone links aesthetics with politics in the context of educational inquiry, an inquiry he reformulates as directed to the larger public, inquiry that is at once fictional and socially committed. In this respect, he has extended and made more complex and provocative the rich legacy he inherited from his mentor, Elliot Eisner. He has honored his own autobiographical and generational commitments as well as demonstrated a perceptive, judicious view of contemporary curriculum scholarship. These essays perform what they ask us to consider, namely a self-reflexive political commitment to social justice, justice for students and for teachers. He asks us as scholars and teachers in the university to reposition ourselves, to decline our roles as polite facilitators of policymakers' pronouncements, in fact to bypass policymakers in an effort to persuade the public to see the schools as they are, the places where our children live much of their childhood, engaged in projects of self-fashioning and world transformation, in a word: education. Tom's loyalty to the school is no knee-jerk gendered reaction to lost influence, but a historically-situated, socially-engaged commitment to concretely-existing individuals, young and old alike. For that he merits not only our sustained applause, but our support.

THINKING QUEER (2000)

There are several points to be made about this remarkable collection of examples of "queer thinking." First, for those of us who identify with the lesbian and gay "community," there is in this volume an affirmation in being represented, in hearing our voices. For that, we all owe a debt of thanks to Susan Talburt and Shirley Steinberg and to the other contributors to this timely book. The appearance of "queer thinking" in the field of education is recent, its formulation in an early stage, even as the political hour feels late. There is an urgency to this work -- people are still dying, being bashed, being discriminated against, still suffering unnecessarily in a myriad of ways, public and private -- which demands that we summon our courage, achieve some measure of solidarity, and press ahead. It feels as if there is momentum, however vague and fragile, and the appearance of this collection supports that.

But this book is not only about politics. In this early phase of conceptual development, it is important to think about everything. After all, it is "everything" -- the straight world -- that is our problem. That is evident here: from the opening of a gay and lesbian office on campus to film to television sitcoms to cartoons and "dyke adventures," whatever occurs to us is legitimate subject matter for queer thinking. The point is to think about "whatever" queerly, not only to legitimate our own experience, but to teach others, both queer others who might feel isolated and intimidated and disempowered *and* straights, many of whom remain quite clueless, not only about us, but about themselves. In this regard the diversity of theme, of point of view, and of intellectual method are all strengths in this collection.

In terms of the broad field of education, there is an escalating movement into cultural studies, an umbrella term under which queer thinking, for many, for the moment, rests. Popular culture has become, it seems, a primary source of the scholarly study of education. In this collection films (*In & Out*), cartoons (*South Park*), television sitcoms (*Ellen*) are all occasions for queer inquiry; in one instance -- "Fierce Dyke Adventures" -- inquiry *is* a cartoon. Subjects perhaps more recognizable to our more conventional colleagues in education -- school uniforms, adolescent literature (portraying lesbians and gay men), reading queerly (in this instance complexity theory), and, as mentioned, a study of the opening of a gay and lesbian office on campus -- are also explicated. The public schools seem, as Karen Anijar notes, "increasingly anachronistic," and the refocusing of scholarly attention away from the school toward the culture at large seems well underway among a number of straight as well as queer scholars.

Anijar's study – deleted from the published version: references here are to the pre-publication manuscript I received - can serve as a sign. In her provocative piece the public schools are in fact a cartoon, that is to say Comedy Central's *South Park*. Calling it campy, if new-right campy (a "weird" concept, as Will of NBC's *Will and Grace* once pointed out, that also describes gay Republicans), Anijar doesn't see what all the (right-wing) fuss is about. While she defends the right of young people to watch it, she focuses on the marketing of the program to introduce her main concern: consumer capitalism and the commodification of, well, everything, including queers. This renders us "consumers" -- not political or civic agents -- and this omniscient apoliticalness is evident, she worries, in queer theory, which evidently Anijar associates with men, given that she dismisses it as little more than a "hermeneutic circle jerk of politicized apoliticalness."

Nor does Anijar have much use for "Tom Hanky of Philadelphia" -- Shirley Steinberg's (1998) critique of the film is pertinent here -- and Karen is left wondering whether "by coming out of the closets and onto the streets a larger cage has been constructed under a capitalist and commodified rubric." Does "becoming conscious of our subject position in a peculiar stew of signification" translate into "a retreat from any notions surrounding egalitarian social justice and democracy"? She wants the gay life "to mean more than cheesy poofs thrown on the pyre of the market." The apparent progress of lesbian women and gay men in America is just that, apparent, as she concludes: "But, the more things change the more things seem to remain, sadly the same."

Glorianne Leck needs no television to find evidence of commodification and standardization. Look no further than school uniforms, a policy proposed by a number of school boards (certainly the case here in south Louisiana), comprised of "representative members of the successful middle and professional class," whose "gender display and work costume ... seems designed to reveal their performance of 'right' attitudes toward work, competition, gender, sexuality, nationalism, self-restraint, and religious conformity" (2000, p. 177). Those school boards who have voted to endorse school uniforms evidently assume that by requiring students "to wear specific costumes of clothing" (2000, 177) they "will reduce inappropriate displays of sexuality in the school setting and will reduce the often extreme social consequences of adolescent fashion competition" (2000, p. 177).

Leck is not persuaded: "Masking may appear to level the playing field, but those educators committed to working with social inequities are likely to find that the mask of a school uniform actually impedes their efforts" (2000, p. 178). Why? Because "they do deny important socially interactive opportunities, and they do mask social cues" (2000, p. 180). She quotes Georg Simmel: "At the same time it [fashion] satisfies in no less degree the need of differentiation, the tendency toward dissimilarity, the desire for change and contrast" (quoted in Leck 2000, 181). As for herself: "Clothes continue to do much to communicate the performance of my sexual, gender, and erotic orientation and my resistance to heteronormativity," and so she decries "the imposition of paper doll clothes called school uniforms" (2000, p. 182).

In a succinct summation of the state of contemporary American culture, Leck notes that "prayer and the lottery appear to be the leading currencies of hope" (2000, p. 190). In the bleak landscape that is the American present, Leck concludes: "I wish to suggest, as one who claims voice as a feminist and a queer, that in the effort by school boards to neutralize the clothing displays of female children and to de-sex the clothing displays of non-heterosexually inclined and differently-gendered children, there is a denial of the historical and individual conditions of each one of us" (2000, p. 194).

Such "denial" is also evident on the big screen, as Shirley Steinberg points out. As she did with *To Wong Foo* ... and other films in her earlier essay on "appropriating queerness" (Steinberg 1998), here Steinberg insightfully critiques Paul Rudnick's *In & Out* (1997), going, as usual, right to the heart of the matter. "Why then," she asks, "is Rudnick so careful to not allow his gay character to have sex" (2000, p. 156)? She answers that the reason has to do with "crossing the heterosexual line of decency," a line that not only offers security to straight viewers, but in her view "defines what gayness might be" (2000, p. 156). Queers in film (she suggests the situation isn't much different on the little screen: television) function primarily to "accessorize and to get laughs" (2000, p. 157). While many queer film-goers may appreciate what appears to be a greater tolerance, Steinberg warns us that "we haven't come a long way, baby, and I am concerned that the public support and acknowledgement for a film such as *In & Out* perpetuates an intolerant tolerance that serves only to re-define in a palatable fashion what queerness should be" (2000, p. 159).

Is there no good news for those of us who think and live queerly? Certainly none in the widely-celebrated "coming out" episode of comedian Ellen Degeneres, as evident in Nancy Lesko's smart analysis. Lesko begins by reiterating Arthur Korker's point that nothing happens in American culture unless it happens on television. Judged with this point in mind, Ellen's television coming out would seem to have been, Nancy notes, "demonstrable progress, worthy of ecstatic celebration" (2000, 161). But there the party ends, as Lesko points out that Ellen proclaimed her lesbian identity only in safe terms, ones that were "very familiar, non-sexual, personalized, and commodified" (2000, p. 165).

Lesko's argument is that in the commodification of Ellen, her lesbian identity was "contained within consumption, monogamous and invisible sexuality, and a middle-class emphasis on a therapeutized self" (2000, p. 165). She recalls Robyn Wiegman and Lynda Zwinger's notion of "heterovisuality" -- "the potential continuity between female homosociality and female homosexuality is disavowed through an intense insistence on a heterosexualized femininity, on the one hand, and through the cultivation of individual narratives of performance and personality on the other" (2000, p. 170) -- to underscore that Ellen's coming out "didn't take us very far" (2000, p. 171). It "may have made us laugh, but questioned little else" (2000, p. 171).

Nor is there much reason to celebrate when we consider lesbian and gay adolescent literature, as Rob Linne does. Linne points out that in adolescent lesbian and gay literature young queer characters are often punished with violence even death, the message being that if you try gay sex something terrible will probably happen to you. Linne makes the sound suggestion that educators make sure they choose: "1) books that illustrate gay empowerment as well as gay victimization; 2) stories that openly explore gay sexuality rather than hiding it as something shameful; and 3) novels that include a colorful multiplicity of character types" (2000, p. 205), and concludes helpfully with a list of suggested readings.

So far, popular culture rules, but the "queendom" is not a happy place. The mood shifts a bit in Marla Morris' intriguing essay where "high" culture makes an appearance, not that "high" culture is guaranteed to give us a rush. Morris summons Dante no less to assert that queer theorists/activists can be, quoting Mandelbaum, "zealously prophetic, politically messianic, indignant, nervous ... theatrical" (quoted in Morris 2000, p. 15). Although students of education have tended to regard theory and activism as separate spheres, Marla merges the two: "I read queer theory as a form of activism and queer activism as a form of theory" (2000, p. 15). Agreeing with Derrida that identity is a "trap," Morris argues that queer representations are "prophetic," as "they announce the coming of an age where sexualities are pluralities, where genders are multitudinous, where subjectivities are like tides of the ocean" (2000, p. 23). That is a powerful image, suggestive of, among other things, the unconscious, a topic in which Deborah Britzman has considerable interest.

Britzman removes queer concerns from the surface of popular culture and the land of identity politics back to the ocean, to use Marla Morris' image. That is, Britzman is interested in nothing less than the very character of sexuality and identity, suggesting that the two are not simply conjoined, and not only at the hip. We are, she suggests, not only estranged from ourselves in terms of consciousness or rationality, but even our semi-conscious desires "slip between the fault lines of recognition and misrecognition, our urges divide in the strange calculus of ignorance and knowledge, and our passions contradict in aim and satisfaction" (2000, p. 33). We know our straight friends are queer and don't get it, but have we considered that we too may misunderstand our desire?

Psychoanalytically, Britzman points out, the very concept of sexuality implies excess; we desire "more than we consciously ask for or even want" (2000, p. 33). Eros is, after Freud, "something between the wish and need" (2000, p. 33). The three forms of resistance to sexuality which interest Britzman are structural, pedagogical, and psychical, this last form an indication that the self is divided from itself. "Can education be sexed?" (2000, p. 35) she asks provocatively. There would seem to be a vague association between knowledge and sexuality, both of which threaten "to ruin innocent lives, or as ... sacred object[s] that require protection, deferral, maturity, and social and legal sanction" (2000, p. 35). Again she asks the provocative question: "Is there any difference between falling in love with ideas and falling in love with a person" (2000, p. 36)? Is it possible to separate the idea from the embodied subjectivity who teaches it?

Britzman would seem to answer no, as "without sexuality, the human would not desire to learn" (2000, p. 38). More generally, "without sexuality there is no curiosity" (2000, p. 39). "The question of sexuality," she writes (or is it the sublimation of sexuality) "is central to the question of becoming a citizen, to crafting a self who can invent, over and over again, the courage to stand up for the self, to feel passionately for the conditions of others, to create a life from the experiments of learning to love and making from this learning to love, a love of learning" (2000, p. 39). The fact that one loves, rather that the gender of the person one loves, may be paramount, as she concludes "the question is not which policy to make on which sexuality but how the strange workings of sexuality can allow for the rethinking of education" (2000, p. 52).

It is the former which preoccupies many, as Susan Talburt knows. Her concern is policy in higher education, and specifically the complex perhaps dialectical relation between policy and identity politics. To study this problem she examines "the highly contentious" (2000, p. 62) opening of a gay-lesbian-bisexual office at a public research university. Talburt is interested in how "institutionalized gay and lesbian identity politics can result in psychologizing gay men and lesbians" (2000, p. 63) and in the process disguise the social and specifically institutional production of identities. In the campus rhetoric she studied, gays and lesbians tended to be represented as white, "women" were coded white and heterosexual, and all "raced" persons were to assumed to be straight. In the opening of the office, identity politics was invoked to characterize gay men and lesbians as a pre-constituted minority group, a set of citizens who pays taxes, is discriminated against, and merits its own office. There appeared, as an additional rationale, what Talburt terms a pathology model of gay and lesbian needs, needs produced by our suffering due to harassment. This displaced the first political rationale in arguments for the establishment of the office.

In a third phase, identity politics, educational equity, and pathology merged as agreement was reached. As a sphere apart from the "real" world, the university was characterized as both responsible for leading and responding to social change. In terms of research on higher education, questions of institutional stasis or transformation might be reframed, Talburt suggests, in terms of the relations of institutional practices to identity-based movements, focusing our attention on how institutional practices both respond to and construct identity.

Clearly, queer thinking may be focused upon extant fields of study, such as higher education in Talburt's essay or upon social research, as when Darleen Opfer sets out to disprove Lipset and Raab (1970) and Hofstadter (1965) thesis that "extremism" and "paranoid politics" result when corporate status displacement becomes anomic status displacement. In other words, when individuals suffer social displacement, particularly of an economic nature, Lipset, Raab, and Hofstadter argued that they then refocus their frustration onto a target-population, which then gets the blame for their change in social status. Sound familiar? Opfer doesn't think so. She suggests that if this theory were true for the contemporary religious right, the incidence of anti-gay action should be declining, as its power seems steady or ascendent. But this is not the case. Opfer argues that the typical fundamentalist engages in anti-queer activism due to specific religious beliefs (something which is accepted in this study but might well be challenged). For this reason, she (generously) concludes that the religious right cannot be dismissed as paranoid or extremist. Not only is the status displacement theory mistaken, employing it now, Opfer worries, provokes more fundamentalists to anti-gay action, and is therefore ill-advised.

Others who think queerly seem unconcerned about the right, or is that because they live in Toronto? For Brent Davis and Dennis Sumara, queer theory involves reconceptualizing an extant area "queerly." Brent and Dennis reframe "complexity theory" as another queer theory and, in particular, employ it to question taken-for-granted ideas of development, education, research, and identity. They aim to render "strange" (an echo perhaps of Maxine Greene's 1973 book) and "queer" those academic discourses, including "complexity theory," that, in their words, "have banished the mark of the troublesome biological body to support an idealized epistemic body" (2000, p. 107). They define complexity theory as a field of inquiry that "examines those phenomena that are self-organizing, adaptive, and dynamic" or, to put the matter another way, "phenomena that are alive or, at least, that we tend to describe with metaphors drawn from vibrant bodies, evolving organisms, and life processes" (2000, p. 107).

Vibrant bodies? Davis and Sumara come to the conclusion that any study of "queer" identities must not begin with "the lived experiences of those who explicitly identify as queer," but with the contentious process of emptying the "heterosexual closet" (2000, p. 123). That closet, while marked "straight," is not. This relational understanding of queer identity mirrors a queer refusal of other binaries, including "mind/body ... theory/practice" (2000, p. 126). Such an understanding of "queer" and of "complexity theory" persuades Brent and Dennis "to find the resources to meet with students, parents, and teachers; to participate in teaching projects; to become involved in community events. This involvement avoids the "critic/criticized" binary, one, which "like the others ... dissolves in complicity" (2000, p. 126). Their refusal to be complicit in the status quo prompts them "to reconsider the unformulated ground, striving to afford less privilege to the formulated figure" (2000, p. 126), which they take to be "nothing short of an ethical imperative as it transforms and conflates the projects of research and education, pushing them both toward a hermeneutic attitude. We are admonished to understand -- and to refuse to allow curriculum events to hang uninterpreted. This matters goes beyond how we approach our research: It is a statement of how we should live our lives" (2000, p. 126). Indeed.

Eric Rofes is interested in vibrant bodies as well. An unrepentant sexual "revolutionary," Rofes continues -- despite what he calls the "excuse" and reality of AIDS -- to "immerse myself in communities that value sex" (2000, p. 132). He describes his own sexual practices as "non-monogamous," "promiscuous," or, thinking of Walt Whitman, very much "democratic" (2000, p. 132) in spirit. "Each day when I wake up, two people move in me: the teacher and the lover" (2000, p. 132). "I hunger for a community of educators who live out our class, gender, race and sex politics, not simply in our teaching or our academic publishing, but in our everyday lives" (2000, p. 133). And so he seeks to "learn from other gay male educators who may face similar barriers, fears, and points of controversy " (2000, p. 133). This won't be easy, as Rofes understands, because "[t]eachers -- including queer teachers -- a notoriously conservative lot." More than a few, he acknowledges, would pronounce his preferences "disgusting." Rofes cites Bourdieu to suggest that such disgust should be "unpacked."

Rofes points out that some have argued that public sex functions in radical and liberating ways, that promiscuity and casual sex may be regarded "as life-affirming practices of bonding and exchanges of pleasure, intimacy, and affection" (2000, p. 138). Nor does he want his sexed body kept out of the classroom: "I've had ... encounters with my undergraduates that have challenged my commitment to including sex and the body in my teaching as something more than distanced, de-personalized intellectual exercise" (2000, p. 147). He ends with a call for dialogue regarding the sacrifices queers have suffered and the implications these sacrifices have for democratic education and social change.

Townsand Price-Spratlen is well aware of sacrifices, gendered and racial. His "autoenthography" focuses on where he lives, at least part of the time: his faculty office, "a political space of multiple dialectics" (2000, p. 216). In particular he focuses on the images has chosen to decorate the office, photographs that provide visitors "with a visual language of various representations of the occupant's identity" (2000, p. 216). Such "workplace images" become moments in the process of "negotiating legacies," or "learning the lessons of history by seeking to understand the contemporary and historical contexts and contributions of [one's] ancestors" (2000, p. 216).

As a gay scholar of African descent, Price-Spratlen negotiates his legacies by exhibiting on his office walls a set of ancestral images he values most. In so doing he makes use of Baldwin's three gifts of language, courage and tenderness (appreciated by Toni Morrison in a passage he quotes to open the piece). There are three photographs displayed on the walls: 1) "Pre-Kindergarten Kisses," a shot of "two young males of African descent embracing each other ... as they smile lovingly, looking into the other eyes" (2000, p. 218), reminding one of Marlon Riggs' declaration at the conclusion of *Tongues United* that "black men loving black men is *the* revolutionary act" (quoted in Simmons 1991, p. 193), 2) a photo of Audre Lorde and 3) of Marlon Riggs. Price-Spratlen rests daily within "the gaze cast by this very special pair of eyes" (2000, p. 219).

When Price-Spratlen looks at the shot of Audre Lorde, he hears a powerful sentence from her 1989 lecture at UCLA: "My poetry calls for an answer from each of you in your lives" (2000, p. 219). The images of Lorde and Riggs affirm for him "a fictive friendship and a lived intimacy" (2000, p. 220) he enjoys with both, inspiring him to "justice-doing," a notion of "liberating activity that challenges human oppression" (2000, p. 222), grounded in, quoting Robert Goss, "the resistance narrative of Jesus, His struggles, death and God's liberative practice" (2000, p. 222). Such "gifts of legacy" inspire him to "move forward, acting on the ever-present duty that my many blessings warmly, kindly impose" (2000, p. 223).

That is a lovely phrase -- "the ever-present duty that my many blessings warmly, kindly impose" -- is it not? Yes we have sacrificed, we have suffered (and suffer still), and it behooves us to remember that being alive -- as many of our comrades are not -- is a duty to remember our blessings, to "move forward" (to borrow Price-Spratlen's language again), in friendship (fictive, sexual, and familial, however unconventionally that last adjective is defined), unafraid, unembittered, willing to hope, determined to have fun. As queer teachers and scholars, it is both our duty and pleasure to think queerly, blessed by those who have gone before, aroused by those around us now, and in fidelity to those who are yet to come.

UNDERSTANDING DEMOCRATIC CURRICULUM LEADERSHIP (1999)

Interest in knowledge for the sake of knowledge,
in thinking for the sake of the free play of thought,
is necessary then to emancipation of practical life
-- to make it rich and progressive.

John Dewey (1910, p. 138)

Understanding has to do with relationships.

Boyd Henry Bode (1940, p. 242)

American efforts to understand the inextricable relationship between democracy and education received their quintessential expression in John Dewey's canonical work on the subject (1916). Nearly a century later we are still straining to teach our constituents and ourselves this simultaneously simple but complicated and profound fact. In our time, the effort has been complicated by what Joe Kincheloe (1999, p. 74) characterizes as the "crisis of democracy." Certainly the sense of powerlessness and political alienation that, for instance, African-Americans and many others have experienced since the nation's birth seems now extended to many heterosexual white men, the nation's historic, prototypical civic subject. Now the straight white man of property also feels adrift in a dead sea of political stasis.

While current conditions require of us educators greater determination, our pedagogical imperative to teach (and to perform in Judith Butler's (1993) not self-evident sense) toward democratization remains. While "praxis" has undergone the same conceptual degradation many popularized concepts suffer -- from meaning something definite to meaning something vague and now meaning not much at all -- it was once a conceptual rallying point for our generation's commitment to democracy and education. Theory and practice, we were sure, would become dialectically interrelated, leading us and our students to higher levels, in Freire's term, in a process of conscientization. There was a certain generational solidarity in that belief, suggested in James Henderson's remark (1999, p. 111) that he has come to view "the American story as inspiring and frustratingly unfulfilled." That is an apt and succinct expression of how many of us feel. Somehow the two -- inspiration and frustration -- keep him, keep us, moving on, still, despite the odds, despite the reality, committed to democracy and education.

James G. Henderson and Kathleen R. Kesson are clearly so committed. This commitment is everywhere evident in this book, "designed," as Henderson (1999,

p. 1) writes, "to support a deepening understanding of democratic curriculum leadership." Henderson (1999, p. 4) quotes John Dewey to remind us that democracy is not just pulling levers on a voting machine, that it "is a way of life. We have yet to realize it is a way of personal life and one which provides a moral standard for personal conduct." Democracy is, of course, tied to freedom. Maxine Greene, Jim notes, "presents a complex, layered understanding of human freedom" (1999, 5). He finds in Nel Noddings's work one of the book's key ideas, that of a caring learning community, what he calls a "forest" idea, as in not being able to see the forest for the trees. "Maintaining this balance between 'forest' and 'trees' is not possible," Henderson (1999, p. 16) explains, "without establishing a rhythm between attention to the details of curricular change and continuing critical reflection on the 'big picture' of this reform effort." To "perform" this rhythm, Henderson and Kesson have selected four critical topics from the tradition of curriculum studies, to be discussed by prominent curriculum scholars: 1) curriculum deliberation by Gail McCutcheon, 2) reflexive systems by Noel Gough, 3) cultural criticism by Joe Kincheloe, and 4) educational mythopoetics by Kathleen Kesson. There is as well a reflection by a schoolteacher named Kerrin McCadden.

It is quite clear that Henderson and Kesson appreciate the complexity of the current situation in the schools. They understand that democratic curriculum reform cannot proceed simply, as on a flowchart, as if procedural consensus could resolve political conflict. In the past but especially now curriculum is the site of political, racial, gendered, and theological dispute. The present situation is so contested, has been claimed by so many and often opposed constituencies that, as Henderson remarks (with understatement), that

> in most settings, such dramatic reform is not possible without a carefully cultivated dialogue between all curriculum stakeholders: educational administrators, teachers, teacher aides, students, students' parents, school psychologists, social workers, community, business, religious leaders and so on. (1999, p. 15)

It is a very crowded room indeed, and one that calls one to cultivate, if one aspires to provide "curriculum leadership," among other things, the art of deliberation.

Joseph Schwab (1978) must be credited with emphasizing the significance of this art, an art associated with disciplined conversation. It surfaces again as major theme in this collection. Understand that "deliberation" is no detached, abstract exchange among Schwab and his University of Chicago colleagues. (Gail McCutcheon concedes her view of "deliberation" is less "formal" than Schwab's.) Given the complex and often contentious character of curriculum, deliberation is now closer to a form of curriculum politics, as McCutcheon (1999, p. 37) acknowledges: "conflict is the engine driving deliberation, and alternatives consist of the fuel." However, the process is not exclusively political; it is also moral. McCutcheon (1999, p. 39) informs us: "deliberation has a moral nature in that it is not a totally objective, value-free enterprise, nor should it be." Moreover: "Deliberation is a social enterprise because the concept of the 'good' democratic society informs collaborative decisions and thus provides an ethical context for all decisions" (1999, p. 40). By depicting deliberation as collaborative and democratic, McCutcheon's model of curriculum leadership echoes certain feminist models of consciousness-raising. Her sense of deliberation has little in common with hierarchical, patriarchal or "top-down" models of curriculum implementation.

How does "deliberation" as a key element in curriculum leadership function in the school as a social system? Noel Gough helps us think about that question, suggesting it might be useful "to think of a system as some kind of organism" (1999, p. 48). But it is not just *any* organism, is it. Noel thinks of the system as a "wild animal" that needs to be "tamed" before it can be made to "do some good" (1999, p. 48). Perhaps the organism Gough has in the back of his mind is the macho male, the somewhat but not entirely mythical coach-promoted to-principal? Yes, that's a stereotype, but the majority of school administrators *are* male, and while we don't tend to think of them as "wild men" perhaps they do, even so, require a little taming. Otherwise they can tend to think the bureaucratic system is, well, theirs. Procedures -- strategies of convenience and efficiency -- sometimes become sacrosanct, as if they were a set of commandments, rather than (as Gough suggests borrowing Gibson's description of cyberspace) the "consensual hallucination" (1999, p. 48) that the bureaucracy in fact is.

It is narrative theory or curriculum understood as storytelling, Gough argues, that "provides us with many critical and creative conceptual tools for both understanding and improving the practice of curriculum leadership" (1999, p. 48). He quotes Madeleine Grumet's famous definition of curriculum as the "collective story we tell our children about our past, our present, and our future" (quoted in Gough 1999, p. 50). Not that this is a finished or unchanging story -- Grumet (1988) employs hermeneutics, autobiography, and feminist theory to show that -- but a social experience, much more, well, I would say conversational (Pinar et al. 1995, p. 848), McCutcheon would say deliberative, and Bill Doll (1993) -- whom Noel credits with making "perhaps ... the most practical contribution to curriculum leadership" (1999, p. 55) -- might say chaotic, if in a different sense than the vernacular. Certainly the point would be not to turn curriculum documents into monuments, as Foucault warned in a different context and Gough nicely reiterates.

From another tradition -- critical theory -- Joe Kincheloe thinks about the problem of curriculum in terms of the present social and political crisis. "The last quarter of the twentieth century," he tells us, "has been marked by a crisis of democracy -- a crisis seldom referenced in the public conversation or in educational institutions" (1999, p. 74). Kincheloe argues for a kind of "critical democracy" which would be characterized by a hermeneutical practice. I think Joe would agree with me that this crisis is also a gendered one, and that much of the reactionary political response of the past thirty years can be understood as (although not reduced to) an effort to reassert while heterosexual male privilege. Mad men don't tend to engage in dialogue. They make accusations, often quote scripture, all the while demanding that things be set aright.

Kathleen Kesson wants things set right too, but she appreciates that both ends and means are not self-evident, but must be decided together, democratically. To reflect on these complicated issues, Kathleen turns to mythopoetics, which point to "the profoundly personal lived experience of human beings, in all of its depth and complexity" (1999, p. 99). This idea -- James Macdonald (1995) was the pioneer here -- includes, Kathleen (1999, p. 93) notes, "autobiography and personal narrative." "Stories are so pervasive throughout the world and throughout history," she continues, "that one might assume, as does curriculum theorist Kieran Egan, that our brains are somehow 'hard-wired' to respond to the narrative form" (1999, p. 92). "In Vermont," Kesson reports, "personal development is one of the primary categories for curriculum development. Currently, the inclusion of the self in the curriculum is most evident in aspects of whole language programs such as journal writing and reader response logs" (1999, p. 93). She points out that "autobiographical work has sometimes been misunderstood as 'asocial,' but scholars, such as Janet Miller (1990), have long emphasized the collaborate and social character of such research" (1999, p. 94). Kesson summarizes well:

> The work of curriculum leaders occurs in complex political networks, which are underpinned by multiple subjectivities, disparate beliefs, and complex webs of meanings. People's visions of what schooling should be are intimately connected with the vision of what constitutes the good life, the viable society. These meanings and beliefs sometimes lie below the surface of consciousness, and it falls to educational leaders to make the tacit, taken-for-granted realities explicit, problematic. It is an uneasy position to be in. (1999, pp. 100-101)

In the concluding chapter of the book, Henderson, Kesson, and Kerrin McCadden reflect on what has transpired herein, namely an effort to elaborate "the meaning of a *caring learning community*" (1999, p. 106). The curriculum of such a community integrates "critical conversation with progressive practice" (1999, p. 109). This means a democratic inclusion of all involved in the educational project, most particularly the practitioner. "By concluding with a practitioner's voice," they write, "we are emphasizing the point that the day-to-day, politically demanding and stressful work of democratic curriculum reform takes place in public schools, not in the minds of curriculum theorists" (1999, p. 107).

Deliberation -- both solo and group as Gail McCutcheon points out -- involves storytelling, what Freire termed "dialogical encounter." This order of conversation is not easily conducted in today's schools. Why? "[T]he potential dynamism of the curriculum deliberation process has been constrained," Kathleen Kesson observes, "because of the discourses of accountability, standards and best practices came to overshadow the discourses of justice, equity, caring, and human development" (Henderson, Kesson and McCadden 1999, p. 114). What to do? "I believe," Kathleen writes, "we must engage in moral conversations and in acts of political solidarity with our colleagues in the field who struggle daily to actualize emancipatory ideals" (Henderson, Kesson and McCadden 1999, p. 117). And this is, it seems to me, what this book does.

That success is evident in the practitioner's piece. A teacher of English in a small city in rural New England, Kerrin McCadden understands the gendered character of the theory-practice relationship. "Like any self-respecting Victorian era woman," she muses, "classroom teachers have been given too much lace to tat and too many knick-knacks to dust to nurture ideas" (Henderson, Kesson and McCadden 1999, p. 119). The pressure she describes is a classic instance of "hyperrationalization" (Pinar et al. 1995, p. 667), an abstraction which McCadden's description renders tellingly concrete. She is clear that a gendered insistence on "productivity" puts an end to curriculum as an authentic and complicated conversation. A different set of images and ideas -- McCadden settles nicely on "generative" -- is required if we are, thinking of Noel Gough's comment, to hallucinate a different social reality. A sense of the "generative," she writes, "threads its way through almost every idea in this book. Even when we are being reminded to deconstruct, it is for the sake of continued change and growth" (Henderson, Kesson and McCadden 1999, p. 125). I agree.

Change and growth may be welcomed, as feminists have shown, that is, when they are self-directed. Change and growth become euphemisms for compliance when they are commanded by others. Those 1970s women's consciousness-raising groups, for instance, were rarely led by men; after all, it was women who labored to find voice, express silenced realities, and discover the solidarity that inheres in the experience of oppression. Freire spoke about "generative themes" emerging the authentic dialogue of the oppressed. Articulating these themes not only heightens the awareness of those who are, in Freire's language, submerged in reality, they enable the participants to understand the provisionality of that reality, how it might be acted upon, transformed. Characterized by deliberation and story-telling, democratic curriculum leadership, is, among other things, such a generative practice. Perhaps we can understand continuing resistance to it -- from within the field as well as from outside -- if we keep in mind it is also a gendered practice.

Recall that, despite the large number of men in the profession, the figure of the schoolteacher, in the American imagination, is female. Especially since the rise of the public school in the nineteenth century, it is women who have tended to go into teaching, especially at the elementary level. That the figure of the American schoolteacher is female is key to unraveling persisting confusions regarding and resistances to the democratization of the theory-practice relationship. This is illustrated by two responses to the observation, made in *Understanding Curriculum*, that a paradigmatic shift has occurred in curriculum studies over the past thirty years. This shift, which Henderson and Kesson mention, was from "curriculum development " toward "understanding curriculum." What does that mean?

In abbreviated form, here are the facts: schools are no longer under the jurisdiction (it was always more professional and political than legal) of education professors. Multiple "stakeholders" (not the least among them the textbook publishers) have created something that tries to look like curriculum consensus but is in fact "gridlock," so that genuine (not just rhetorical) reforms -- let alone revolutions -- in practice are unlikely, certainly unlikely to be led by university-based curriculum scholars and researchers. This is not to say that we in the university have, for instance, lost interest in teachers or in schooling, or that we had been seduced by subjects more interesting and exciting (although some students of cultural studies might say that). The simple if for some inassimilable truth is that our influence has decreased over the past thirty years, not only due to a more complicated and contentious political and cultural terrain in which curricular issues are now situated, but as well due to a certain devaluation of education professors generally, following not only those attacks from the arts and sciences professors in the 1950s (Arthur Bestor [1953] was the most visible I suppose) and which have continued up through the present time, for instance Adler (1982), Bloom (1987), and Hirsch (1987).

Our devaluation intensified during the Kennedy administration's curriculum reform movement in the 1960s, the leaders of which were discipline-based practitioners in the university (such as physicists), not curriculum developers in schools of education. These two developments -- an increasingly complex and multiply influenced school situation (from the right-wing, etc.) plus a devaluation in the political stock of education and (specifically) curriculum professors -- plus a third and sometimes related development -- a movement toward "theory" and scholarly understanding rather than bureaucratic proceduralism (imprinted in the infamous Tyler rationale) -- resulted in a reconceptualized field of curriculum studies.

Because traditional curriculum development was no longer an option for curriculum generalists by the 1970s, and not wanting to be left looking for something to do (as Schwab entitled his 1983 essay), we formulated ways for the traditional concerns of the field -- such as asking the fundamental curriculum question, What knowledge is of most worth? -- to re-expressed, this time via teachers' interpretations of the textbooks chosen by others. Interpretation involved, as it turned out -- and as this volume indicates -- deliberation and story-telling, all laced with politics, race, and gender. Phenomenology (including hermeneutics) as well as post-structuralism, autobiography and biography, aesthetics, theology, international developments as well as strictly institutional concerns thematize contemporary scholarly efforts to understand curriculum. Now we understand that the curriculum is not only school-district guidelines, textbooks, and objectives. Now we understand that curriculum is that "complicated conversation" in which teachers and students engage each other as well as the textbook material, in, as this book succinctly puts it, a caring learning community.

Now the responses to these observations have been peculiar and revealing. They underline, I believe, the gendered character of the theory-practice relationship. If we are to understand the inextricable relations between democracy and education, we are obligated, it turns out, to challenge patriarchy. For if the figure of the American schoolteacher is female, the figure of the American college professor is male. For "theory" -- associated with the university -- to acknowledge that "practice" -- associated with the school -- is no longer able or willing to accept/follow its dictates and advice, amounts to acknowledging that women are no longer dependent upon or require men. Nothing works better than an acknowledgement like that to persuade some straight white men that it's time to quote scripture. And in one form or another, that is precisely what critics have done.

One kind of response to the history of the field reported in *Understanding Curriculum* has been reminiscent of those (often) southern preachers who resort to quoting the Old Testament to support his (usually "his") idea of "tradition." One critic actually quoted from the 1862 Morrill Act that established new agricultural and mechanical colleges with explicit vocational missions. This is an odd version of a sacred text, but it was cited as if it were: to show the errors of the contemporary field. So it was written, so it shall be: we in the university must never abandon our charge to inform "practice." A second kind of response has been, well let's say, more New Testament, in which the reviewers concluded their essay by "witnessing." They recounted how they had traveled among the multitudes (i.e. schoolteachers) with timeless curriculum ideas, thereby raising them up from, well, if not the dead maybe from routine, two fates not so very different when all is said and done.

What provoked the preaching, some of it in the category of "old time religion" and some of it a more new-testament-style tale of salvation? Why would critics misread this reporting of the facts as a kind of theory deserting practice, or as a heretical distortion of tradition? If we keep in mind that the figure of the American schoolteacher is female and that the figure of the American college professor is male, the puzzle becomes clarified. One current of it is, I suppose, a sense of male loyalty to the female, not wanting to leave her in the lurch, wanting to be helpful. A few male curriculum scholars' wives are in fact schoolteachers; to speak of theory and practice parting company must feel to them a little like, if not a divorce, at least a separation. But another current -- and here is the locus of the anger, the preaching -- is a reassertion of heterosexual male privilege. It is our job -- as professionals, i.e. "men" -- to tell teachers, i.e. women, what to do; theory must guide practice. More than a few practitioners ask us to tell them what to do, although I think that is often an expression of resistance to the privileged and gendered site of theory, pointing out as it sometimes does that we experts do not always know what to do in schools.

To suggest that we men have lost our historic position of privilege with schools, that now both scholars *and* practitioners must reflect *together* on education -- in theoretically informed ways -- as something of "equals," well this implies an equality of partnership between men and women that is yet to be realized in American society at large, and certainly not in curriculum studies. Some injured men -- ah, a crisis of democracy is it? -- resort to the Old Testament, citing nineteenth century legislation that, presumably, consecrates our position as head of the (school)household. Others inspire crestfallen readers with tales of preaching to masses, converting them, by the power of the word, to new life. Behind both reactionary responses lies a reassertion of traditional sex roles and in particular the privileged location of the heterosexual white male, as these are encoded professionally and intellectually in the theory-practice relationship.

So "understanding democratic curriculum leadership" runs up against not just right-wing crazies, but our close colleagues who are not eager to abandon what

139

seems to them ordained, if not by nature, if not by God, then at least by the Morrill Act. I applaud Jim Henderson and Kathleen Kesson for fighting the good fight, for insisting on democratization despite these profoundly anti-democratic currents. "Deliberation" and "story-telling" as elucidated here are nearly unknown arts, in the university as well as in the school, where, as Kerrin McCadden understands, "classroom teachers have been given too much lace to tat and too many knick-knacks to dust to nurture ideas" (Henderson, Kesson and McCadden 1999, p. 119). Democratization is a gendered as well as political and pedagogical aspiration. When we deliberate and tell stories, let us speak of a day when traditional and unjust divisions of labor are memories only, when men regard women not as practice to be guided, but as equal and respected colleagues engaged in that complicated conversation with our children that is the curriculum.

THE LURE OF THE TRANSCENDENT (1999)

During the autumn of 1969 I was privileged to study with Dwayne Huebner at Teachers College. It was a long ride from Port Washington, Long Island, where I was teaching English at Paul D. Schreiber High School, first via the Long Island Railroad to Manhattan, then on the subway uptown to Teachers College. But what an event it was. In a large room with seventy others, I watched an extraordinary figure in the distance speaking a tongue few of us grasped, but which we all found compelling. We knew we were in the presence of a most remarkable and learned man.

Paul Klohr, in whose class I had been introduced to curriculum theory the summer before, had advised me to study with Dwayne Huebner. Huebner is one of the most important figures in the field, he had said. Twenty-five years later, now that I know the field, I realize how right Paul was. In the fall of the 1969, Dwayne Huebner became a central figure in my "field," my stumbling, eccentric but determined efforts to find my way intellectually at the end of a revolutionary decade. Politics had led me to high-school teaching, but in 1969 I had no faith left in SDS or a second American revolution, and little left in the country, a country, I concluded after the Kent State murders, I had completely misunderstood. In this distressed state of mind, I met Dwayne Huebner.

It was the combination of his quiet, intense, undefeated manner and breathtaking scholarly scope that first heartened, then inspired, me. Huebner became central to my field; more importantly, he became central to *the* field. This fact is, I think, still under appreciated today. Philip Jackson has performed the extraordinarily useful and important service of writing a short history of curriculum studies in his introduction to the 1992 *Handbook of Research on Curriculum*. In it he discusses the "giants" in the field: Bobbitt, Dewey, Tyler, Schwab. Missing, I contend, is Dwayne Huebner.

Consider the following: a decade before political issues would consume a wing of the field, Huebner was writing about the importance of political theory to curriculum studies. Fifteen years before phenomenology would emerge as an important discourse in the field, Huebner was studying Heidegger and Jaspers. Nearly a decade before Joseph Schwab judged the field moribund, Huebner declared that the field lacked vitality. And twenty years before religious and theological studies would constitute a major sector of curriculum scholarship, Huebner was studying transcendence while teaching courses at the Union Theological Seminary in New York. In 1982 Huebner left Columbia's Teachers College for Yale's Divinity School to focus upon religious studies more specifically, but he has returned to us, first in 1993 in his powerful analysis of spirituality and curriculum (1999, pp. 401-416), and now in this collection (1999).

In *Understanding Curriculum*, I situated Dwayne Huebner's work historically, emphasizing the ways it foreshadowed the Reconceptualization of the field in the 1970s. Now that I have been collecting his essays and introducing his work, it has become clear to me that Jackson's short history of the field is too short. It is now clear to me, and I am confident you will agree as you work your way through this volume, that Huebner's importance to the field is great. It is greater, for instance, than Schwab's. His influence on and significance for what would follow positions him alongside Tyler, although one must be quick to add that Huebner's influence is altogether salutary. Additionally, the intellectual character of contribution is altogether more complex and provocative than either Tyler's or Schwab's. While it will seem to some audacious or unnecessary to make such this claim, it needs to be made. Someday, I feel confident, Huebner will be recognized as more important than Tyler in the history of the field. Let us turn our attention, albeit in an introductory way, at what -- over a thirty-five year career -- Dwayne Huebner has accomplished. Remarkable is only the first word that comes to mind.

As early as 1950s, Huebner was challenging the hegemony of the Tyler Rationale, published only a few years earlier (Tyler 1949). At Teachers College, Columbia University, Huebner taught a course in curriculum theory (with Arno Bellack) which relied on non-Tylerian foundations. First offered in 1957, this course on curriculum theory was part of the doctoral core in the Department of Curriculum and Teaching at Teachers College, not only the first department in the field (established in 1938), but at this time probably the premier department as well. Bellack approached curriculum problems through analytic philosophy; Huebner worked through phenomenology and political science. (Ten years later Huebner would introduce phenomenology to the field at large [Huebner 1999, pp. 131-142]. Phenomenology and political theory now comprise two major sectors of curriculum scholarship: understanding curriculum as phenomenological and political text.] Huebner's and Bellack's collaboration would surface in print: in 1960 the two men reviewed the research on teaching. Their conclusion pointed to the agenda Huebner would undertake in the years to follow: "Too few of the studies referred to here move from empirical data to an evaluation of the concepts used to organize these data" (Bellack and Huebner 1960, p. 254).

The fundamental rethinking of concepts toward which this conclusion points would begin to appear two years later. In a collection entitled *Curriculum Crossroads*, Dwayne Huebner wrote "Politics and Curriculum" (1999, pp. 15-22), in which he discusses the value of political science in the study of curriculum problems. His examination of curriculum in terms of democratic ideology, control of resources, power, and slogans sets his paper apart from the others in the collection; it foreshadowed what would become a major scholarly initiative in the field.

In 1962, in the midst of the structures-of-disciplines movement, mainstream curriculum scholars must have read Huebner's essay with disbelief. Huebner seems to understand the naiveté of his audience, their need for him to explain himself. He asks: why make the move to political science in the first place? He begins his answer by noting, seven years before Schwab would make the same claim famous, that "the attempt [to look at curriculum with concepts from political science] seems justified by the present inadequate state of curriculum theory which is overwhelmed by problems, and suffering from a lack of intellectual vitality" (1999, p. 15).

Such insight must have seemed heresy to many readers, still smiling in a false security that the field was fine. Did Huebner's analysis escape the attention of his colleague at the University of Chicago? While Huebner was saying, in effect, that the field was moribund, Schwab was busy working on the structure of the disciplines. "Certainly the educational enterprise," Huebner says with uncharacteristic understatement, "is loaded with political action" (1999, p. 15). The structure-of-the-disciplines movement was itself, needless to say, a testimony to that fact.

At this early date Huebner (1962) understands that all the hoopla at ASCD meetings (for instance) regarding the democratic character of education was mostly that. Always sensitive to this constituency, however, he puts the matter pedagogically:

> The democratic ideology used by educators, however, falls into the never-never land of wishful thinking. On the one hand, it approaches, never quite reaching but often replacing, a religious ideology.... On the other hand, the prevailing democratic conception never quite realizes the dimensions of a political ideology, for it fails to deal with conflict and struggle and the phenomenon which resolves both -- power. (1999, pp. 15-16)

Note that Huebner employs the notion of power -- fifteen years before a succeeding generation of education scholars would eagerly seize upon the concept -- referring to the work of Arendt, Merriam, Tillich, and Lasswell. There is as well a discussion of "educational elites" and "educational ideologies," buzzwords among leftist curriculum scholars in the late 1970s and early 1980s.

Power circulates, it is not possessed, Foucault has taught us. Recalling Albert Schweitzer, Martin Buber, Erich Fromm, Nicholas Berdyaev, Jose Orega y Gasset, and Ernest G. Schachtel, Huebner discusses intersubjective "circulation," i.e. "forms of relating to others." For him the central question is "what may transpire?" (1999, 75). Half a dozen years before Freire would popularize the "dialogical encounter," Huebner explicates such encounter; he suggests it involves "a form of transaction which maintains the maximum freedom of each [person]" (1999, p. 76). And years before Rorty (1989, 1991) would make it a centerpiece of his philosophy of culture and politics, Huebner dwells upon "the nature of conversation" (1999, 78). Also in this early essay he foreshadows his later interest in language, discussing the "limitations of functional language" (1999, p. 87), and the importance of "valuing religious and aesthetic language" (1999, p. 88). Then he moves to the work of Karl Jaspers who recognized the centrality of communication for the development of "selfhood" (1999, p. 89). Lest his reader think he is advocating a form of political quietism or social withdrawal, he points out that the educator must become "aware of his limited, and limiting, thought patterns and language systems for shaping value and legitimizing action" (1999, p. 90). It is a landmark paper, well in advance of scholarship that would dominate the field in the late 1970s.

Next Huebner turns his attention to the "art of teaching" (1999, pp. 23-35). Several years before Elliot Eisner (1971a, 1971b, 1972) would popularize art (specifically connoisseurship) as a metaphor for curriculum evaluation, Huebner understood that curriculum and teaching were aesthetic text. Also during these early years of the decade he was working on Heidegger, long before that name became known to curriculum students; Huebner sketched phenomenological notions of knowledge, curriculum, and the classroom in three powerful papers (1999, pp. 36-73). His phenomenological interest was developed and extended in papers that would follow, culminating in his important 1967 "Curriculum as Concern for Temporality" (see Huebner 1999, pp. 131-142).

In his 1966 "Curriculum as a Field of Study" Huebner advanced four radical propositions. First, he observed that conceptions of curriculum tended to be tied to "technique." They are not linked to the human spirit. Second, the field suffered from an overdependence upon values conceived as goals or objectives. Relatedly, the field suffered from an overdependence upon learning as the primary expression of human temporality. Third, correction of this primitive and simplistic conception of curriculum could be achieved partially by the design of an educative environment conceived as valued educational activity. Fourth, Huebner insisted that curriculum design was inherently a political process by means of which the curricular worker sought to attain a just environment. Extending the work he had done earlier, Huebner (1966a, p. 112) endorsed art as a model of curriculum theory and design:

> Is it possible, now that we are partially freed from vision-hindering busywork, that we can begin to make efforts to grasp the overall design of curriculum and to see how man's evolving techniques can be made subservient to man's evolving spirit? Educational environment and activity in the schools are symbolic of what man is today and what he wants to be tomorrow. The design of these symbols is a great art. The study of curriculum should be a preparation for this artistry.

One might think a career had been capped at this point. After all, he had scooped both Schwab and Eisner, declaring the field moribund in 1962, and introducing art, as well as political and social theory, by 1963, and theology and phenomenology by 1967. Realizing perhaps that he had swept away the traditional field of curriculum development, at least as Tyler understood it, he moved to outline the elements of what would become the new field.

In "The Tasks of the Curricular Theorist" in which Huebner (1999, pp. 212-230) made three important points which would be developed further in the decade after the Reconceptualization. First, he noted that curricularists operated in human history, with other human subjects, in actual human environments. This complexity can be seen in the individual biographies of students and educators. Second, the curriculum theorist is responsible through language and through environmental design to generate new language and environmental forms. Huebner's notion of environment included the school building, materials, and people -- all structuring "elements" of educational experience. Third, he argued that it is in praxis, through political engagement and pedagogical work in the world, where education takes place. Huebner (1999, p. 228) wrote:

> What are the tasks of curriculum theorists? As is true of all theorists his task is to lay bear the structure of being-in-the-world and to articulate this structure through the language and environmental forms he creates. His responsibility is for the forms he creates and uses, that they may be controlled by him rather than controlling him.

Here Huebner is anticipating other sectors of contemporary curriculum scholarship, twenty years in advance of their maturation. Note that years before Herbert Kliebard's influential scholarship Huebner is calling for curriculum history. History is expressed in individual biographies, and in one breath he has pointed simultaneously to efforts to understand curriculum as historical and biographical/autobiographical text. His concept of environmental design is material -- including architecture and artifacts -- as well as social and intersubjective. He grounds educational experience in the world, at once an ontological and political concept. And a decade before it would become a buzzword, Huebner calls for *praxis*.

The political interest indicated in the last sentence is developed further in his tour-de-force "Poetry and Power: The Politics of Curricular Development" (1999, pp. 231-240). In this gripping statement (I was among those who heard him speak), Huebner asserted his view that educators are lost, that they will remain lost as long as they accept the promise of a "quick fix" through slogans and bandwagons, as long as *teachers* do not act to change the educational world. Such action, he pointed out, requires risk-taking. Huebner advocated three rights: 1) there must be "unconditional respect for the political, civil, and legal rights of the young as free people participating in a public world" (1999, p. 235); 2) the student has "the right of access to the wealth in the public domain -- I mean primarily the knowledge, traditions, skills that shape and increase a person's power in the public world" (1999, 236); and 3) the right of "each individual, regardless of age, to participate in the shaping and reshaping of the institutions in which they live" (1999, p. 238). Huebner (1999, pp. 238-239) concluded: "The school is but a manifestation of public life. As educators we must be political activists who seek a more just public world. The alternative of course is to be school people -- satisfied with the existing social order -- the silent majority who embrace conservatism." It is a conservatism that would position them in "gracious submission."

Huebner's rejection of the traditional role of curriculum developers in favor of politically inspired actors engaged in seeking "a more just public world" inspired an entire generation of curriculum scholars. Efforts in the late 1970s and 1980s to understand curriculum politically, phenomenologically, aesthetically, and theologically can be directly traced to Huebner's groundbreaking scholarship in the 1960s and early 1970s. In 1975 Huebner reflected on his own journey:

> Throughout this contact with diverse philosophical and theological traditions, the basic operating assumptions of curriculum thought bothered me. How could one plan educational futures via behavioral objectives when the mystical literature emphasized the present moment and the need to let the future care for itself? The thread that ran through my questions and my searching was an intuition that an understanding of the nature of time was essential for understanding the nature of education.... The journey has been lonely at times, but the direction feels right even though it seems veiled in a "Cloud of Unknowing." I am convinced that the curriculum person's dependency on scientific thought patterns, even though they have not found their way into practice as they should, has broken the linkage with other very great and important intellectual traditions of the East and the West which have profound bearing on the talking about the practice of education. (Huebner 1975, p. 215)

Among the traditions upon which Huebner called were phenomenology and theology.

Huebner's (1970) earlier assertion of self-definition would thematize the reconceptualized field. He embraced the concrete, institutional interest Schwab had claimed: "I am a curriculum person. I happen to be concerned with the nitty gritty of schooling: what goes on in classrooms" (1970, p. 169). Second, he points to language and discourse, both of which would preoccupy the contemporary field, when he wrote: "We have oversimplified the relationship between the design of educational environments and the language with which we talk about them" (1970, pp. 178-179). Huebner's statements would lay the path for contemporary studies, a path partly in the practical everyday life of schools and partly in theoretical issues of language, discourse, and textuality.

In 1982 Huebner left Teachers College, Columbia University for the Yale University Divinity School. That is not the end of our story. Just as his educational theory is important for students of theology, his essays in religious education speak strongly to students of education. He defined his interest in the religious and the spiritual broadly. In a 1985 paper on spirituality and knowing for the 94th Yearbook of the National Society for the Study of Education (1999, pp. 340-352), he begins with the OED, where he finds that "spirit" is derived from the Latin word for breath and breathing ... "spirit refers to that which gives vitality" (1999, p. 343). Noting that this idea holds broad significance, he stresses that: "Talk of the 'spirit' and the 'spiritual' in education need not, then, be God talk... Rather, the talk is about lived reality, about experience and the possibility of experiencing" (1999, p. 344). "Various modes of knowing," he points out, "are suffused with the spiritual (1999, p. 348). Indeed, "Education is only possible because the human being is a being that can transcend itself" (1999, p. 345).

In a second provocative essay that also appeared that year, Huebner (1999, pp. 358-368) explored the relationship between education and religion. They are, in his view, separable. He explains that:

Religious language could be used as metaphor to look at speak about educational events and phenomena.... In fact, that very process of transferring religious language to education strikes me as being foreign to what I am about, and in part would distort the story of my own life as educator.... Most of my professional career has been a search for more adequate and powerful ways to describe education. (1999, p. 358)

Religious or theological language helps one to do just that. He does acknowledge that: "Over the years I have been led more and more directly into studies of and work in theological and religious education" (1999, p. 358).

It is not only religion and education that are intertwined. Later in this essay he suggests how the political, the phenomenological, and the theological all inhabit what is educational:

Education is the lure of the transcendent -- that which we seem is not what we are, for we could always be other. Education is the protest against present forms that they may be reformed and transformed. Education is the consciousness that we live in time, pulled by the inexorable Otherness that brings judgment and hope to the forms of life which are but the vessels of present experience. (1999, p. 360)

In what seems today a brilliant Lacanian move, he says: "Content is otherness" (1999, p. 362). Huebner has, however, theology not psychoanalysis in mind.

Content he understands very broadly; it includes the pedagogical practice of encountering otherness, even that most transcendent of Others, God. In a 1987 essay on the religious education and the presence of God (1999, pp. 388-395), he writes: "In the minds of some, religious education is a time set-aside. It has become a place, such as Sunday school .... However, it need not be time ... set aside .... Religious education can be a way of practicing the presence of God" (1999, p. 388). What does that entail? "Practicing that presence," he explains, "requires more or less constant awareness of or reference to God in our life" (1999, p. 389).

What is religious education? In statements that echo his earlier work on the significance of human encounter and relationship as well as transcendence to educational experience, he answers:

Here, then, is our agenda for religious education. It is one of scrutinizing the fabrics of relationships that we have, those of intimacy and those of community, and of asking how God is present or absent in those relationships. And then, with the help of our religious traditions, imagining how we can practice the presence of God in these relationships of intimacy and community. (1999, p. 392)

He concludes by returning to the interrelatedness of his life-long interests:

> The religious part of the religious educational work before us is to help
> ourselves and others practice the presence of God in all our doings in this
> world. The educational part of the religious educational work before us is to
> overcome those habits -- whether they are habits of mind, of language, of
> social convention -- that substitute our diverse idols for God's presence in our
> midst, and to establish new habits more adequately grounded in God's realm
> and God's covenant with us. (1999, p. 395)

In May 1993, a 70-year old Dwayne Huebner returned to the curriculum field in an
importantly synoptic essay focused on the spiritual in curriculum (1999, pp. 401-
416). Huebner's paper was in response to an invitation to speak in New Orleans to
a seminar on spirituality and curriculum, sponsored by three near-by universities,
and organized by LSU Professor William E. Doll, Jr. In a powerful reading,
Huebner returned to many of the themes that had preoccupied him -- and the field -
- over a lifespan. Huebner appreciates that the problem of the field remains one of
language. He acknowledges that, while not dominant in the scholarly field,
technical language remains embedded in the schools, i.e. in the talk of school
people. To some extent he blames the field he left for the present predicament of
educators, lost in the technical, pseudo-scientific language of bureaucratic
legitimation that erases not only the spiritual but the imagination as well. In a "we"
that includes educators and especially educational psychologists, he reminded us
that: "We have forgotten or suppressed that imagination is a foundation of our
givens" (1999, p. 401).

Evoking a notion of educational journey that he had employed over two decades
ago (1975), he dismissed once again the language of educational psychology, and
especially that of learning theory: "'Learning' is a trivial way of speaking of the
journey of the self" (1999, p. 405). It is this pseudo-scientific and profoundly
distorting language that had led Huebner to become skeptical of mainstream
research: "Several years later I began to question the educator's dependency on the
research enterprise" (1999, p. 402). In part, it is that pretense of certainty
associated with the social and behavioral sciences fields which is so reprehensible.
It is awareness that there is a "beyond" to our knowledge that is the beginning of
the theological: "It is a 'moreness' that takes us by surprise when we are at the
edge and end of our knowing" (1999, p. 403). What other damage had technical
language done as he looks back at thirty years? Huebner (1999, p. 411) answered:

> Similarly, the significance of the word "study" has been destroyed. Students
> study to do what someone else requires, not for their own transformation, a
> way of 'working' on their own journey, or their struggle with spirit, the
> otherness beyond them. Just as therapy is work -- hard work -- but important
> for the loosening of old binds and discovering the new self; so too should
> education as study be seen as a form of that kind of work.

Next Huebner moves to teachers and teaching. Sounding not only theological but
phenomenological, Huebner (1999, p. 411) reminded the audience that: "teaching
is a vocation.... A vocation is a call." Indeed, the vocation of teaching, he

continued, involves three aspects: "Three voices call, or three demands are made on the teacher. Hence the life that is teaching is inherently a conflicted way of living. The teacher is called by the students, by the content, and by the institution within which the teacher lives.... Spiritual warfare is inherent in all vocations" (1999, p. 411). Given the complexity of this calling, Huebner (1999, p. 413) understands that: "The pain of teachers, unable to respond to the call of some students, is often too much, and they seek relief by hardening their hearts." How can teachers respond to the demands of their profession? Huebner (1999, p. 415) tells us:

> It is also quite clear to me that it is futile to hope that teachers can be aware of the spiritual in education unless they maintain some form of spiritual discipline. This needs to be of two kinds. Given the inherent conflicts involved in teaching, and the inherent vulnerability of their vocation, teachers need to seek out communities of faith, love, and hope.... The second discipline is a disciplining of the mind, not in the sense of staying on top of all the educational research and literature, but in the sense of developing an imagination that has room for the spiritual, such that when you look out over the educational landscape you see not only what is there and recognize your call to respond with love, truth and justice; but so you can also see the principalities and powers, the ideals and the spiritual possibilities hidden behind all of the forms and events that are taken for granted.

Here Huebner has pointed to the core of understanding curriculum, especially as theological text. He enables us to appreciate that finally our struggle to teach and to study with others and with God is precisely that: a call for labor, for discipline, sustained by faith, love, and resolve. The effort to understand curriculum as theological text is not a separate specialized sector of scholarship; it is call to live with others morally and transcendentally: "The need is not to see moral and spiritual values as something outside the normal curriculum and school activity, but to probe deeper into the educational landscape to reveal how the spiritual and moral is being denied in everything" (Huebner 1999, p. 414). In seeing how the moral is denied we glimpse how we might work toward its realization.

Dwayne E. Huebner returned to the curriculum field on November 20, 1993, on the campus of Loyola University in New Orleans, but it was clear he had never left us. As this abbreviated and overly simple introduction to his work makes clear, he and a very few others -- such as his friend and colleague James B. Macdonald (1995) -- helped create the world contemporary curriculum scholars now inhabit and labor to recreate as educators and theoreticians. His generative influence has been evident in many discourses, including the political, the phenomenological, the aesthetic as well as the theological. Huebner may have left the field in grief and indignation over what has happened to the schools, perhaps because he was unable to find solace in the emerging scholarly field which his own work had made possible, and certainly in order to focus more exclusively on religious education. His journey has been remarkable, highly significant for two fields of study. Clearly one of the most important minds the field of curriculum has known, Dwayne

Huebner may well be judged by future historians of the field as *the* most important. It seems so to me.

"I AM NOT YET" (1998)

On Thursday June 27, 1996, Maxine Greene spoke at Louisiana State University (not for the first time), to an overflow crowd packed into the old Hill Memorial Library. She had been invited to speak about her "present passions." What were they, as she faced her 80th year? "I ask myself," she seemed to confide to us, as if there were two − not one hundred − people in the room, "what is the meaning of what I have done?" Surveying the current scene, she is, she says, somber. In a time characterized by the continued deterioration of the nation's schools, the degradation of the public sphere generally, when the progressive project itself seems a memory, "what," she asked herself, looking at us, "has my work meant?" There was no hint of self-pity: only the feeling-filled, engaged voice of a serious intellectual.

It was the clear to us that morning, listening to her, that her past does not hold her attention for long. It is the future that draws her, the future that calls to her. She is rewriting, she tells us, her first book, *The Public School and the Private Vision* (and asked me not to include discussion of the original version in *The Passionate Mind of Maxine Greene*). She continues a rigorous schedule of public speeches and professional obligations, including teaching. It is late morning now, and she has been speaking for an hour. As she draws near to what feels like the end of the speech, she pauses and looks at us. "Who am I?" she poses, partly to us, partly to herself. She answers: "I am who I am not yet." "Not yet" ... the phrase still hangs in the air around me. Maxine Greene *is ... not yet*. Her own sense of incompletion, of what is not yet but can be, inspires us to work for a future we can only imagine now. You will see that inspiration at work in the essays collected here (Pinar 1998a).

The intimacy of our relationship to Maxine -- an intimacy shared by others who have heard and read her -- will be evident in these essays also. To introduce them I want to say something about Maxine Greene in a more public sense. Yes, she is a distinguished philosopher of education, probably the most important of her generation. Her work is very widely known, her name -- along with Paulo Freire's -- among the most recognized worldwide by those interested in education. She is a former president of the American Educational Research Association, the first woman so honored in thirty-one years. Within philosophy of education (see Kohli 1995) she has triumphed despite "paradigm wars" and gender trials. Her victories there and at Teachers College have not always come automatically. But this is not an occasion to speak to the internal history of her career. I hope to contribute to our reflection upon her public accomplishment by going outside the field of education for a moment. I note first of all that she is an intellectual, a serious public intellectual; it was to this fact I spoke in the Ayers-Miller collection (Pinar 1998b).

In this volume I wish to suggest a related characterization, still as intellectual, but more specifically as a New York public intellectual. To do that, I will recall Susan Sontag, one of the most important and accomplished public intellectuals in the New York tradition.

There are risks: the two figures are quite different in many respects. There are, however, certain resonances between aspects of Sontag's work -- particularly her sense of herself as a public intellectual -- and Greene's. My aim is not to make a comparative argument, but rather to help us see Maxine Greene more vividly, outside our private feelings for her, by focusing on Susan Sontag. Because Maxine Greene is unique -- no one can copy her singular, virtuoso interweaving of philosophy, literature, and social theory -- we lack a suitable context from within the field of education to characterize her, to appreciate her, to grasp her achievement. I want the juxtaposition to point directly at that final element, as Maxine Greene's achievement is great.

SUSAN SONTAG

Like Maxine Greene, Susan Sontag arrived on the New York intellectual scene in the early 1960s. It was the end-time for a certain form of American intellectual culture and the figure -- what has been termed the public intellectual -- it supported. Sontag's early essays, collected in *Against Interpretation* (1966), argued on behalf of avant-garde tastes, criticized what she took to be the parochialism of American arts and criticism, and demanded a new intellectual agenda. Calling for a "new sensibility," Sontag seemed to express and even lead much of what would later be dismissed as "the Sixties." In the 1960s, Sontag achieved a media exposure hitherto rare in American intellectual life. In a decade of rapid cultural shifts as well as political, gender, and racial radicalization, Susan Sontag assumed an iconic significance (Kennedy, 1995). Stanley Aronowitz (1982, p. 13) declared that Sontag "has become the major American example of the Critic as Star." While her reputation is no longer that of the avant-garde radical, the aura of the *enfant terrible* remains, as she remains, Liam Kennedy (on whose work I am relying here) asserts, "one of the last of a kind, and no less a legend (1995, p. 2)"

The intellectual role Sontag has often self-consciously performed is that of the generalist or "writer-intellectual" (Beyer 1980, 43). Her studies of thought and culture -- wide-ranging, marked by changing personal taste and interest -- include essays on historical events, "camp", science-fiction, pornographic literature, photography, fascist aesthetics, cancer, and AIDS. She has explicitly endorsed the generalist figure of the intellectual, acknowledging both Americans (Paul Goodman and Harold Rosenberg) and Europeans (Roland Barthes and Walter Benjamin) as models. Introducing the 1966 American edition of Barthes's *Writing Degree Zero*, Sontag (1970, p. xi) was discussing herself as well as Barthes when she wrote: "Only if the ideal of criticism is enlarged to take in a wide variety of discourse, both theoretical and descriptive, about culture, language and contemporary consciousness, can Barthes plausibly be called a critic." For Sontag, the work of the contemporary intellectual requires this expanded concept of "criticism" (Kennedy 1995).

"The deepest structure in the culture and ideology of intellectuals," Alvin Gouldner (1979, p. 33) once observed, "is their pride in their own autonomy." Sontag exhibited such a pride as an independent thinker and champion of critical intelligence. It is a role she sometimes imagined -- as has Edward Said (1996) -- as a condition of intellectual "exile." Anticipating Said (1996), Sontag imagined the intellectual as a kind of "amateur" unrestricted by disciplinary and professional allegiances. This formulation of her intellectual self-image, Kennedy (1995) insists, is crucial to an understanding of her work: "I think of myself as self-created, that's my working illusion" (quoted in Cott 1979, p. 53). This longheld "illusion" -- as Kennedy (1995, p. 4) characterizes it -- is one that might have been born during what she has described as her "very solitary and very bookish childhood" (quoted in Kennedy 1995, p. 4). It may have to do as well with the struggles of a woman in a predominantly male intellectual world (Kennedy 1995).

New York intellectual culture at mid-century was typified by intellectual men who were generalists: Edmund Wilson, Paul Goodman, and Harold Rosenberg. There were as well important literary critics, such as Lionel Trilling, Irving Howe, Mary McCarthy, and Philip Rahv, who also exhibited an interest in diverse contemporary topics in their writings. These were critics who, in Howe's words, "found a way to pay attention to a particular text and also comment on the larger cultural context in which these texts had appeared" (Cain 1989, p. 561). Many wrote to express the moment, an ambition deriving, for some, from 1930s leftist political movements as well as from the practical demands of small-journal publication. Stylistically, they exhibited a preference for the essay, "develop[ing] a characteristic style of exposition and polemic.... The kind of essay they wrote was likely to be wide-ranging in reference, melding notions of about literature and politics.... It is a kind of writing highly self-conscious in mode, with an unashamed bravura and display" (Howe 1971, pp. 240-241).

New York intellectuals had a strong sense of European cultural models, and not only due to ethnic inheritance (several were or were children of Jewish immigrants). Himself a New York intellectual, Daniel Bell (1989, p. 131) described these individuals as "self-invented," keen to play down family origins and stimulated by a "hunger for culture." This cosmopolitan sense of culture -- typically New York -- might be characterized as "an admixture of Marxism and modernism ... though by the 1950s Freud show[ed] more influence than Marx" (Kennedy 1995, 8-9).

New York intellectuals tended to associate intellectuality with critical inquiry as an activity as well as the general breath of the cultural critic's interests. Intellectual labor was construed as "critical contention and interventionism" which seeks "an immediate relation to public issues" (Kennedy 1995, p. 9). Harold Rosenberg (1970, p. 10) explained: "If criticism ... waits for aesthetics and history to reassert themselves, it avoids the adventure of playing a part in events."

Sontag owes much, Kennedy (1995) points out, to this New York model of engaged intellectuality; it has, in part, formed her commitments to intellectual generalism and cultural criticism, her insistence upon critical autonomy, and her reliance upon the essay form. However, while very much influenced by the critical and ideological commitments of the postwar generation, Sontag has also challenged these. In so doing she exhibited a strong sensitivity to cultural and political shifts of the 1960s. But this sensitivity did not detach her from those earlier preoccupations associated with high modernism important earlier in the century.

The "mind as passion" and the "body in pain" are key motifs in Sontag's work. These themes emerge from certain ideas associated with high modernism: the negative, the transcendent, transgressive, the authentic, the difficult, the silent. "The ethical task of the modern writer," she writes, "is not to be a creator but a destroyer -- a destroyer of shallow inwardness, the consoling notion of the universally human, dilettantish creativity, and empty phrases" (1983, p. 131). She accepts this task as morally serious, as a correlative of the principle of negation she admires in modernist thinking. "All possibility of understanding," she states, "is rooted in the ability to say no" (Sontag 1977, 1979, 23). The necessity of negation informs both the style and the content of her own writings. As Kennedy (1995, p. 10) observes: "Her remarkably self-reflexive prose dramatizes the activity of mind as an antinomian or dialectical play of ideas and valorizes the restlessness of the self-critical intellect." "In the passion play of thought," Sontag (1987 [1969], p. 80) wrote, "the thinker plays the roles of both protagonist and antagonist." Sontag self-consciously manipulates the essay form, especially its performative features, enabling her to experiment with ideas. As Kennedy (1995) notes, Sontag favors disjunctive forms of argument; aphoristic and epigrammatic modes of critical expression are evident throughout her writing.

Sontag's role as a New York public intellectual has come to seem to some as somewhat dated in recent years. The ideals of autonomy and responsibility that support the figure of the free-floating public intellectual came to be questioned, especially by academic cultural critics (see, for instance, Leitch 1992). For decades, now, independent intellectual activity is considered as being in terminal decline, overwhelmed by the pressure of professionalization and institutionalization which have given rise to a "new class" of intellectual specialists -- technical experts, policy advisers, and academic theoreticians (Gouldner 1979; Jacoby 1987; Ross 1989; Said 1996). There has been a fundamental restructuring of the intellectual terrain; the role of the public intellectual has faded. The New York intellectual, characterized by a general and contestatory critique of culture and politics, has not completely disappeared, but this figure has been increasingly difficult to imagine within an intellectual public sphere that has become increasingly polycentric and politically polarized (Kennedy 1995).

In the 1990s Sontag was regarded as something of an eccentric in American intellectual life, as one of "the last intellectuals" (Jacoby 1987) in the New York tradition. Her commitment to the generalist role and her sense of a common culture that is responsive to rational thought and argument seems to many anachronistic given the fragmentation of the public sphere in the United States over the last thirty years. Thomas Bender (1993, p. 144) argued that such an intellectual can no longer assume a public:

> [A] plurality of audiences [exists] within a public culture that is essentially cosmopolitan and contested. In the past a fragment of the public, the educated middle-class audience... was able to pose with success as the whole. Today, the public is at once increasingly representative, and more fragmented, making it harder to find, to reach, and to define. The intellectual no longer has an unselfconscious "we" relationship to the public.

In place of a common culture there is a plurality of cultures and tastes, and the generalist can assume no sure constituency under such conditions. Todd Gitlin (1990, p. 222) observed that "general thought is so distinctive a taste, now, as to qualify as a special interest alongside personal computing, running, and so on at the serious newsstand." As the public sphere becomes increasingly polycentric intellectuals will probably limit their thinking to localized and specialized problems and communities. However, as Liam Kennedy (1995, p. 129) concludes,

> the universalizing public intellectual has not disappeared and many continue to find a large, differentiated audience. Sontag stands as a singular if not sole example. She is not the last intellectual, but an intellectual who has made public her own ambivalent, speculative, and provocative thoughts on the decline of the new.

An extraordinary American intellectual, Susan Sontag brings to mind another.

MAXINE GREENE

Like Sontag, Maxine Greene brought a new sensibility to the academic field of education, our own equivalent of the "public sphere," fragmented as it is into specialized, even balkanized, terrains. Not content to remain within philosophy of education (see Kohli 1998), Maxine Greene has assumed a "generalist" or "writer-intellectual" identity, emphasizing the genre of the essay. Like Sontag, Greene has engaged many of the major intellectual influences of the twentieth century in the West, as Marla Morris (1998), for instance, explains. Like Sontag, Maxine's aesthetic sense is highly developed. Her commitment to the arts is complete, witness the essays by Donald Blumenfeld-Jones, Mary-Ellen Jacobs (1998), Carol Jeffers (1998), Rebecca Luce-Kapler (1998), Patrick Slattery/David Dees (1998), and Susan Stinson (1998). There seems to be a strong, if submerged, autobiographical element in Greene's work too, and this becomes somewhat discernible when we place her autobiographical statement (chapter 1) next to her texts. Maxine's scholarship also stimulates autobiographical reflection, witness the essays by Robert Graham (1998), Wendy Kohli (1998), Nancy Lesko 91998), Kathleen O'Gorman (1998), Anne Pautz (1998), Susan Stinson (1998), and Denise Taliaferro (1998).

Just as Sontag experimented with an expanded notion of "criticism," Maxine Greene has performed an expanded idea of scholarship, as the Tom Barone (1998),

155

Alan Block (1998b), Brent Davis/Dennis Sumara (1998), and Paula Salvio (1998) chapters testify. Her virtuoso performances -- composed from literature, philosophy and theory (social, feminist, racial) -- dissolve traditional disciplinary boundaries, disclosing not only extraordinary depth but a breathtaking intellectual range as well. Like the New York intellectuals and Susan Sontag in particular, Maxine also seems to conceive of intellectuality as very much a matter of political engagement, critical inquiry, and cultural criticism, as the Jon Davies (1998), Jesse Goodman/Julie Teel (1998), James Giarelli (1998), James Henderson/Janice Hutchison/Charlene Newman (1998), and Nancy Lesko essays testify. And, too, Greene has relied upon the essay as the vehicle through which to convey her passionate mind (Greene 1995, 20). Finally, like Sontag, Maxine seems to many of us "the last intellectual" in the broad field of education. After all, to whom would we point as a successor? Like Sontag, Maxine Greene is a legend.

Because Maxine is so vivid for us, such an embodied presence - Mary-Ellen Jacobs (1998), Nancy Lesko (1998), Susan Stinson (1998), among others, speak to this point - I wanted to start the book with her own autobiographical voice. From her autobiographical voice I wanted us to return to the texts; they are gifts from her to us. Through four books Maxine has inspired an entire generation of scholars to think in politically engaged and powerfully interdisciplinary ways, as these essays make clear. As indebted as we are to her, as fond of her as we are, we must remember, however, that we do not know her in any definitive or final fashion, that she -- as an intellectual, as a scholar, as an individual -- is not finished. As she said in June 1996, "I am ... not yet." To emphasize this sense of her singularity, of her temporality as an intellectual, as a woman, as an singular individual, to underline her autobiographical as well as public intellectual voice, I choose that phrase to subtitle this collection of gifts from us to you, Maxine.

To make these essays a gift to you is not only to admire you in public, but to reflect in sometimes concrete sometimes abstract ways about your work: the four books, the themes we see laced throughout your work, the influences of others we see in your texts, and finally what we discern as your influence on the series of specialized areas which comprise, in part, the broad field of education. And so I invited the contributors to make statements on these four topics.

If we have succeeded in this endeavor, that success will not be indicated by your personal pleasure -- although we want that -- but by an intensification of public interest in your work. We want even more readers to know what you have done, know your intellectual leadership, your educational vision. If more of us teach your books, if more prospective and practicing teachers know their "landscapes of learning," how to "release their imagination," know what freedom is, then we will be gratified indeed. We realize that the task of intensifying interest in your work is not finished with this volume and with the Ayers-Miller volume that preceded it. I hope there appear a dozen books on your contribution during the next few years. What a hopeful sign that would be for the twenty-first century, for those of us who, like you, are not yet.

CURRICULUM THEORY AS A PRAYERFUL ACT
(1995)

Twelve years ago, at the relatively young age of 58, James B. Macdonald died. Given the traditionally ahistorical character of the field, it is probable that there are younger scholars working today who do not remember Macdonald's work as a source for theirs. Reread these papers. You will see that they either anticipated or coincided with the appearance of thematically similar essays. Not a little of the scholarship that has followed his merely provides detail to his foundation. It is an event of great importance that James Macdonald's son – Bradley Macdonald, a professor of political science at Colorado State University – has collected his father's most memorable and influential papers. The field will be grateful to you, Brad Macdonald. And the field will thank Joe Kincheloe and Shirley Steinberg for publishing this collection in their Counterpoint Series.

Who was James B. Macdonald? Macdonald's ground-breaking scholarship provoked the Reconceptualization of the U.S. curriculum field, influencing an entire generation of curriculum scholars (Searles, 1982; Holland and Garman, 1992; Pinar, Reynolds, Slattery, Taubman, 1995). Like the other major curriculum scholar of the 1960s and 1970s – Dwayne E. Huebner – Macdonald received his Ph.D. from the University of Wisconsin-Madison, advised by Virgil Herrick.

Macdonald's first university position was as Assistant Professor in Curriculum and Extension at the University of Texas-Austin during the 1956 – 1957 academic year. From 1957 – 1959 he served as Assistant Professor in Elementary Education at New York University. From 1959 – 1963, Macdonald was Associate Professor and Director of School Experimentation and Research at the University of Wisconsin-Milwaukee. He was a Professor in the Department of Curriculum and Instruction, and the Department of Educational Policy Studies at the University of Wisconsin during the period of 1963 – 1966. From 1966 – 1972 Macdonald served as Professor of Curriculum and Social and Philosophical Foundations of Education at the University of Wisconsin-Milwaukee. From 1972 until his death on November 21, 1983, Macdonald was Distinguished Professor of Education at the University of North Carolina at Greensboro (Brubaker and Brookbank, 1986). Macdonald's contribution was acknowledged by an international conference in his honor (Apple 1985; Grumet 1985; Huebner 1985; Molnar 1985; Pinar 1985; Spodek 1985; Burke 1985; Wolfson 1985a, b).

In an autobiographical reflection which prefaced his essays collected in *Curriculum Theorizing: The Reconceptualization* (2000 [1975]), Macdonald wrote:

Personally, my own work in the field in retrospect is best explained to myself as an attempt to combine my own personal growth with a meaningful social concern that has some grounding in the real world of broader human concerns. Thus, education has served as a societal pivotal point to explore myself and the broader human condition in a meaningful context. (1975a, p. 3)

This integration of the subjective and the social is strikingly evident throughout Macdonald's remarkable career. For instance, as early as 1964 he discussed the relationship between society and the individual, and specifically the ways in which society defined individuals. He called for a new image that could shape schools in general and the curriculum in particular. He called those schools which recognized a new image of children as self-actualizing as "reality-centered." This early essay would mark the beginning of his enormous contribution to the Reconceptualization of curriculum studies. Macdonald (1964, p. 47) wrote:

We simply mean that the school does not exist primarily to inculcate our cultural heritage, not principally to develop role players for society nor primarily to meet the needs and interests of the learners. The school exists to bring learners in contact with reality, of which out society, ourselves, and our cultural heritage are parts.

During the 1960s Macdonald challenged the supremacy of the structure-of-the-disciplines approach to curriculum development (although he was supportive of Schwab's later work on the practical). In addition, he challenged what he characterized as socially and psychologically oriented curriculum theory, positing another concept in which these become elements. The point of this concept – reality-centeredness – is to rationalize a curriculum in which the student can be free to develop his or her own thinking and values, and to encourage creative responses to reality (Burke 1985). It was frontier work that would be continued and extended over the remaining twenty years of his important career.

These concerns are discernible in Macdonald's 1966 essay, entitled "Learning, Meaning and Motivation: An Introduction." Here he discussed the problems associated with the structure-of-the-disciplines movement and urged a concern for the person. Macdonald challenged directly the former:

There is, after all, no reason to suspect that the reformulation of content alone in the schools will suffice to counter the loss of self, the dehumanization and depersonalization of people living in a technological society such as ours. Further, there is no reason to suspect that the structure of the disciplines can by magic of organization reduce the threat of nuclear holocaust, bring justice and equality to all people or provide a basis for freedom from poverty for all. (Macdonald and Leeper 1966, pp. 5-6)

This acknowledgement would help provoke the Reconceptualization of the 1970s (the paradigm shift from curriculum development to understanding curriculum), resulting in the field in which we work today.

A second major statement by Macdonald on the primacy of the person was published in *Precedents and Promise in the Curriculum Field* (Robison 1966). Dwelling on the theme of dehumanization, Macdonald advocated a person-oriented curriculum:

We will create our own image of ourselves through the ways we structure and relate to our own world. This image is in dire peril of becoming characterized by a partially ordered and conditioned set of regimented performances in the modern age. What we must strive for is to make men what they ought to be – complete human beings. (quoted in Robison 1966, p. 52)

School structure was dehumanizing. What was necessary was a reconceptualization of what school and curriculum could be, the cultivation of self-conscious and complete human beings. Again, early on Macdonald sounded a challenge that would be repeated over and over again in the 1970s.

At the 1967 Ohio State University Curriculum Theory Conference, chaired by Paul R. Klohr, Macdonald's paper was noteworthy. On this occasion, he delineated between "framework" and "engineering" theories at work in curriculum. Framework theorists were said to interpret curriculum issues by means of "aesthetic rationality," a concept Macdonald borrowed from Herbert Marcuse (1964), the well-known critical theorist whose work was widely read during the 1960s. Macdonald argued that aesthetic rationality pointed to the human capacity to cope rationally with the world on an intuitive basis. The individual must return to the world as experienced for insights that enabled one to transcend one's present systems of thought and to move to new paradigms or fresh perspectives.

Macdonald focused on the danger of the engineering theorists, predominant at that time. In this 1967 statement, one finds the heart of the political theory so influential in the decades to follow. Indeed, Macdonald's concerns foreshadowed those of nearly an entire generation of curricularists: "The danger of our present 'systems approach' to human behavior is that as we gain greater control over ourselves, the systems concept will become so useful in solving our problems of efficiency and effectiveness that we shall be in grave danger of losing contact with reality through 'aesthetic rationality.'" Further: "Schooling will be reduced to objectification of this systematic process [efficiency and effectiveness]. This process is already demonstrable in other aspects of our society. It is especially obvious in the realm of our national economic security policies" (Macdonald 1967, p. 168). The "system approach" – a succinct characterization of the Tyler Rationale and its behavioristic offspring such as performance objectives – would not prove popular due to its success but due to its failure. The more it failed, the more its use was intensified. The objectification process, including the objectification of students into categories (gifted, etc.) of the interpersonal process would further bureaucratize educational institutions.

Calling for a very different field, Macdonald (1967, 166) began by acknowledging that curriculum theorizing is "a challenging undertaking." At this stage, and quite beyond the mainstream thinking of the period, Macdonald (1967, p. 166) discerned that "there appears to be framework theorists and engineering theorists. Both may be needed." Framework theorists are those interested in later, non-technical issues, and he identified himself with this group: "This paper will focus upon theory as the development of frameworks from which designs can be generated rather than theory as the testing of designs," which represented a form of "technological rationality" (1967, p. 166). In technological rationality:

> phenomena are identified as separate objects (always in transaction or flux); common qualities are abstracted, related to one another, and put into system. The danger of using the technological rationality in human behavior is that, in our desire to gain control, understand, and predict, we may (and perhaps already have) come to see ourselves as objects or the representation of these objects that we find useful for our purposes .... We will then become what Marcuse called one-dimensional. (1967, pp. 166–167)

Macdonald then discussed the notion of "aesthetic rationality [which] is meant here to mean man's [sic] capacity to cope rationally with the world on an intuitive basis – to return to the world for insights which will enable him to transcend his present systems of thought and move to new paradigms ... or fresh perspectives" (1967, pp. 167-168). In contrast to technological rationality, which is "closed," aesthetic rationality "is a rationality of means applied to ends which are always open" (1967, p. 168). Macdonald (1967) then moved directly to the field of curriculum:

> Obviously, if education is to escape a similar entrapment (as a weapons delivery system locks us into nationalism, and an arms race), theorizing in curriculum must remain broad enough in scope to include the use of aesthetic rationality – this means specifically, that the systems metaphor is not enough and must be used carefully.... The central question is whether theory and theorizing are neutral or committed. Yet, its [curriculum theory's] central utility may well be the creation of forms which lead to interpreting curriculum phenomena, not so much to solving curriculum problems by applying scientific generalizations. At present, the most appropriate role for curriculum theory is probably an interpretive role.... Theory in curriculum has an essentially heuristic role. Curriculum theory should be committed, not neutral. It should be committed to human fullness in creation, direction, and use. All of man's rational potential should be committed to the processes and goals in curriculum theorizing.... Curriculum theorizing is an act of disciplined thinking. It is disciplined by the vertical awareness of curriculum theory as it has developed historically and by the horizontal awareness of man's contemporary status of development in various formal disciplines.... Rather than place emphasis only upon the discipline of technical reason, curriculum theory should be disciplined by the total rational potential of man [sic], both aesthetic and technological. (1967, pp. 168-169)

This was a major paper, one that went well beyond public curriculum debates (although correctly locating them in national defense issues) to the very character of thought employed in curriculum research. He rejected rationalistic and technical systems of theorizing as distorting and finally inhuman, endorsing an aesthetic rationality which holds political, historical, and technological potential. Note that Macdonald suggested an interpretative role for curriculum theory, once that in fact the field would take up a decade later, i.e. the project to understand – not only develop – curriculum.

In another seminal paper first published in 1971 entitled "Curriculum Theory," James Macdonald foreshadowed the movement to reconceptualize the field by laying out three categories of curriculum theorists, a scheme I employed in my mapping of the field (Pinar 2000 [1975]; Giroux, Penna, and Pinar 1981; Pinar and Grumet, 1988). Extending the notion of "framework" theorist that he had developed in 1967, Macdonald wrote that:

> One group (by far the largest) sees theory as guiding framework for applied curriculum development and research and as a tool for evaluation of curriculum development.... A second "camp" of oftentimes younger (and far fewer) theorizers is committed to a more conventional concept of scientific theory. This group has attempted to identify and describe the variables and their relationships in curriculum. The purpose of this theory is primarily conceptual in nature, and research would be utilized for empirical validation of curriculum variables and relationships, rather than as a test of the efficiency and effectiveness of a curriculum prescription. A third group of individuals look upon the task of theorizing as a creative intellectual task which they maintain should be neither used as a basis for prescription or as an empirically testable set of principles and relationships. The purpose of these persons is to develop and criticize conceptual schema in hope that new ways of talking about curriculum, which may in the future be far more fruitful than present orientations, will be forthcoming. At the present time, they would maintain that a much more playful, free-floating process is called for by the state of the art. (Macdonald 2000 [1975b], p. 6)

After a decade of Reconceptualization, this third group would come to dominate the field.

In yet another major paper, this one delivered at the 1973 University of Rochester Curriculum Theory Conference and entitled "A Transcendental Developmental Ideology of Education" (1974), Macdonald began by citing the limitations of developmental models in curriculum and in education generally. In the context of a reference to Freire, Macdonald pointed to the development of the autobiographic (which he termed romantic) and the political discourses (which he linked with earlier reconstructionist discourses) that would become influential in Reconceptualization. Macdonald (1995 [1974], p. 70) wrote:

> We still do not generally recognize this radical thrust in curriculum thinking, but the growing edge of writing in the past five to ten years leans toward a resurgence of romanticism and a renewal of past reconstructionist terms of the radical tradition. *Neither ... is the same as its predecessor.* [emphasis added]

161

Those who have contested the concept of Reconceptualization irresponsibly ignore Macdonald's appreciation of the distinctiveness of the post-1960s scholarship.

Macdonald goes on to note that the political or radical criticism of the autobiographic emphasis upon the individual asserts that it is a conservative reassertion of the status quo, i.e. of conservative political theory. He (1995 [1974], p. 72) wrote:

> [A] radical ideology claims that liberal developmental ideology and romantic ideology are embedded in the present system. That is, the emphasis upon the individual and his unfolding or developing necessitates acceptance of the social structures as status quo in order to identify in any empirical manner the development of the individual. Thus, developmental theory is culture and society bound, and it is bound to the kind of a system that structures human relations in hierarchical dominance and submission patters and alienates the person from his activity in work and from other people.

However, like the developmental/psychological view, the radical perspective was flawed as well.

> Yet I find this [radical] view limiting in its materialistic focus, and I suspect that it is grounded fundamentally in the Industrial Revolution and reflects the same linear rationality and conceptualizing that characterizes the rise of science and technology.... The world today is not the same, and a different reading of history is needed to help make sense of the contemporary world.... The radical-political perspective as a home for curriculum thinking does not adequately allow for the tacit dimension of culture: it is a hierarchical historical science that has outlived its usefulness both in terms of the emerging structure of the environment and of the psyches of people today. (Macdonald 1995, p. 73)

This critique of Marxism would become loud with the arrival of poststructuralism in the field not ten years later (Pinar et al. 1995, 283; see, also, Taubman 1979, 1982; Daignault and Gauthier 1982).

Then Macdonald the visionary surfaced. He (1995 [1974], p. 75) wrote that "today's technology is yesterday's magic." He continued:

> Technology is in effect an externalization of the hidden consciousness of human potential. Technology ... is a necessary development for human beings in that is the means of externalizing the potential that lies within. Humanity will eventually transcend technology by turning inward, the only viable alternate that allows a human being to continue to experience oneself in the world as a creative and vital element. Out of this will come the rediscovery of human potential. (Macdonald 1995 [1974], p. 75)

Political and economic analysis cannot, to borrow Jean-Paul Sartre's concept, "totalize" culture, society, and history. Rather, political and social theory represents:

a radical social adjunct to conceptual culture. Now we are facing the opening of doors of perception in human experience, not as the minor mystical phenomena that have appeared throughout history, but as a large-scale movement of consciousness on the part of our young. A multimedia world is perceptual, not linear, in the utilization of concepts, but patterned concepts are received upon impact as perceptual experience. The psychological attitude born in this culture is a psychology of individuation, not individualism or socialism.... Thus the conscious attitude of integration is one of acceptance, of ceasing to do violence to one's own nature by repressing or overdeveloping any part of it. This Jung termed a "religious" attitude, although not necessarily related to any recognizable creed. (Macdonald 1995 [1974], pp. 75-76, 82)

Macdonald's thought represents a major contribution to the U.S. curriculum field. First, we have here a rather comprehensive curriculum theory, one rooted in the historical world as well as in the history of curriculum discourses. It contains within it the major theoretical elements of the field's history, and it has made them over in a view of complexity and moral power. Second, as Melva Burke (1985) has chronicled, Macdonald's career spans what some might call the four theoretical moments of the field: scientific thinking, personal humanism, sociopolitical humanism, and transcendental thought. For Macdonald curriculum theory was fundamentally a creative act. Perhaps his view is summarized in his statement that "curriculum is an exciting venture for persons whose dispositions lead them in this direction. There is an article of faith involved...[because it is] 'the study of how to have a world'" (Macdonald, 1975b, p. 12).

In a videotaped autobiography Macdonald identified four stages of his intellectual development. The first stage was scientism, which he eventually felt excluded too much – especially affect. From scientism Macdonald moved to what he termed person-centered humanism, and third to what he termed sociopolitical humanism. His fourth and final stage was transcendentalism, with its significant secular and religious implications and its call for cultural revolution. He believed that each stage was necessary and important to his study of what he considered the key question in curriculum: How shall we live together? (Brubaker and Brookbank 1986; Macdonald, 1986).

The path-breaking work of James B. Macdonald not only challenged the traditional field during the 1960s and 1970s, it suggested a thematic route for Reconceptualization in the 1970s. Its thematic outlines would be political and autobiographic, and would include European traditions such as phenomenology and theology. What sounded like "faint voices" in the 1960s and like sheer speculation in the very early 1970s would turn out to be "fact" by 1980. This swift movement from the traditional to the reconceptualized field was, in part, a consequence of the scholarship of James B. Macdonald.

In the early 1980s, Macdonald sketched the outlines of the relations between gender and curriculum, collaborating with his wife Susan Colberg Macdonald. They pointed to the scale of the problem of sexism and the links among sexism, world armaments, and the environmental crisis. The Macdonalds connected politics, economics, and culture with the production of gendered personalities in the family and the school. They distinguished between the "agentic" or agency-oriented personality (typically male), and the "communal" one (typically female), concepts which generally parallel the gender distinctions drawn by object relations theorists (Grumet 1988). These psychoanalytic theorists typify contemporary man (in countries like the U.S.) as achieving independence at the price of relationship and intimacy, and the contemporary woman as sometimes submerged in relationship at the cost of independence and autonomy. These psychological constellations of self-formation support and express political inequalities.

The Macdonalds (1988) argued that sexism permeates all aspects of the school, including its organization, status hierarchy, and curriculum. They noted that concepts such as behavioral objectives, behavior modification, competency analysis, instructional systems, and so on, support agency-oriented value orientations. The so-called hidden curriculum reproduces familial sex-role stereotyping at worst, and fails to challenge the gender status quo at best. No aspect of school life seems to escape these influences. What course of action is possible? The Macdonalds suggested that "social engineering" was inappropriate and ineffective. Rather, incremental social action, taken in individual ways according to what is possible at each institutional site, offers hope for long-term change. In addition, scholarship (especially theoretical work) is necessary to justify and explicate what must be done. The Macdonalds suggested that the school must be reconceived to support a concept of "sociability" or community, in which patterns of independence, relationship, and intimacy could be lived by both sexes within the institution. At stake, the Macdonalds insisted, is not only gender equity in the school but the survival of the planet.

James B. Macdonald's scholarly range was very remarkable. The reader of this collection will find citations not only from curriculum specialists, but from social theorists, poets, and scholars in the humanities and arts as well. For instance, Macdonald illustrated and amplified his ideas by drawing upon the work of Adler, Apple, Berger, Blake, Bloom, Bruner, Buber, Castaneda, Coleman, Dewey, Elkind, Freidenberg, Freire, Freud, Fromm, Goodlad, Goodman, Habermas, Heisenberg, Herrick, Huebner, Illich, Jackson, James, Jung, Klein, Kliebard, Koestler, Kohlberg, Langer, Lefebvre, Mann, Marcel, Marcuse, Marx, McLuhan, Miel, Mills, Myrdal, Nietzsche, Phenix, Polanyi, Ricoeur, Rogers, Schwab, Soleri, Steiner, Stratemeyer, Tolstoy, Tyler, Watts, Whitehead, and Yeats, among others. To give you an impressionistic sense of the conceptual range of his interests – as well as their presence in 1990s scholarship – prepare to find the following concepts in this collection: embeddedness, self, culture, identity, meaning, listening, empathy, unspoken assumptions (i.e. hidden curriculum), technology, gender, bureaucracy, depersonalization, morality, human development, transcendence, romance, powerlessness, inwardness, individuation, being, Zen, Christianity, ecology, mathematics, aesthetics, imagination, mind, body, love, ideology, dialogue, scholarship, understanding, psychoanalysis, science, hermeneutics, objectivism, scientism, emancipation, life-world, consumption, power, politics, economics, language, democracy, multiculturalism, bisexuality, decadence, community, God, goodness, values, anarchy, passion, and always the school. Macdonald's modest self-presentational style could not hide the scope, rigor, and integrity of his scholarly accomplishment.

Throughout his career, James Macdonald argued against the traditional structures of curriculum research that excluded the ethical dimension of education. From several perspectives, Jim explored curriculum from a "utopian impulse for justice, equity, and fairness." He wrote:

> Education [is] a moral enterprise rather than simply a set of technical problems to be solved within a satisfying conceptual scheme....Thus, the struggle for personal integration, educational integrity, and social justice go on, necessitating a constant reevaluation of oneself, one's work and one's world – with the hope that with whatever creative talent one possess will lead toward something better that we may all share. (1975a, p. 4)

He concluded that "the act of theorizing is an act of faith, a religious act.... *Curriculum theory is a prayerful act*" (Macdonald 1995 [1981], p. 181).

A prayerful act, an act of faith. Perhaps before any of us, James B. Macdonald knew how profoundly we were moving away from the take-for-granted and the everyday. His work and presence were openings to worlds not here, worlds many have turned against as impractical. But Macdonald knew that to give up praying to that world, dreaming of that world, is to collapse defeated into this one, is to abandon hope of our redemption, and the redemption of our children. In a world and a field sometimes contracted by stinginess, blinded by loss of vision, and embittered by loss of heart, James B. Macdonald's life and career offers us a powerful and clear vision of a new world. Let us celebrate his monumental achievement by reading and rereading his essays, and proceeding, with his help, toward that new world.

DREAMS, A DAUGHTER AND HER SON

ON THE EDUCATION OF THE IMAGINATION (1995)

To the Lighthouse and Back is, as Mary Aswell Doll herself says, a very strange book. Like Robert Musil, I say that in strangeness resides reality and truth. Certainly you will find both reality and truth in these pages. Not the mundane, so-called practical truth of teaching, but the truth of the night, of literature, of lived experience, becomes disclosed. This truth is, however, not removed from the world; it is always wed to the text. "I speak to the text" (1995, p. 8), Mary begins, and among the texts to which she speaks in Virginia Woolf's breathtaking achievement *To the Lighthouse*. Indeed, by entitling this book *To the Lighthouse and Back*, Doll reveals her loyalty to the text, demonstrating that the inner world is inner only because it is profoundly related to the public world. Why does she choose *To the Lighthouse*? "The reason I will never not-teach this book, *To the Lighthouse*, is that I never understand it enough" (1995, p. 14). And may I say that you the reader may make the same judgment about this book. I have read it – as a whole and as separate essays – several times, and each time I make new notes, excited to learn something I did not know, and want to use in my own writing. For me, this is perhaps the greatest praise I can make regarding a colleague's work: that I take notes, that I learn from it. And I have always learned from Mary Aswell Doll, a close friend for twenty years now. Reading her is like, in her phrase, a "waking dream exercise"(1995, p. 16) in which one is moved into the body via the mind. "The word is flesh," Mary (1995, p. 28) reminds us, "I think of my body as unleavened bread." And we, as readers, are unleavened bread, conversing with ourselves as we speak to Mary speaking to us. This is a profound sense of education as comedy not tragedy: "A key word for such a postmodern poetics of Comedy might be conversing" (1995, p. 30), she suggests. Conversing with each other, and with ourselves: "Why on earth," she asks, "do we not make self-relating one of the focal points of pedagogy" (1995, p. 32)? Why on earth indeed. In exploring the self-self relation, the world becomes more complicated, more interesting. Mary writes: "Far be it from teachers to invoke passion with their subjects! ... *[W]ithout* an erotic component, teaching becomes mechanical, calculating, and abstract" (1995, p. 48). Eros is feminine: "Eros in the classroom would welcome the principles of the evolving Feminine: paradox, fluidity, sojourn, and body" (1995, p. 49). Like Derrida, Doll is interested in loosening the grip of western reason, and that possibility has to do with "Eros's power over logocentricism" (1995, p. 52). And where is this power? I believe it is in the body: "we must read body" (1995, p. 132), she tells us. Each of these extraordinary sentences waits for you within these pages. Who is this person Mary Aswell Doll? Bergamo "insiders" have known of her for years. She is a gifted poet, literary theorist, Beckett scholar, and, on the side as it were, an important curriculum theorist. As I reviewed her curriculum scholarship, I thought of three thematic areas: children's dreams, being a daughter, and the education of the imagination.

CHILDREN'S DREAMS

In a study published in 1988, Doll (1988b) reported themes she discerned in the dreams of 90 children (ages 4–12). In over half of these dreams, the image of the "monster" was prominent. Often half vegetable, half animal, the monster would appear in the dreamscene suddenly. Not danger but its size and the suddenness of appearance required the dreamer's attention. Indeed, the child was never in danger from the monster. Doll (1995, p. 100) explained:

> The monster's metaphoric function in dreams should be taken seriously ... not because the monster is awful, but because it inspires awe; not because it is problematic but because it gives images to thought. And its presence leads thought down to the springs of memory and imagination.

She concluded that "what was important to the child was that the monster seemed to be the agent by which the child was transported to another world, felt as being back or down or in" (1995, p. 99).

Doll noted that the image of monster has mythological importance, citing famous mythological monsters (and their combatants) such as Beowulf and Grendel, Hercules and the Nemean lion, David and Goliath. But Doll observed that in the dreams of these children a different, non-combative encounter occurs. In these dreams the monster invites the child to accompany it to its "place." "For the monster," Doll (1995, p. 100) explains, "in taking the child to its place, is allowing the child to experience utter Otherness. And the child's reluctance to slay the beast would seem to indicate an openness to Otherness."

Etymologically, the French root of monster is "monere," meaning to warn and to remind (see 1995, p. 102). In this sense the monster suggests a reminder of what is being forgotten from daily life. The Latin root – "monstrum" – means evil omen, portent, prodigy, suggesting the danger associated with such reminders. Finally, Doll reported that the location of many of these children's dreams are in the world, including the school. In this regard Doll wrote: "Civilization, as Freud knew so well, is the breeding ground for horror" (1988b, p. 93). She adds: "Like a thief at the gates, the unconscious slips through the cracks of conscious control" (Doll 1982, p. 198).

Dreams present a dialogue with the "primal mind" (1995, p. 99). In describing their dreams, children are expressing

> The power of generative metaphor to change utterly that which presents itself as hideous. For the child who has no power to change world events or parents' attitude and behaviors, this inner power of generative dream

metaphors is wonderfully healing. Expressing the monster either in words or pictures releases some of the hold our social codes have in rigidifying though into stereotypes, dogmas, and other literalisms. Dreams, even (particularly?) nightmare monsters, invite twice seeing – a wisdom our ancestors knew. (1995, p. 106)

For Mary Aswell Doll, education should not only "lead out," (*educare*); it should "lead in" (1982, p. 201). Such an education of the imagination requires dreaming more deeply in order to discover, or recover, one's inner world (Doll, 1990).

A DISTANT DAUGHTER

Mary Aswell Doll believes that the sphere of the imagination may be more real than everyday experience. To educate the imagination, she writes, one must distantiate oneself from what she terms our "literal" selves. Writing autobiographically may help, oddly it may seem, to achieve this distance. The interweaving of Doll's scholarship and her life – indicated in her speech at her and her son's alma mater at his commencement – became clear in a 1990 study which includes autobiographical remembrance of her mother and father. Both parents occupy noteworthy places in American literary history:

I come to my topic autobiographically. I am a distant daughter, who came to know my mother only when my mother was 82 and I was 42. My mother, an extraordinary editor of the 40s and 50s, was much loved by the literati. She had heard Ezra Pound read T. S. Eliot's *The Wasteland* in Paris, had lived downstairs from Truman Capote on Nantucket when he finished his first novel, *Other Voices Other Rooms*; had been one of Eudora Welty's first editors while fiction editor of *Harper's Bazaar* magazine; and had swum in the nude with Jean Stafford on (pardon the pun) Bear Island, Maine. (1995, p. 66)

While her mother was appreciative of her fellow artists, she had little time for Mary:

The fact is that I did not live with my mother. She had had a nervous breakdown shortly after I was born.... I grew up with my father, and together with my brother, commuted to my editor-mother on alternate weekends ... On the week-ends I would have cokes with Truman [Capote] nearby at the Beekman Towers, see Danny Kaye movies with Eudora [Welty] ... I tell this story to situate it in the matrix of my unconscious: in my mother, my alma mater. I loved those week-ends and I hated them. (1995, p. 66-67)

Even though Mary lived with her father, he may have been more distant than her mother. His distance may have resulted from his distance from himself, from his dreamlife, his unconscious. She tells us that it may be true that adult men were once as close to their unconscious minds and as freely dreaming as adult women and as children can be now. Doll recalls the Legend of Gilgamesh, a myth older than the Homeric poems, earlier than the transcriptions of the Bible. This legend tells the story of a hero-adventurer who found nourishment in dreams, suggesting that the dreamer-hero is an archetype, expressing a doubled relationship between an outer kindly, civilized self and an inner, wild self. Mary comments: "It is no wonder that such a seeker should find his doubled self in the outer world and would, thereby, become a whole person" (1995, p. 71). Then she returns to the memory of her father:

> Through reading this ancient epic I came to understand and appreciate the relationship my editor-father had with his most famous writer, Thomas Wolfe. The two men were opposite in significant ways – my father (Southern, born in early October 1900, Harvard-educated, mother-dominated; editor; conservative) Thomas Wolfe (Southern, born in early October, 1900, Harvard-educated, mother-dominated; writer; drinker, womanizer) .... The second half of the Gilgamesh epic is really the story of desperate grief and desperate, unrealistic searching. My father was a diminished person after the death of Thomas Wolfe, in 1938, only months after they had met, 2 years before I was born. I grew up with my father's grief. All during my life with my father he was preoccupied, searching for his lost companion, unable to come to terms with the loss of his double, the other more complete half of his self. (1995, p. 72)

This (re)search for completion, which Doll undertook here by involving the memory of her parents, is a primary element of an autobiographical curriculum. And dreams become an essential element in such a curriculum. "I wish to propose," Doll (1995, p. 65) tells us, "a curriculum that places the dream as a center point." In another place her enthusiasm for dreamwork is stronger. She writes: "Dreams can heal, prophesize, compensate, illuminate. Their power is immense ... Dreams can re-mind us of what we need to put back into our minds. If we are, as I propose, to educate the imagination, what better way to this than to dream the dream forward" (1995, pp. 72-73).

Doll weaves themes of dreams, family, teaching, and death in a 1988 study of her teaching during the time of her brother's dying of AIDS. Her son's school truancy underlines the intensity of this period, a time interrupted by frequent trips across the continent (the family lived in California at the time) to be with her dying brother. In a lyrical voice, Mary brings us closer to our own experience of death and dying as she narrates her own experience to this period. Writing a story enables her son Will to convert mourning into affirmation of life; a dream provides a passage through this labyrinth of emotion. "My brother taught me the rudiments of life during his dying," Mary confides (1995, p. 142). "When I returned to my teaching I knew I had to teach differently if I were to remain authentic about this death experience" (1995, p. 142). Such authenticity comes through dwelling in one's experience, admitting the experience of death as well as of life.

"SLEEP WELL"

In her commencement address to the Cambridge School, Mary Aswell Doll notes that she had stood there before. She is a graduate of the Cambridge School, as would be her son this day. Both Mary and Will lived in the same dormitory room, separated by a generation. She tells the audience: "The very fact that I stand before you today is a repetition. I lived my first year on campus in White Farm, just as Will did. On the second floor, as Will did. First in the room at the top of the stairs in the hallway, like Will. Then in the room directly to the left of the stairs, like Will" (1995, p. 94). Repetitions are an essential feature of education understood autobiographically. Themes are repeated, sometimes in different form; dreams repeat "problems" and issues until the dreamer manages to "solve" them, to move through them. Mary invites her listeners to think about their lives as circular:

> Lives, I suggest, can be linear or they can be circular. I invite you graduates
> to consider the journey on which you are about to embark – out from school
> and into the world – not only as a linear adventure, single points pointing
> outward only – but as a circle, points looping dynamically from within: your
> outer journey roundly connected to the spiral of your inner self, the center
> geyser of your being. (1995, pp. 92-93)

Concluding her commencement address Mary Aswell Doll summarizes her provocative, highly significant and singular scholarship. Reminding her listeners that dreams represent the reality of their lives, and that lives are circular, themes repeated, and passages revealed, she bids good-bye: "And so, dear graduates, I bid you go your way, sleep well, and remember these lines from T. S. Eliot: 'We shall not cease from exploration, and the end of all our exploring/ Will be to arrive where we started/ And know the place for the first time'" (quoted in Doll 1995, p. 97).

And now you may know this place for the first time. I invite you to participate in this wonderful "waking dream exercise," in the extraordinary, mythic, and lived world that Mary Aswell Doll so vividly portrays. We are waiting for you.

LIFE HISTORY AND THE SCHOOL SUBJECTS (1995)

The Making of Curriculum can be situated at the intersection of three important contemporary discourses: history, politics and life history. Indeed, Ivor Goodson writes: "Exploring curriculum as a focus allows us to study, indeed exhorts us to study, the intersection of individual biography and social structure ... Our methods therefore have to cover the analysis of individual lives and biographies as well as of social groups and structures" (1995, p. 59). Goodson promoted the use of life history as early as 1981. This discourse (which includes autobiographical studies as well as biographical studies) has developed rapidly – in part due to his seminal contribution – so that today it is a primary curriculum discourse.

That same year Ivor Goodson was arguing for the centrality of curriculum history, especially of the school subjects. And while historical discourses have also become central to the contemporary field, as late as 1989 Goodson could still rightly remind us: 'It is time to place historical study at the center of the curriculum enterprise' (1989, p. 138). He employs history and life history to correct the regrettable tendencies toward abstraction (which now may be termed tendencies towards master-narratives) evident in so much educational scholarship in the 1970s and early 1980s. For instance, referring to Michael F.D. Young (although he could just have easily been discussing the American reproduction theorists who so uncritically appropriated Young's and related British scholarship), Goodson notes: "Certainly the most undeveloped aspect of *Knowledge and Control* in respect to school subjects is the scrutiny of the process whereby unspecified dominant groups exercise control over presumably subordinate groups in the definition of school knowledge" (1995, p. 162). Goodson's historical research, as students of Goodson's *oeuvre* know, not only corrects these early errors; it represents an original line of scholarship. He makes convincing arguments for the historical study of school subjects, the so-called "preactive" phase of curriculum, and gives intriguing British examples, including rural and European studies, and geography. His study of geography, for instance, allows him to say:

> The establishment of geography – how geography was rendered a discipline –
> was a protracted, painstaking and fiercely contested process. The story is not
> of the translation of an academic discipline, devised by ("dominant") groups
> of scholars in universities, into a pedagogical version to be used as a school
> subject.... Far from this socialization in dominant institutions being the major
> factor creating the pattern we have examined, it was much more
> consideration of teachers' material self-interest in their working lives. (1995,
> pp. 177,180)

Not only are the reproduction theorists corrected, so are philosophers of the curriculum such as Hirst, Peters, and Phenix:

> The philosophical perspective has provided support for the view that school subject derives from forms of fields of knowledge or "disciplines." Of course, once a school subject has brought about the establishment of an academic discipline base, it is persuasively self-fulfilling to argue that the school subject receives intellectual direction and inputs from university scholars. This version of events simply celebrates a *fait accompli* in the history of the school subject and associated disciplines. (1995, p. 180)

Like all interdisciplinary scholars, Goodson makes clear that life history only makes sense within political analysis that only makes sense within historical narrative. Each of these strands of scholarship are interwoven in a perspective of originality and maturity, as evident in the following statements near the conclusion of *The Making of Curriculum*:

> Life history and curriculum history are focal in this reconceptualization of our studies.... We can see how such discursive formation functions through the way in which the debate over curriculum and schooling is constructed, conducted and organized. We can illustrate also how this is underpinned by the structuring of material interests. (1995, 197, pp. 199–200)

As this book makes plain, Ivor Goodson is one of the most important scholars at work in the field today. His originality, his interdiscursive sophistication, and his thematic emphases locate him as the "cutting edge" of the reconceptualized field. In the new field history and life history are ascendant discourses: they are important now and will become more so. Goodson's historical focus is unique, informed by life history and politics. His interest in life history is informed by politics and history. And his political theory is embedded in history and life history, thereby escaping the collapsing political sector of scholarship in the new field. Political curriculum theory as we have known in the past twenty years may disappear after its defeat at the hands of feminist and racial theory, post-structuralism and life history, but the political dimensions of curriculum study will reassert themselves in more convincing and complex forms. And Goodson's scholarship will be central to these new forms.

Ivor F. Goodson's scholarship is of great interest to all students of curriculum, especially Americans. We must attend to it carefully. This new edition of *The Making of Curriculum* is one very fine place to start.

THE SIGNIFICANCE OF THE SOUTH (2007)

Rage muted becomes nostalgia for a place that never was.

Reta Ugena Whitlock (2007, p. 132)

And can never be.

Soon after arriving in Louisiana it became obvious that there was an idea that had brought me there. Reassembling it from casual comments made by LSU administrators, I discerned there was an expectation that I was bringing with me advanced concepts of education that would enable the state to surge ahead economically. Quite aside from the simplistic assumption that there is any obvious causal relationship between education and prosperity, the idea seemed to me simultaneously self-hating and saturated with the hatred of others. It was self-hating as it implied local Louisianans couldn't figure things out on their own.[1] The idea seemed politically reactionary as it implied limited local responsibility for three centuries of assault on poor whites and all blacks. In effect, we Yankee experts were to clean up the mess three centuries of white racism and elitism had institutionalized.

As impossible – as obnoxious – was the idea that brought me to Baton Rouge in 1985, it forced upon me a set of considerations I had not before fully faced. Promptly – with help – I started to study southern history and culture, study structured by race.[2] The 1991 collection on "place" (Kincheloe and Pinar 1991) was the initial report of that study of the South, followed by a 1993 collection in which I theorized curriculum as racial text (Castenell and Pinar 1993). From that preliminary work I focused on the gender of racial politics and violence (2001), then on the genealogy of whiteness (2006a).

During my twenty years at LSU I encouraged several of my brightest Ph.D. students to undertake studies of the South. Susan Edgerton (1991, 1996) was the first to accept this invitation; Ugena Whitlock was among the last (see also Casemore [in press], Jewett 2006, Ng-A-Fook [in press]). As an emerging specialization within the academic field of education, Southern curriculum studies holds great significance not only for curriculum studies, but for teacher education, the "foundations" of education, as well as for history, literature, and, of course, Southern Studies. I claim the same for the present volume.

CONDEMNATION AND CRUCIFIXION

What I am *doing* is a Southern reconstruction.

Reta Ugena Whitlock (2007, p. 169)

The institutionalization of rage, revenge, and resurrection –Whitlock works these concepts in chapters 3 and 4 – typifies the political history of the American South. Political violence has fueled the present political ascendancy of the Confederacy.[3] Not only for the sake of the South, but for the sake of the United States, last century's failed Reconstruction must again be undertaken. This time reconstruction cannot be conducted by the federal (Confederate) government. If it occurs at all, reconstruction will occur through the political, intellectual, and psychological labor of the South's own progressives. Due to the very personalism of Southern culture that Whitlock describes and performs, progressives have tended suspend their activism for the sake of family and friends.[4] For good reason: when Southern progressives – consider the case of George Washington Cable (see Pinar 2001, p. 92), for instance – did take unpopular stands, their lives were threatened. While physical death is less likely now than in Cable's time, the price of activism remains high.

Despite the price, Reta Ugena Whitlock remains in love with the South. *Because* she loves the South she confronts its nostalgia. "I will not fight any longer for a Lost Cause," she tells us, "but will continue to look to the South for causes worth fighting for" (2007, p. 2). One cause is the hearts and minds of Southern school children. One central site of that struggle is the school curriculum, as conservatives have long known.[5] Focused on the curriculum – the meaning of the past for the present and our prospects for the future – Whitlock appreciates that political culture both informs and is informed by what students study. Because it is "culture" white Southerners imagine they are "protecting" when they vote for conservative candidates, culture is one sphere that must be reconstructed. The reconstruction of culture occurs through the education of the public.

Wryly, Whitlock (2007, p. 15) acknowledges that "reconstruction is a volatile word in the context of Southern studies." Not only the word's association with events 140 years ago is in play here, the very construct of reconstruction contests the conservatism to which so many white Southerners cling. Recall that social reconstruction (and not just of the South) was the primary educational aspiration of many progressives 75 years ago, progressives still vilified by conservative politicians and scholars (see, for instance, Ravitch 2001).

Social reconstruction requires the racial restructuring of the South. Whitlock works to unravel the knot that is white racism, its compact and convoluted interconnections with home, family, class, and church. By confronting whites (and in particular, neo-Confederate white men), Whitlock contributes to the dissolution of whiteness and to the racial restructuring of the South and the nation.

For Southerners, the site of confrontation between an unreconstructed past, a reactionary present, and a progressive future is not only the lunch-counter, the bus, the school: it is the home. "Home is not a sanctuary," Whitlock (2007, p. 82) appreciates, no "place of safety and comfort. It is a place of reconstruction, of the working through. Home is where Whitlock asserts both her religious fundamentalism and her queer identity. "Fundamentalism is my native tongue," she tells us, "and I speak it now, but queerly" (2007, p. 91).

No curse of the Covenant, Whitlock's speaking in tongues performs the labor of reparation.[6] It is labor simultaneously intellectual and spiritual:

I therefore want to reveal the complexities, paradoxes, anomalies of spirit and desire that I bear witness to as a queer fundamentalist—not a fundamentalist, not a lesbian woman void of other identity experiences, not a critic with an overdetermined attachment to one theoretical discourse, perspective, or ground for thinking—but as a person with truly problematic and contradictory identifications and desires. (2007, p. 87)

Demonstrating Aoki's (2005 [1985/1991], p. 232) crucial concept of "creative tensionality," Whitlock (2007, p. 87) teaches "ethically from within the tension of these contradictions." Declining to abandon her faith, her sexuality or her home, embracing contradiction and tension: Ugena testifies to the reciprocity of psychic and social reconstruction through reparation.[7]

It is precisely the complexity of tension that is suppressed in the literalism many fundamentalists – Christian, Islamic - embrace. In their insistence on certainty, on a bifurcated world of good and evil, many U.S. fundamentalists vacate the earth in an anti-intellectual, treasonous "rapture" in which the fate of the nation is a casualty of individual "salvation." While the United States has suffered religious extremists from its genocidal genesis, it was only during the "radical" racism of the late nineteenth-century South – the apex of lynching – that religious fundamentalism spread throughout the South. Historian Joel Williamson (1984) argues that the latter was a function of the former.

Not only Southern fundamentalism follows from nineteenth-century radical racism. I argue that many contemporary white Southerners' "conservative" values - Black and Black (1992, p. 9) list "traditional family values, the importance of religion, support for capital punishment, and opposition to gun control" and I would add opposition to abortion and to civil rights for lesbians and gay men - preserve traces of earlier racist recalcitrance. The reactionary rage that animates some white southerners' engagement with these issues provides the clue to the presence of the past. While southern "conservatism" cannot be reduced to residues of racial hatred – it is broader and more complex than that – it cannot be understood apart from it either. What Lillian Smith understood to be true in the South over fifty years ago reverberates still:

Southern tradition, segregation, states' rights have soaked up the fears of our people; little private fantasies of childhood have crept there for hiding, unacknowledged arsenals of hate have been stored there, and a loyalty covering up a lack of self-criticism has glazed the words over with sanctity. No wonder the saying of them aloud can stir anxieties until there are times when it seems we have lost our grasp on reality. (Smith 1963 [1949], p. 135)

It is nothing less than the reconstruction of "reality" that is at stake in the curriculum development[8] Whitlock has undertaken.

COMMUNION

[C]onversation is inextricably linked to communion.

Reta Ugena Whitlock (2007, p. 160)

Speaking the language of Christian fundamentalism, Ugena Whitlock reminds her fellow fundamentalists that human hatred – whether in the form of homophobia, racism, sexism, classism, or ageism - destroys spirituality. "Celebrating the agency of all people," she admonishes, "strengthens the spirit—both our individual and collective spirits" (2007, p. 112). Appealing for openness, trust and dialogue, Whitlock (2007, p. 113) calls for unity in diversity: "When we begin and end with love, we confront discomfort, fear, and rage with openness, not narrowness; peace, not violence." Whitlock is not only sagacious; she is savvy, for in Foucaultian terms, such language constitutes a reverse discourse (see Savran 1998, p. 55).

A "reverse" discourse, Didier Eribon (2004, 312) explains, "speak[s] on its own behalf, demand[s] that its legitimacy ... be acknowledged, often in the same vocabulary, using the same categories by which it was ... disqualified." "What takes place," Eribon (2004, p. 313) continues, "might be a reappropriation of the meanings power has produced in order to transform their value." In the mouths of conservatives, calls for openness, trust, and dialogue are insincere platitudes in the service of political manipulation and indoctrination. In reclaiming Christianity as a potentially progressive force (as, historically, it was for many African Americans: see Pinar 2001, p. 1138), Whitlock "reverses" this insincerity, rendering "communion" no fetishistic displacement of community (in favor of a cannibalistic incorporation of the body of the Father), but an educational restructuring of privilege and possession. "The language of fundamentalism," Ugena knows, "is a powerful tool" (2007, p. 164).

Unlike the oedipal politics of the enraged straight son, the "misfit" queers the South by haunting it, not in the service of nostalgia, but of reconstruction. In Flannery O'Connor's stories, Ugena tells us, "the Misfit functions to disrupt, and with this rift comes grace" (2007, p. 117). Grace and redemption carry a "price," Whitlock reminds, still using biblical language, and that price is death. "For the South," she asserts, significantly,

> this means focusing on the death through which grace, and Southern reconstruction, may occur. The South must lay to rest the Lost Cause - through which there will be neither resurrection nor remission of Southern sins. (2007, p. 118)

In the liberation of death - in the "shattering of the white Southern self" - a "new communion of reconstruction" constitutes resurrection, not of the lost cause, but of the democratic cause the South rejected and the North has never realized (2007, p. 125). By occupying "spaces between sin and redemption," Whitlock (2007, p. 126) continues, the subjectivity of the misfit "troubles truths about good and evil, right and wrong, salvation and damnation."

Concluding the book – it constitutes, I submit, an intellectual breakthrough (see Axelrod 1979) in Southern Studies - Ugena is reminded of James Macdonald's (1995, p. 173) "hermeneutic quest" in which curriculum theory is likened to a moment in the meditative hermeneutic cycle. So conceived, Macdonald (1995, 181) explained, "the act of theorizing is an act of faith, a religious act.... What defines [both theory and pedagogy] is the spirit and vision that shines through the surface manifestations" (quoted in Whitlock 2007, p. 20).

Inspired by Macdonald, Whitlock writes that "the spirit of curriculum is an *inspirited* curriculum" (2007, p. 163), not only a spiritual and phenomenological concept (see Aoki 2005 [1987], p. 359), but a profoundly political one as well. For Whitlock, the inspirited curriculum is one "invigorated with the daily practice of making meaning and transgressing social codes" (2007, p. 163). Adopting Appiah's concept of cosmopolitanism, she suggests, may enable teachers provide "a curricular forum so that we — strangers all — may, as singular and social citizens of the cosmos, come to the realization that we matter to each other" (2007, p. 163). In such a forum, the study of the South becomes an educational opportunity for communion wherein "Southerners might acknowledge one another and engage one another in conversation about progressive social, cultural, and political movement" (2007, p. 164). It is conversation populated by the past:

> Communion is a common sharing of mourning in the search for hope. In remembrance of bodies lynched, for example, there might be a radicalized communion in which forgiveness is sought, reparation paid. Spiritual and social reparation, ultimately, is the price of Southern restoration, and it is one that some white Southerners are loathe to pay. (2007, p. 166)

Whitlock is one white Southerner ready to pay, one white Southerner who invites other white Southerners to join her in reparation.

Sometimes subtly, sometimes baldly, often humorously, Reta Ugena Whitlock faces her Pharisees and declines both crucifixion and condemnation, offering us instead communion through complicated conversation. In teaching as a misfit, Whitlock disrupts the sacrilegious ceremonies of conservatism and reclaims the – her - South, reconstructing the Confederate States of America as the future home for the progressive United States of America the Declaration of Independence promises us all.

NOTES

INTRODUCTION

[1] I am referring to matters concerning the academic disciplines, not to disciplinarity as normalization and surveillance, phenomena often associated with modernization (see, for instance, Hardt and Negri 2000, 23) and with homosexual disavowal (see Hope 1994, 194, n. 20).

[2] Not all social reconstructionists expressed skepticism toward disciplinarity. Gerald Ponder (2006, 244) reports that George Counts was not enthusiastic about curriculum integrated around large themes as were Rugg and others. He retained a great deal of faith in the viability and usefulness of the academic disciplines and their related school subjects. He did, however, emphasize the need for social orientation in subject matter and instructional method.

[3] The other four included 1) specific competencies/technology, 2) human traits/processes, 3) social functions/activities, and 4) individual needs and interests/activities.

[4] Brent Davis (2005, 131) thinks in terms of "recursive elaboration" rather than in terms of "sitting atop a mound of past work." He links antecedent scholarship to present acts of *improvisation* and goals of *improvement* (2005, 131-132), the former concept reminiscent of Aoki's reference to jazz (2005 [1990], 367ff.) and the latter to "advancement," if we delete the ameliorative orientation the noun connotes to students of Kliebard. Davis (2005, 132) acknowledges that "This realization does not free me from the responsibility to be attentive to who said what when – in fact, it seems to amplify the need to be familiar with what has come before – but it is liberating in that it highlights the importance of a repetition. Not a mindless mimicking, but a mindful reiteration." This seems to be a fine phrase for the labor of the synoptic text today, quite in contrast to Davis' cynical revision of historicity as "territoriality" (see 2005, 131). Indeed, one must demonstrate one's work is "different" (2005, 131); otherwise it is a mindless reiteration. As Donna Trueit (2005, 95), also writing of complexity theory, writes, the point of (for her, chaos and complexity theories, for me scholarship generally, historical scholarship in particular) is "to help us to think about and to deal with, change – not by rearranging what is present, but by looking for what was not there before ... to be creative."

[5] Like the stereotype of traditional housewives complaining about their day at home with the kids, some schoolteachers complain to their evening-course college professor "husbands" about their daytime trouble with their students, claiming curricular primacy for those complaints over the books listed on the syllabus. The gender of participants' occupational location takes precedence over the actual anatomy of individuals involved. Schoolteachers (gendered female in the popular imaginary) and education professors (gendered male in the popular imaginary, if female within the academy) are, I have argued, trapped in a bad marriage (see 2004a, 172ff.).

[6] Education professors are not the only ones to suffer this fate; see Menzies and Newson (2006, 13). For me, one sign of an academically strong academic institution is that its organizational noise is inaudible.

[7] That Schwab's emphasis upon concepts and methodologies is more appropriate to scientific traditions is unsurprising, given his disciplinary training in genetics (see Pinar et al. 1995, 193).

[8] Verticality is the complement of the regressive phrase of the method of *currere*, during which the life history of one's ideas can be re-experienced (see Pinar 2004a, 36).

[9] In this sense, verticality can also be understood as a form of "historical consciousness" (see Seixas 2004, 10). For a study of the significance of biographical studies, see Kridel 1998; Kridel and Bullough 2007.

[10] As I will acknowledge in the main text, there are readers who will be wondering if commitments to disciplinarity do not mean withdrawal from political engagement with the world. In part, it is this question that prompts me to call upon Spivak's notion of "planetarity" (later in the introduction) to suggest that the structures of subjectivity the structures of disciplinarity cultivate portend ways of being-in-the-world that are characterized by engagement and sustainability. That said, I want to affirm that intellectuals – when they tell the truth, not simply do the work of the state and its

bureaucracies – are also activists. The critical and detailed attention to a specific text is also attention to the cultural and political context in which the text was composed and appears (see Cain 1989, 561). Nothing can replace the indispensable labor of intellectuals - writing, thinking, speaking, reporting – "whose effects have been both unique and indispensable" (Lazarus 1999, 187). Because these effects cannot be quantified, those trained in social science tend to dismiss these effects as inconsequential. Because intellectuals have been politically marginalized in the U.S., those working in America tend to imagine their practices are inconsequential, when the rage and hysteria of the right-wing over the curriculum demonstrates the contrary.

[11.] See: http://www.edcollege.ucf.edu/esdepart/cirs/main.cfm)

[12.] See: http://pkp.sfu.ca/about

[13.] For a brief discussion of their significance, see Pinar et al. 1995, 177-185. In my introduction to his collected works (Huebner 1999), I argued that Huebner belongs alongside Bobbitt, Tyler, and Schwab. This is, regrettably, a minority view.

[14.] My candidate for this key post was Professor William H. Schubert. Schubert enjoys the stature - intellectual, moral, disciplinary - prerequisite to the project. Other members might include, I suggested, Professor Craig Kridel, the Director of the University of South Carolina's Museum of Education, the coauthor of a new book on the Eight-Year Study (Kridel and Bullough 2007), and by anyone's calculation, one of key curriculum historians working today. The participation of retiring AAACS President – Janet L. Miller (2005) – would ensure the expansion of the canon to include key "founding mothers" (Sadovnik and Semel 2002; Crocco, Munro, Petra and Weiler 1999) - and of a promising junior scholar – such as Professor Denise Taliaferro Baszile (2006) – would also help ensure a fair and just referencing of historical and contemporary scholarship prerequisite to expertise in curriculum studies. The AAACS General Membership accepted my proposal and these nominations.

[15.] See: http://www.m-w.com/dictionary/founded

[16.] In my view, "study" qualifies for such a concept.

[17.] Discussing pre-Socratic meanings of poiesis, Donna Trueit (2005, 87) suggests that "each *poietic* reenactment involves pulling the past into the present, recollection, and re-presenting with variation, since each performance was intended to improve upon the past, to have a sense of novelty." I draw a distinction between novelty and advancement. Novelty does mean "new," but it can connote something ornamental rather than fundamental. Rather than refashioning the present for the sake of amusement or adornment, intellectual advancement must "midwife" what it "not yet" into the present by teaching us what we did not before understand. That is what the over-used concept of "transformation" implies, is it not: that all participants now understand their – the – situation in terms they did not before, thereby providing passages to what is to come.

[18.] There remains a socialist movement of workers in 35 countries:
http://www.socialistworld.net/index.html

[19.] See the Editorial Statement of the Journal of the American Association for the Advancement of Curriculum Studies (retrieved on March 9, 2007, from
http://www.uwstout.edu/soe/jaaacs/statement.htm):
The American Association for the Advancement of Curriculum Studies (AAACS) supports at least two notions of advancement that emerge out of its historical location and its relationship with the International Association for the Advancement of Curriculum Studies (IAACS).
As conceptualized in relation to local configurations within the United States, advancement refers to the importance of maintaining a formal curriculum studies field. This field emerged historically within the larger discipline of education, and now permeates several disciplines. It entails rigorous attention to cultural issues and methodological concerns involved with understanding curriculum as many kinds of texts, including, but significantly extending beyond, curriculum-as-administrative-text. The importance of this conceptualization of advancement extends to institutional issues at the tertiary level. This includes, for example, consideration of the politics of placement, of where, when, and how curriculum studies exists as an independent arena of research and teaching as well as an organizing concept within or across departments.

Advancement as it is conceptualized in relation to IAACS' mission refers to the importance of placing curriculum studies in an international frame of reference. This can entail, among other things, examinations of how the field of curriculum studies exists and operates in particular locales, analyses of curriculum histories in cross-national perspective, and investigations into the relationships among curriculum formation, epistemology, ontology, governance, and state-formation in international perspective.

The intellectual advancement of U.S. curriculum studies requires, then, serious and sustained attention to scholarly production within and outside the United States. To support such serious and sustained attention, JAAACS, an on-line journal, will publish research essays that critique and contextualize (theoretically, historically) new scholarship, interweaving past and present ideas in the field, On occasion two or more new books and/or essays/articles will be juxtaposed to suggest new trends, pointing out distinctions among points of view. With the book(s) and article(s)/essay(s) situated at the illusory center, JAAACS research essays will explore not only ideas in these texts but also their relations to culture, society and the historical moment. In attending to the complicated conversation that is the present and past scholarship of curriculum studies worldwide, JAAACS research essays will make a significant contribution to the advancement of U.S. curriculum studies.

[20.]Since the publication of *Understanding Curriculum* (Pinar et al. 1995), wherein, employing a poststructuralist schema, we identified eleven primary curriculum discourses, efforts to understand curriculum as historical text, as political, as racial, as a gender text, as phenomenological, as deconstructed/poststructuralist/postmodern, as autobiographical, as aesthetic, as theological, as institutional, and as international text. The order of my listing here honors the centrality of curriculum history by placing it first; it registers my faith in the promise of internationalization by listing it last.

CHAPTER 1

[1.]The text is: Jardine, David W., Friesen, Sharon, and Clifford, Patricia (2006). *Curriculum in abundance*. Mahwah, NJ: Lawrence Erlbaum.

[2.]Post-structuralism is a movement in literary criticism and philosophy originating in France in the late 1960s. In no minor way derived from Martin Heidegger's *Being and Time* (1927), post-structuralism suggested that language is not a transparent medium that connects one directly with a "truth" or "reality" outside it but, rather, a structure or code whose elements derive their meaning from their contrast with one another and not from any explicit connection with an "outside" – in the present context, non-relational - world. See Pinar et al. 1995, chapter 9, for its history in curriculum studies.

[3.]Rather than being "skinned" by the curriculum, Dennis Sumara and Brent Davis (1998, 76) recommend "unskinning" the curriculum, "simultaneously removing and imposing boundaries."

[4.]Recall that Madeleine Grumet [1988] postulated curriculum *as* contradiction.

[5.]There's a cup in this text, but it doesn't runneth over, and, moreover, it's Styrofoam. Jardine associates it not with a morally bankrupt, i.e. politicized, Christianity, but, rather, with "a perfect example of a Cartesian Substance: something that is bereft of any relations" (2006, 273). The essential, self-enclosed, socially isolated Christian "soul" is indeed bereft of earthly relations; it is with the loin-clad son on the cross and his ill-tempered irresponsible Father with "whom" the believer is, presumably, related, and then through "gracious submission."

CHAPTER 9

[1.]This is my insertion in Watson's words. See Plant, R. (1986). *The Pink Triangle: The Nazi War against Homosexuals*. New York: Henry Holt and Co. Also: Heger, Heinz (1994). *Men with the Pink Triangle: The True, Life-and-Death Story of Homosexuals in the Nazi Death Camps*. [Introduction by Kalus Muller. Trans. by David Fernback.] Los Angeles: Alyson.

CHAPTER 19

[1] There was little in the scholarly literature in the mid-1980s to articulate a progressive curriculum of place, including for the South. In the collection of essays (Kincheloe and Pinar 1991) introducing the concept of "place" to curriculum studies, I pointed to the educational significance of regional studies generally, as my co-editor – Joe Kincheloe, then teaching in Louisiana, too (now teaching in Canada, as am I) – emphasized critical theory in understanding curriculum as a form of social psychoanalysis.

[2] It was, for me, a return to race. As a senior at Ohio State in 1968, I had enrolled in an experimental urban education program taught by Professor Donald R. Bateman (see Bateman 1974). In that program I was introduced to the work of Paulo Freire, began tutoring in the inner city of Columbus, and prepared to join the pedagogical regiment of the revolution (or so I hoped). As my anxious white mentor teacher watched, I taught black eighth-graders Richard Wright's *Black Boy* and Eldridge Cleaver's *Soul on Ice*. Nixon had been elected president that fall, and soon I realized my role in black liberation was, well, more complicated than I had first appreciated. For a dozen years afterward I focused on the politics and phenomenology of subjectivity, on what later (and through an identity politics prism) would be called whiteness studies. It would take the facticity of Louisiana to force me to confront my own racialization.

[3] The denial of basic human rights (presumably guaranteed by the Geneva Accord) to prisoners at Guantanamo, the invasion of Iraq (and its misrepresentation to the American public), the torture at Abu Ghraib: these headline the violence abroad perpetuated by the Republican (the neo-Confederate) Party. Domestically, the refusal to raise the minimum wage, the anti-gay initiatives (most famously focused on the issue of marriage), exploiting the fear of terrorism and mindless flag-waiving typify the violent tactics of "conservatives" determined to destroy democracy for the sake of God and country (not the USA, I am arguing, the CSA). George W. Bush becomes intelligible as a Confederate – not American – President. Whitlock uses a botanical metaphor to depict the political influence of the South, namely that it "spreads like kudzu through the rest of America." The vine is home-grown, of course, not Asian, and much worse than a nuisance.

[4] A character in Lillian Smith's *Strange Fruit* personifies the problem of the Southern progressive. After a lynching,

> Prentiss Reid, editor of *The Maxwell Press*, sat late in his office. Yellow sheets of paper lay in front of him, covered with pencil marks. The town's religious skeptic, the admirer of Tom Paine, the man who fought Prohibition, who had dared raise questions in 1917 about the persecution of aliens, had drawn a blank for tomorrow's editorial. "Anything you say now will do more harm than good. That's the trouble. Always the trouble! Say what you think, make a gesture, you stir up a mare's nest. Make things worse that they were before - So they say."

> He lit a cigarette; stared the bookshelf above his desk. *Holy Bible, Common Sense, Age of Reason, Rights of Man.* Four books worn from handling. Pages marked, words underlined, comments scribbled in the margins. There was no man in Maxwell who could with so much ease cite Holy Writ in an argument as could the town's infidel; and none who could quote whole pages from Tom Paine as causally as if from a talk with a friend. (Smith, 1972 [1944], 364-365)

What will this progressive Southerner say about the lynching of an innocent black man? Reid rationalizes his inaction; instead of criticizing his fellow Southerners, he blames the North.

> Prentiss Reid lit another cigarette; stared into the wall, shrugged, wrote rapidly for a few minutes. ".... [B]ut what's done now is done. Bad, yes. Lawlessness and violence are always bad. And this particular form smacks of the Dark Ages. It hurts business, it hurts the town, it hurts the county, it hurts everybody in it. But it's time now to get our minds on our work, get back to our jobs, quit this talking. Those who participated in the lynching were a lawless bunch of hoodlums. We don't know who they are. They ought to be punished. But who are

they? No one seems to know.... As for northern criticism. There will be plenty. All we can say is: if the dam Yankees can handle these folks better than we who've had more than two hundred years' practice, let them try it. Lord knows, they're welcome to try it. Up there. And we might ask them how about their own gangsters? And how about East St. Louis and Chicago?" (Smith, 1972 [1944], 367)

These are references to the famous 1917 East St. Louis (see Pinar 2001, 672) and 1919 Chicago race riots. For Reid, they are excuses to rationalize silence.

[5.] From evolutionary theory (linked by Southerners to godlessness) to African American history and culture (linked by Southerners to the Communism) to religious (in)tolerance and now gay and lesbian history and (again, 80 years after the Scopes Trial) to evolutionary theory (see Good 2005), Southerners have led the way in denying school children access to the truth (see Zimmerman 2002).

[6.] Freud's construction of the primal scene, Ned Lukacher (1986, 44) points out, represents an effort to define the "work of reparation in terms of the affirmation of the ineluctability of difference and deferral." Supplementing financial payments, reparation – in particular, unraveling the knot of whiteness - becomes an ongoing "undecidable intertextual event that is situated in the differentiated space between historical memory and imaginative construction, between archival verification and interpretative free play" (1986, 24). For me (Pinar 2006a), race is the curse of the Covenant; reparation requires restructuring the relationship between (white, heavenly) father and (sublimated, religious) son.

[7.] Quoting Fanon (1968, 247) - "the consciousness of the self is not the closing of the door to communication, but guarantees it" – Nigel Gibson (2003, 189) points out that "this 'self which does not close the door to communication develops by undergoing mediation (and therefore self-negation) and only then embraces the other in mutual recognition." In religious and educational (rather than Marxist) terms, Whitlock acknowledges the same reconstructive reciprocity between the subjective and social.

[8.] After the Reconceptualization, curriculum development is an intellectual – not bureaucratic – labor of study and teaching (Pinar 2006b).

REFERENCES

Adler, Mortimer (1982). *The paideia proposal.* New York: Macmillan.

Allen, Louise Anderson (2001). *A bluestocking in Charleston: The life and career of Laura Bragg.* Columbia: University of South Carolina Press.

Althusser, Louis (1993). *The future lasts a long time and the facts.* [Edited by Olivier Corpet & Yann Moulier Boutang. Translated by Richard Veasey.] London: Chatto & Windus.

Anderson, Amada (2006). *The way we argue now: A study in the cultures of theory.* Princeton, NJ: Princeton University Press.

Anderson, James D. and Watkins, William H. (2005). *Black protest thought and education.* New York: Peter Lang.

Aoki, Douglas Sadao (2002, Spring). The price of teaching: Love, evasion, and the subordination of knowledge. *JCT 18* (1), 21-39.

Aoki, Ted T. (1990). Sonare and videre: Questioning the primacy of the eye in curriculum talk. In George Willis and William H. Schubert (Eds.), *Reflections from the heart of educational inquiry: Understanding curriculum and teaching through the arts* (pp. 182-189). Albany, NY: State University of New York Press.

Aoki, Ted T. (2003). Locating living pedagogy in teacher "research": Five metonymic moments. In Erika Hasebe-Ludt and Warren Hurren (Eds.) *Curriculum intertext: Place/language/pedagogy* (pp. 1-9). New York: Peter Lang.

Aoki, Ted T. (2005 [1978]). Toward curriculum inquiry in a new key. In William F. Pinar and Rita L. Irwin (Eds.), *Curriculum in a new key* (pp. 89-110). Mahwah, NJ: Lawrence Erlbaum.

Aoki, Ted T. (2005 [1981]). Toward understanding curriculum: Talk through reciprocity of perspectives. In William F. Pinar and Rita L. Irwin (Eds.), *Curriculum in a new key* (pp. 219-228). Mahwah, NJ: Lawrence Erlbaum.

Aoki, Ted T. (2005 [1983]). Curriculum implementation as instrumental action and as situational praxis. In William F. Pinar and Rita L. Irwin (Eds.), *Curriculum in a new key* (pp. 111-123). Mahwah, NJ: Lawrence Erlbaum.

Aoki, Ted T. (2005 [1985/1991]). Signs of vitality in curriculum scholarship. In William F. Pinar and Rita L. Irwin (Eds.), *Curriculum in a new key* (pp. 229-233). Mahwah, NJ: Lawrence Erlbaum.

Aoki, Ted T. (2005 [1986]. Interests, knowledge and evaluation: Alternative approaches to curriculum evaluation. In William F. Pinar and Rita L. Irwin (Eds.), *Curriculum in a new key* (pp. 137-150). Mahwah, NJ: Lawrence Erlbaum.

Aoki, Ted (2005 [1987]). Inspiriting the curriculum. In William F. Pinar and Rita L. Irwin (Eds.), *Curriculum in a new key: The collected works of Ted T. Aoki* (pp. 357-365). Mahwah, NJ: Lawrence Erlbaum.

Aoki, Ted (2005 [1990]). *Sonare* and *videre*: A story, three echoes and a lingering note. In William F. Pinar and Rita L. Irwin (Eds.), *Curriculum in a new key: The collected works of Ted T. Aoki* (pp. 367-376). Mahwah, NJ: Lawrence Erlbaum.

Aoki, Ted T. (2005 [1991a]). Layered understandings of orientations in social studies program evaluation. In William F. Pinar and Rita L. Irwin (Eds.), *Curriculum in a new key* (pp. 167-186). Mahwah, NJ: Lawrence Erlbaum.

Aoki, Ted T. (2005 [1991b]). Five curriculum memos and a note for the next Half century. In William F. Pinar and Rita L. Irwin (Eds.), *Curriculum in a new key* (pp. 247-261). Mahwah, NJ: Lawrence Erlbaum.

REFERENCES

Aoki, Ted T. (2005 [1991c]). The sound of pedagogy in the silence of the morning calm. In William F. Pinar and Rita L. Irwin (Eds.), *Curriculum in a new key* (pp. 389-401). Mahwah, NJ: Lawrence Erlbaum.

Aoki, Ted T. (2005 [1991d]). Bridges that rim the Pacific. In William F. Pinar and Rita L. Irwin (Eds.), *Curriculum in a new key* (pp. 437-439). Mahwah, NJ: Lawrence Erlbaum.

Aoki, Ted T. (2005 [1992]). Layered voices of teaching: The uncannily correct and the elusively true. In William F. Pinar and Rita L. Irwin (Eds.), *Curriculum in a new key* (pp. 187-197). Mahwah, NJ: Lawrence Erlbaum.

Aoki, Ted T. (2005 [1993]). The child-centered curriculum: Where is the social in pedocentricism? In William F. Pinar and Rita L. Irwin (Eds.), *Curriculum in a new key* (pp. 279- 289). Mahwah, NJ: Lawrence Erlbaum.

Aoki, Ted T. (2005 [1993]). Legitimating lived curriculum. In William F. Pinar and Rita L. Irwin (Eds.), *Curriculum in a new key* (pp. 199-215). Mahwah, NJ: Lawrence Erlbaum.

Aoki, Ted T. (2005 [1996]). Imaginaries of "East and West": Slippery curricular signifiers in education. In William F. Pinar and Rita L. Irwin (Eds.), *Curriculum in a new key* (pp. 313-319). Mahwah, NJ: Lawrence Erlbaum.

Aoki, Ted T. (2005 [2000]). Language, culture, and curriculum. In William F. Pinar and Rita L. Irwin (Eds.), *Curriculum in a new key* (pp. 321-329). Mahwah, NJ: Lawrence Erlbaum.

Aoki, Ted T. (Ed.).(n.d.). *Voices of teaching*. Monograph, Volume 1. Program for Quality Teaching. Vancouver, British Columbia, Canada: British Columbia Teachers' Federation.

Appel, Stephen (1999). (Ed.). *Psychoanalysis and pedagogy*. Westport, CT: Bergin & Garvey.

Appiah, Kwane Anthony (2006). *Cosmopolitanism: Ethics in a world of strangers*. New York: W.W. Norton & Company.

Asher, Nina (2002). (En)gendering a hybrid consciousness. *Journal of Curriculum Theorizing, 18* (4), 81-92.

Asher, Nina (2005). At the interstices: Engaging postcolonial and feminist perspectives for a multicultural education pedagogy in the South. *Teachers College Record, 107* (5), 1079-1106.

Axelrod, Charles David (1979). *Studies in intellectual breakthrough*. Amherst, MA: University of Massachusetts Press.

Apple, Michael W. (1985). There is a river: James B. Macdonald and curricular tradition. *JCT, 6*(3), 9-18.

Aronowitz, Stanley (1982, November). Opposites detract: Sontag versus Barthes for Barthes' Sake," *The Village Voice Literary Supplement*, 13-14.

Atwell-Vasey, Wendy (1998a). *Nourishing words: Bridging private reading and public teaching*. Albany: State University of New York Press.

Atwell-Vasey, Wendy (1998b). Psychoanalytic feminism and the powerful teacher. In William F. Pinar (Ed.), *Curriculum: Toward new identities* (pp. 143-156). New York: Garland.

Axelrod, Charles David (1979). *Studies in intellectual breakthrough*. Amherst, MA: University of Massachusetts Press.

Ayers, William C. and Miller, Janet L. (Eds.) (1998). *A light in dark times: Maxine Greene and the unfinished conversation*. New York: Teachers College Press.

Bagley, William (1905). *The educative process*. New York: Macmillan.

Bagley, Carl, Cancienne, and Babst, Gordon Albert (Eds.) (2002). *Dancing the data*. (Lesley College Series in Arts and Education, v. 5). New York: Peter Lang Publishing.

Baker, Bernadette M. (2001). *In perpetual motion: Theories of power, educational history, and the child*. New York: Peter Lang.

Baker, Bernadette M. (2002a). Disorganizing educational tropes: conceptions of dis/ability and curriculum. *Journal of Curriculum Theorizing, 18*(4): 47–80.

Baker, Bernadette M. (2002b). The hunt for disability: the new eugenics and the normalization of schoolchildren. *Teachers College Record, 104*: 663–703.

Banks, James A. (1997). *Educating citizens in a multicultural society*. New York: Teachers College Press.

188

Banks, James A. (2005). *Cultural diversity and education: Foundations, curriculum, and teaching.* [Fifth edition.] Boston: Allyn & Bacon.

Barone, Thomas (1998). Maxine Greene: Literary influences. In William F. Pinar (Ed.), *The passionate mind of Maxine Greene* (pp. 137-147). London: Falmer.

Barone, Thomas E. (2000). *Aesthetics, politics, and educational inquiry: Essays and examples 1979-1997.* New York: Peter Lang.

Barrington, Judith (1997). *Writing the memoir: From truth to art.* Portland, OR: The Eighth Mountain Press.

Barthes, Roland (1986). *The rustle of language.* New York: Hill and Wang.

Baszile, Denise Taliaferro (2006). A fire Inside: A critical meditation on the importance of freedom dreams. *JCT 22* (3), 7-25.

Bateman, Donald R. (1974). The politics of curriculum. In William F. Pinar (Ed.), *Heightened consciousness, cultural revolution, and curriculum theory: The proceedings of the Rochester conference* (pp. 54-68). Berkeley, CA: McCutchan.

Bell, Daniel (1989). The intelligentsia in American society. In *The winding passage: Essays and sociological journeys 1960-1980* (pp. 119-137). Cambridge, MA: Abt Books.

Bell, Quentin (1972). *Virginia Woof: A biography.* New York: Harcourt Brace Jovanovich, Inc.

Bellack, Arno and Huebner, Dwayne E. (1960, June). Teaching. *Review of Educational Research, XXX* (3), 246-257.

Benavot, Aaron and Truong, Nhung (2006). Introduction. In Aaron Benavot and Cecilia Braslavsky (Eds.) *School knowledge in comparative and historical perspective: Changing curricula in primary and secondary education* (pp. 1-11). New York: Springer.

Bender, Thomas (1993). *Intellect and public life: Essays on the social history of academic intellectuals in the United States.* Baltimore: Johns Hopkins University Press.

Berliner, David and Biddle, Bruce (1996). *The manufactured crisis: Myths, fraud and the assault on America's public schools.* Cambridge, MA: Perseus.

Bersani, Leo (1987). Is the rectum a grave? *October 43,* 197-222.

Bersani, Leo (1995). *Homos.* Cambridge, MA: Harvard University Press.

Bestor, Arthur (1953). *Educational wastelands: The retreat from learning in our public schools.* Urbana, IL: University of Illinois Press.

Beyer, Monika (1980), A life style is not a life: An interview with Susan Sontag. *Polish Perspectives, XXIII, IX,* 42-46.

Black, Earl and Black, Merle (1992). *The vital South: How presidents are elected.* Cambridge, MA: Harvard University Press.

Block, Alan (1997). *I'm only bleeding: Education as the practice of social violence against the child.* New York: Peter Lang.

Block, Alan (1998a). Curriculum as affichiste: Popular culture and identity. In William F. Pinar (Ed.), *Curriculum: Toward new identities* (pp. 325-341). New York: Garland.

Block, Alan A. (1998b). "And he pretended to be a stranger to them...." In William F. Pinar (Ed.) *The passionate mind of Maxine Greene* (pp. 14-39). London: Falmer.

Block, Alan A. (2002). "If I forget thee ... thou shall forget": The difficulty of difficult memories. In Marla Morris and John A. Weaver (Eds.), *Difficult memories* (pp. 25-44). New York: Peter Lang.

Block, Alan A. (2004). *Talmud, curriculum, and the practical: Joseph Schwab and the Rabbis.* New York: Peter Lang.

Block, Alan A. (2006). Personal communication.

Blomgren, Constance (2003). Terra incognita. In Erika Hasebe-Ludt and Warren Hurren (Eds.) *Curriculum intertext: Place/language/pedagogy* (pp. 33-37). New York: Peter Lang.

Bloom, Allan David (1987). *The closing of the American mind.* New York: Simon & Schuster.

Blumenfeld-Jones, Donald (1998). What are the arts for? Maxine Greene, the studio and performing arts, and education. In William F. Pinar (Ed.) *The passionate mind of Maxine Greene* (pp. 160-173). London: Falmer.

Bobbitt, Franklin (1918). *The curriculum.* New York: Houghton Mifflin.

REFERENCES

Bode, Boyd Henry (1940). *How we learn*. Boston: C. D. Heath & Co.

Boler, Megan (1999). *Feeling power*. New York: Routledge.

Bowers, C. A. (1995). *Educating for an ecologically sustainable culture*. Albany: State University of New York Press.

Bowers, C.A. (2000). *Let them eat data: How computers affect education, cultural diversity and the prospects of ecological sustainability*. Athens: University of Georgia.

Bowers, C. A. (2006). *The false promises of constructivist theories of learning: A global and ecological critique*. New York: Peter Lang.

Bowers, C. A. and Apffel-Marglin, Frédérique (Eds.) (2004). *Re-thinking Freire: Globalization and the environmental crisis*. Mahwah, NJ: Lawrence Erlbaum.

Brantlinger, Ellen A. (Ed.) (2005). *Who benefits from special education: Remediating (fixing) other people's children*. Mahwah, NJ: Lawrence Erlbaum.

Britzman, Deborah P. (1995). Is there a queer pedagogy? Or, stop reading straight. *Educational Theory 45* (2), 151-165.

Britzman, Deborah P. (1998). *Lost subjects, contested objects: Toward a psychoanalytic inquiry of learning*. Albany, NY: State University of New York Press.

Britzman, Deborah (2000). Precocious education. In Susan Talburt and Shirley Steinberg (Eds.) *Thinking queer* (pp. 33-59). New York: Peter Lang.

Britzman, Deborah P. (2003). *Practice makes practice*.[Revised edition.] Albany: State University of New York Press.

Britzman, Deborah (2006). *Novel education: Psychoanalytic studies of learning and not learning*. New York: Peter Lang.

Brubaker, D. and Brookbank, G. (1986). James B. Macdonald: A bibliography. *Journal of Curriculum and Supervision, 1*(3), 215-220.

Burke, Melva (1985). The personal and professional journey of James B. Macdonald. *JCT, 6*(3), 84-119.

Butche, Robert W. (2000). *Image of excellence: The Ohio State University School*. New York: Peter Lang.

Butler, Judith (1993). *Bodies that matter: On the discursive limits of "sex."* New York and London: Routledge.

Cain, William (1989, autumn). An interview with Irving Howe. *American Literary History* 1(3), 554-564.

Camus, Albert. (1971 [1956]). *The rebel: An essay on man in revolt*. New York: Knopf.

Cannella, G. S., & Viruru, R. (2004). *Childhood and postcolonization: Power, education, and contemporary practice*. New York: RoutledgeFalmer.

Caputo, John (1987). *Radical hermeneutics: Repetition, deconstruction and the hermeneutic project*. Bloomington, IN: Indiana University Press.

Carlson, Dennis (1998). Who am I? Gay identity and a democratic politics of self. In William F. Pinar (Ed.) *Queer Theory in Education* (pp. 107-119). Mahwah, NJ: Lawrence Erlbaum.

Carpenter, William B. (1886). *Principles of mental physiology*. London: Kegan Paul.

Carson, Terry (Ed.). (1988). *Toward a renaissance of humanity: Rethinking curriculum and instruction*. Edmonton, Alberta, Canada: World Council for Curriculum & Instruction.

Casemore, Brian (in press). *The autobiographical demand of place: Curriculum inquiry in the American South*. New York: Peter Lang.

Castenell, Jr., Louis A. and Pinar, William F. (Eds.) (1993). *Understanding curriculum as racial text: Representations of identity and difference in education*. Albany: State University of New York Press.

Chalmers, F. Graeme (2004). Painting me into a corner? In Rita L. Irwin and Alex de Cosson (Eds.) *A/R/Tography: Rendering self through arts-based living inquiry* (173-183). Vancouver, Canada: Pacific Educational Press.

Chambers, Cynthia (2003a). "As Canadian as possible under the circumstances": A view of contemporary curriculum discourses in Canada. In William F. Pinar (Ed.), *International handbook of curriculum research* (pp. 221-252). Mahwah, NJ: Lawrence Erlbaum.

Chambers, Cynthia (2003b). On being a disciple of memoir. In Erika Hasebe-Ludt and Warren Hurren (Eds.) *Curriculum intertext: Place/language/pedagogy* (pp. 103-109). New York: Peter Lang.

Chandler, James (n.d.) Critical disciplinarity. Retrieved from: http://criticalinquiry.uchicago.edu/issues/v30/30n2.Chandler.html on December 19, 2006.

Chodorow, Nancy J. (1978). *The reproduction of mothering*. Berkeley: University of California Press.

Christian, Barbara (1997). Fixing methodologies. In Elizabeth Abel, Barbara Christian, and Helene Moglen (Eds.), *Female subjects in black and white* (pp. 363-370). Berkeley: University of California Press.

Clandinin, D. Jean and Connelly, F. Michael (2004). *Narrative inquiry: Experience and story in qualitative research*. San Francisco, CA: Jossey-Bass.

Connelly, F. Michael, He, Ming Fang and Phillion, JoAnn (Eds.) (in press). *Sage handbook of curriculum search*. Thousand Oaks, CA: Sage.

Cott, Jonathan (1979, October 4). Susan Sontag: The Rolling Stone Interview. *Rolling Stone*, 46-53.

Crary, Jonathan (1990). *Techniques of the observer: On vision and modernity in the nineteenth century*. Cambridge, MA: MIT Press.

Cremin, Lawrence A. (1961). *The transformation of the school: Progressivism in American education, 1876-1957*. New York: Alfred A. Knopf.

Crocco, Margaret Smith, Munro, Petra and Weiler, Kathleen (1999). *Pedagogies of resistance: Women educator activists, 1880-1960*. [Foreword by Nel Noddings.] New York: Teachers College Press.

Cuban, Larry (2001). *Oversold and underused: Computers in the classroom*. Cambridge, MA: Harvard University Press.

Daignault, Jacques (1992). Traces at work from different places. In William F. Pinar and William M. Reynolds (Eds.), *Understanding curriculum as phenomenological and deconstructed text* (pp. 195-215). New York: Teachers College Press.

Daignault, Jacques and Gauthier, Clermont (1982). The indecent curriculum machine. *JCT, 4*(1), 177-196.

Davies, Jon (1998). *The Dialectic of Freedom*. In William F. Pinar (Ed.) *The passionate mind of Maxine Greene* (pp. 39-45). London: Falmer.

Davis, Brent (2004). *Inventions of teaching: A genealogy*. Mahwah, NJ: Lawrence Erlbaum.

Davis, Brent (2005). Interrupting frameworks: Interpreting geometries of epistemology and curriculum. In William E. Doll, Jr., M. Jayne Fleener, Donna Trueit, and John St. Julien (Eds.) *Chaos, complexity, curriculum, and culture* (pp. 119-132). New York: Peter Lang.

Davis, Brent and Sumara, Dennis J. (1998). Thinking about thinking: Maxine Greene on cognition. In William F. Pinar (Ed.) *The passionate mind of Maxine Greene* (pp. 247-253). London: Falmer.

Davis, Brent and Sumara, Dennis (2000). Another queer theory: Reading complexity theory as a moral and ethical imperative. In Susan Talburt and Shirley Steinberg (Eds.) *Thinking queer* (pp. 105-129). New York: Peter Lang.

Davis, Brent, Sumara, Dennis, and Luce-Kapler, Rebecca (2000). *Engaging minds*. Mahwah, NJ: Lawrence Erlbaum.

de Cosson, Alex (2004). The hermeneutic dialogue: Finding patterns midst the aporia of the artist/researcher/teacher (Rewrite #10 in this context). In Rita L. Irwin and Alex de Cosson (Eds.) *A/R/Tography: Rendering self through arts-based living inquiry* (pp. 127-152). Vancouver, Canada: Pacific Educational Press.

Deleuze, G. (1995). *Negotiations 1972-1990*. [Trans. M. Joughin]. New York: Columbia University Press.

Deleuze, Gilles and Guattari, Félix (1987). *A thousand plateaus: Capitalism and schizophrenia*. [Trans. and foreword by Brian Massumi.] Minneapolis: University of Minnesota Press.

Deleuze, Gilles and Guattari, Félix (1989). *Anti-Oedipus: Capitalism and schizophrenia*. [Trans. R. Hurley and H. R. Lane]. Minneapolis: University of Minnesota Press.

REFERENCES

Delgado, Richard and Stefancic, Jean (2001). *Critical race theory: An introduction*. New York: New York University Press.

Dewey, John (1910). *How we think*. Boston: D. C. Health & Co.

Dewey, John (1916). *Democracy and education*. New York: Macmillan Company. [Reprinted 1966, the Free Press].

Dimitriadis, Greg and McCarthy, Cameron (2001). *Reading & teaching the postcolonial: From Baldwin to Basquiat and beyond*. New York: Teachers College Press.

Doerr, Marilyn (2004). *Currere and the environmental autobiography: A phenomenological to the teaching of ecology*. New York: Peter Lang.

Doll, Mary Aswell (1982, Winter). Beyond the window: Dreams and learning. *JCT 4*(1), 197-201.

Doll, Mary Aswell (1988a). *Beckett and myth: An archetypal approach*. Syracuse, NY: Syracuse University Press.

Doll, Mary Aswell (1988b, Spring). The monster in children's dreams. *JCT 8*(4), 89-99.

Doll, Mary Aswell (1990, October). *Educating the imagination: A curriculum proposal*. Paper presented to the Bergamo Conference, Dayton, Ohio.

Doll, Mary Aswell (1995). *To the lighthouse and back*. New York: Peter Lang.

Doll, Mary Aswell (1998). Queering the gaze. In William F. Pinar (Ed.), *Queer theory in education* (pp. 287-298). Mawah, NJ: Lawrence Erlbaum.

Doll, Mary Aswell (2000). *Like letters in running water: A mythopoetics of curriculum*. Mahwah, NJ: Lawrence Erlbaum.

Doll, Mary Aswell (2002). Portraits of anti-semites. In Marla Morris and John A. Weaver (Eds.), *Difficult memories* (pp. 191-208). New York: Peter Lang.

Doll, Mary Aswell, Wear, Delese, and Whitaker, Martha L. (2006). *Triples takes on curricular worlds*. Albany: State University of New York Press.

Doll, Jr., William (1993). *A post-modern perspective on curriculum*. New York: Teachers College Press.

Doll, Jr., William E. (1998). Curriculum and concepts of control. [Assisted by Al Alcazar.] In William F. Pinar (Ed.). *Curriculum: Toward new identities* (pp. 295-323). New York: Garland.

Doll, Jr., William E. (2002). Ghosts and the curriculum. In William E. Doll, Jr. and Noel Gough (Eds.), *Curriculum visions* (pp. 23-70). New York: Peter Lang.

Doll, Jr., William E. (2005). The culture of method. In William E. Doll, Jr., M. Jayne Fleener, Donna Trueit, and John St. Julien (Eds.) *Chaos, complexity, curriculum, and culture* (pp. 21-75) New York: Peter Lang.

Doll, Jr., William E., Fleener, M. Jayne, Trueit, Donna, and St. Julien, John (Eds.) (2005). *Chaos, complexity, curriculum, and culture*. New York: Peter Lang.

Dollard, John, et al. (1939). *Frustration and aggression*. New Haven, CT: Yale University Press.

Dunlop, Rishma (1999). *Boundary bay: A novel*. Vancouver, British Columbia: University of British Columbia, unpublished Ph.D. dissertation. [Published in 2000 by Staccato Chapbooks.]

Edgerton, Susan H. (1991). Particularities of "otherness:" Autobiography, Maya Angelou, and me. In Joe L. Kincheloe and William F. Pinar (Eds.), *Curriculum as social psychoanalysis: The Significance of place* (pp. 77-97). Albany, NY: State University of New York Press.

Edgerton, Susan H. (1996). *Translating the curriculum: Multiculturalism into cultural studies*. New York: Routledge.

Egan, Kieran (1990). *Romantic understanding: The development of rationality and imagination, ages 8-15*. New York: Routledge.

Egan, Kieran (1992). *Imagination in teaching and learning*. Chicago: University of Chicago Press.

Eisner, Elliot W. (1971a, May). How can you measure a rainbow? *Art Education, 24*, 36-39.

Eisner, Elliot W. (Ed.). (1971b). *Confronting curriculum reform*. Boston, MA: Little, Brown & Co.

Eisner, Elliot W. (1972). *Educating artistic vision*. New York: Macmillan.

Eisner, Elliot W. (1979). *The educational imagination: On the design and evaluation of school programs*. New York: Macmillan.

Ellsworth, Elizabeth (1997). *Teaching positions: Difference, pedagogy, and the power of address*. New York: Teachers College Press.

English, Fenwick (1999). *Deciding what to teach and test: Developing, aligning and auditing the curriculum*. Thousand Oaks, CA: Corwin Press, Inc.

Eppert, Claudia (1999). Learning responsivity/responsibility: Reading the literature of historical witness. Toronto: University of Toronto, Ontario Institute for Studies in Education, Ph.D. dissertation.

Eribon, Didier (2004). *Insult and the making of the gay self*. [Trans. Michael Lucey.] Durham, NC: Duke University Press.

Fanon, Frantz (1968). *The wretched of the earth*. [Preface by Jean-Paul Sartre. Trans. by Constance Farrington.] New York: Grove Press. [Originally published by François Maspero éditeur, Paris, France, under the title *Les damnés de la terre*, 1961.]

Ferneding, Karen (2004). *Questioning technology*. New York: Peter Lang.

Felman, Shoshana (1993). *What does a woman want? Reading and sexual difference*. Baltimore: Johns Hopkins University Press.

Fleener, M. Jayne (2002). *Curriculum dynamics: Recreating heart*. New York: Peter Lang.

Fowler, Leah (2006). *A curriculum of difficulty: Narrative research in education and the practice of teaching*. New York: Peter Lang.

Fox, Seymour, Scheffler, and Marom, Daniel (Eds.) (2003). *Visions of Jewish education*. Cambridge: Cambridge University Press.

Franklin, Barry (Ed.) (2000). *Herbert Kliebard and the promise of schooling*. New York: Teachers College Press.

Freire, Paolo (1968). *Pedagogy of the oppressed*. New York: Seabury.

Gallagher, Catherine and Greenblatt, Stephen (2000). *Practicing new historicism*. Chicago: University of Chicago Press.

Garrison, Jim (1997). *Dewey and eros: Wisdom and desire in the art of teaching*. New York: Teachers College of Press.

Gastambide-Fernandez, Rubén A. and Sears, James T. (Eds.) (2004). *Curriculum work as a public moral enterprise* (pp. 119-126). Lanham, MD: Rowman & Littlefield.

Gauthier, Clermont (1992). Between crystal and smoke: Or, how to miss the point in the debate about action research. In William F. Pinar and William M. Reynolds (Eds.), *Understanding curriculum as phenomenological and deconstructed text* (pp. 184-194). New York: Teachers College Press.

Gay, Geneva (2000). *Culturally responsive teaching: Theory, research, and practice*. New York: Teachers College Press.

Giarelli, James M. (1998). Maxine Greene: The literary imagination and the sources of a public education. In William F. Pinar (Ed.) *The passionate mind of Maxine Greene* (pp. 174-178). London: Falmer.

Gibson, Nigel C. (2003). *Fanon: The postcolonial imagination*. Cambridge: Polity.

Gilmore, Leigh (1994). *Autobiographics: A feminist theory of women's self-representation*. Ithaca, NY: Cornell University Press.

Giroux, Henry A., Penna, Anthony, and Pinar, William F. (Eds.). (1981). *Curriculum and instruction: Alternatives in education*. Berkeley, CA: McCutchan.

Gitlin, Todd (1990). Sociology for whom? Criticism for whom? In Herbert J. Gans (Ed.), *Sociology in America* (pp. 214-226). Newbury Park, CA: Sage Publications.

Good, Ron (2005). *Scientific and religious habits of mind: Irreconcilable tensions in the curriculum*. New York: Peter Lang.

Goodman, Jesse and Teel, Julie (1998). The passion of the possible: Maxine Greene, democratic community, and education. In William F. Pinar (Ed.), *The passionate mind of Maxine Greene* (pp. 60-75). London: Falmer.

Goodson, Ivor (1988). *International perspectives in curriculum history*. Boston, MA: Routledge & Kegan Paul.

193

REFERENCES

Goodson, Ivor F. (1989). Curriculum reform and curriculum theory: A case of historical amnesia. *Cambridge Journal of Education 19*(2), 131-141.

Goodson, Ivor (1995). *The making of curriculum*. [Second edition.] New York: Routledge.

Goodson, Ivor F. (2005). *Curriculum, pedagogy and life works: The selected works of Ivor Goodson*. London: Routledge.

Gough, Noel (1999). Understanding curriculum systems. In James G. Henderson and Kathleen R. Kesson (Eds.) *Understanding democratic curriculum leadership* (pp. 47-69). New York: Teachers College Press.

Gough, Noel (2003). Thinking globally in environmental education: Implications for internationalizing curriculum inquiry. In William F. Pinar (Ed.), *International handbook of curriculum research* (pp. 53-72). Mahwah, NJ: Lawrence Erlbaum.

Gouldner, Alvin (1979). *The future of intellectuals and the rise of the new class*. New York: Seabury Press.

Grant, Agnes (1995). The challenge for universities. In Marie Battiste and Jean Barman (Eds.), *First Nations education in Canada: The circle unfolds* (pp. 208-223). Vancouver: University of British Columbia Press.

Greene, Maxine (1973). *Teacher as stranger*. Belmont, CA: Wadsworth.

Greene, Maxine (1978). *Landscapes of learning*. New York: Teachers College Press.

Greene, Maxine (1981). Response to a predecessor. *Educational Researcher 10*(3), 5-6.

Greene, Maxine (1988a). The artistic-aesthetic and curriculum. *Curriculum Inquiry 6*(4), 283-296.

Greene, Maxine (1988b). *The dialectic of freedom*. New York: Teachers College Press.

Greene, Maxine (1995). *Releasing the imagination*. San Francisco: Jossey-Bass.

Greene, Maxine (1995). What counts as philosophy of education? In Wendy Kohli (Ed.), *Critical conversations in philosophy of education* (pp. 3-23). New York: Routledge.

Greene, Maxine (2001). *Variations on a blue guitar: The Lincoln Center Institute lectures on aesthetic education*. New York: Teachers College Press.

Greene, Naomi (1990). *Pier Paolo Pasolini: Cinema as heresy*. Princeton: Princeton University Press.

Grumet, Madeleine R. (1985). The work of James B. Macdonald: Theory fierce with reality. *JCT, 6*(3), 19-27.

Grumet, Madeleine R. (1988). *Bitter milk: Women and teaching*. Amherst: University of Massachusetts Press.

Grumet, Madeleine R. (1990). Voice: The search for a feminist rhetoric for educational studies. *Cambridge Journal of Education, 20*(3), 277-282.

Hampton, Eber (1995). Towards a redefinition of Indian education. In Marie Battiste and Jean Barman (Eds.), *First Nations education in Canada: The circle unfolds* (pp. 5-46). Vancouver: University of British Columbia Press.

Hardt, Michael and Negri, Antonio (2000). *Empire*. Cambridge, MA: Harvard University Press.

Hasebe-Ludt, Erika and Hurren, Wanda (Eds.) (2002). *Curriculum intertext: Place, language, pedagogy*. New York: Peter Lang.

Henderson, James G. (1999). The journey of democratic curriculum leadership: An overview. In James G. Henderson and Kathleen R. Kesson (Eds.) *Understanding democratic curriculum leadership* (pp. 1-22). New York: Teachers College Press.

Henderson, James G. and Kesson, Kathleen R. (Eds.) (1999). *Understanding democratic curriculum leadership*. New York: Teachers College Press.

Henderson, James G. and Kesson, Kathleen (2003). *Curriculum wisdom: Educational decisions in democratic societies*. Prentice-Hall.

Henderson, James G., Hutchison, Janice, and Newman, Charlene (1998). Maxine Greene and the current/future democratization of curriculum studies. In William F. Pinar (Ed.) *The passionate mind of Maxine Greene* (pp. 190-212). London: Falmer.

Henderson, James G., Kesson, Kathleen R., and McCadden Kerrin A. McCadden (1999). Three personal reflections. In James G. Henderson and Kathleen R. Kesson (Eds.) *Understanding democratic curriculum leadership* (pp. 106-126). New York: Teachers College Press.

194

Graham, Robert J. (1998). Of friends and journeys: Maxine Greene and English education. In William F. Pinar (Ed.) *The passionate mind of Maxine Greene* (pp. 213-221). London: Falmer.

Heidegger, Martin (1962). *Being and time.* [Trans. J. Macquarrie & E. Robinson.] New York: Harper & Row.

Hirsch, E. D. (1987). *Cultural literacy: What every American needs to know.* Boston, MA: Houghton Mifflin.

Hirsch, Jr., E. D. (1999). *The schools we need: And why we don't have them.* New York: Anchor Books.

Hlebowitsh, Peter S. (2005a). Generational ideas in curriculum: A historical triangulation. *Curriculum Inquiry 35*(1), 73-87.

Hlebowitsh, Peter S. (2005b). More on "generational ideas" (a rejoinder to Ian Westbury and Handel Kashope Wright). *Curriculum Inquiry 35*(1), 119-122.

Holland, Patricia and Garman, Noreen (1992). Macdonald and the mythopoetic. *JCT, 9*(4), 45-72.

Hofstadter, Richard (1965). *The paranoid style in American politics and other essays.* New York: Alfred A. Knopf.

Hope, Trevor (1994). Melancholic modernity: The hom(m)osexual symptom and the homosocial corpse. *Differences 6*(2+3), 174-198.

Howe, Irving (1971). *Decline of the new.* London: V. Gollancz.

Huebner, Dwayne E. (1966). Curriculum as a field of study. In H. Robison (Ed.), *Precedents and promise in the curriculum field* (pp. 94-112). New York: Teachers College Press.

Huebner, Dwayne E. (1970). Status and identity: A reply. In C. Bowers, I. Housego and D. Dyke (Eds.), *Education and social policy* (pp. 169-179). New York: Random House.

Huebner, Dwayne E. (1975). Autobiographical statement. In William F. Pinar (Ed.), *Curriculum theorizing: The reconceptualists* (pp. 213-215). Berkeley, CA: McCutchan. [Reissued in 2000 as *Curriculum theorizing: The reconceptualization* by Educator's International Press.]

Huebner, Dwayne E. (1999). *The lure of the transcendent.* Mahwah, NJ: Lawrence Erlbaum.

Hurren, Wanda (2003). Auto'geo'carto'graphia' (a curricular collage).In Erika Hasebe-Ludt and Warren Hurren (Eds.) *Curriculum intertext: Place/language/pedagogy* (pp. 111-121). New York: Peter Lang.

Irwin, Rita L. (1995). *A circle of empowerment: Women, education, and leadership.* Albany: State University of New York Press.

Irwin, Rita L. (2003). Towards an aesthetic of unfolding in/sights through curriculum. *Journal of the Canadian Association for Curriculum Studies, 1*(2), 63-78 Available at: http://www.csse.ca/CACS/JCACS/V1N2/essays.html 16 pgs

Irwin, Rita L. and Alex de Cosson, Alex (Eds.). (2004). *A/r/tography: Rendering self through arts-based living inquiry.* Vancouver, B.C.: Pacific Educational Press.

Jackson, Philip (1992). Conceptions of curriculum and curriculum specialists. In Philip Jackson (Ed.), *Handbook of research on curriculum* (pp. 3-40). New York: Macmillan.

Jackson, Philip W. (2002). *John Dewey and the lessons of art.* New Haven, CT: Yale University Press.

Jacobs, Mary-Ellen (1998). Confinement, connection and women who dare: Maxine Greene's shifting landscapes of teaching. In William F. Pinar (Ed.), *The passionate mind of Maxine Greene* (pp. 81-88). London: Falmer.

Jacoby, Russell (1987). *The last intellectuals.* New York: Basic Books.

jagodzinski, jan (1997a). *Pun(k) deconstruction: Experifigural writings in art & art education.* Mahwah, NJ: Lawrence Erlbaum.

jagodzinski, jan (1997b). *Postmodern dilemmas: Outrageous essays in art & art education.* Mahwah, NJ: Lawrence Erlbaum.

jagodzinski, jan (Ed.) (2002). *Pedagogical desire: Authority, seduction, transference, and the question of ethics.* Westport, CT: Bergin & Garvey.

Jardine, David (1992). Reflections on education, hermeneutics, and ambiguity: Hermeneutics as a restoring of life to its original difficulty. In William F. Pinar and William M. Reynolds (Eds.), *Understanding curriculum as phenomenological and deconstructed text* (pp. 116-127). New York: Teachers College Press.

REFERENCES

Jardine, David W. (1997). Their bodies swelling with messy secrets. In Terry Carson and Dennis Sumara (Eds.) *Action research as a living practice* (pp. 161-166). New York: Peter Lang Publishing.

Jardine, David W., Friesen, Sharon, and Clifford, Patricia (2003a). *Back to the basics of teaching and learning: "Thinking the world together."* Mahwah, NJ: Lawrence Erlbaum.

Jardine, David W., Friesen, Sharon, and Clifford, Patricia (2003b). "Behind every jewel are three thousand sweating horses": Meditations on the ontology of mathematics and mathematics education. In Erika Hasebe-Ludt and Warren Hurren (Eds.) *Curriculum Intertext: Place/Language/Pedagogy* (39-49). New York: Peter Lang.

Jardine, David W., Friesen, Sharon, and Clifford, Patricia (2006). *Curriculum in abundance.* Mahwah, NJ: Lawrence Erlbaum.

Jay, Martin (1993). *Downcast eyes: The denigration of vision in twentieth-century French thought.* Berkeley: University of California Press.

Jay, Martin (2005). *Songs of experience: Modern American and European variations on a universal theme.* Berkeley: University of California Press.

Jeffers, Carol S. (1998). From both sides of the looking glass: Visions of imagination, the arts, and possibility. In William F. Pinar (Ed.), *The passionate mind of Maxine Greene* (76-80). London: Falmer.

Jewett, Laura M. (2006). *A delicate dance: autoethnography, curriculum, and the semblance of intimacy.* Baton Rouge: Louisiana State University, unpublished Ph.D. dissertation.

Kafala, Ted and Carey, Lisa (2006). Postmodern movements in curriculum theory: The logic and paradox of dissensus. *JCT 22*(1), 25-43.

Kennedy, Liam (1995). *Susan Sontag: Mind as passion.* Manchester and New York: Manchester University Press.

Kesson, Kathleen R. (1999). Toward a curriculum of mythopoetic meaning. In James G. Henderson and Kathleen R. Kesson (Eds.) *Understanding democratic curriculum leadership* (pp. 84-105). New York: Teachers College Press.

Kincheloe, Joe L. (1999). Critical democracy and education. In James G. Henderson and Kathleen R. Kesson (Eds.) *Understanding democratic curriculum leadership* (pp. 70-83). New York: Teachers College Press.

Kincheloe, Joe L. and Pinar, William F. (Eds.) (1991). *Curriculum as social psychoanalysis: The significance of place.* Albany: State University of New York Press.

Kliebard, Herbert (1986). *The struggle for the American curriculum 1893-1958.* Boston, MA: Routledge & Kegan Paul.

Kliebard, Herbert (2000 [1975]). Metaphorical roots of curriculum design. In William F. Pinar (Ed.) *Curriculum studies: The reconceptualization* (pp. 84-85). Troy, NY: Educator's International Press. [Originally published in Pinar (Ed.), *Curriculum theorizing: The reconceptualists* (84-85). Berkeley, CA: McCutchan.]

Kliebard, Herbert (1999). *Schooled to work: Vocationalism and the American curriculum, 1876-1946.* New York: Teachers College Press.

Kliebard, Herbert (2002). *Changing course: American curriculum reform in the 20th century.* New York: Teachers College Press.

Klohr, Paul R. (1967). This issue. *Theory into Practice, 6*(4), 165.

Kohli, Wendy (1995). Contextualizing the conversation. In Wendy Kohli (Ed.), *Critical conversations in philosophy of education* (pp. xiii-xvi). New York: Routledge.

Kohli, Wendy (1998). A situated philosopher. In William F. Pinar (Ed.) *The passionate mind of Maxine Greene* (180-189). London: Falmer.

Krall, Florence R. (1994). *Ecotone: Wayfaring on the margins.* Albany, NY: State University of New York Press.

Kridel, Craig (Ed.) (1998). *Writing educational biography.* New York: Garland.

Kridel, Craig (1999). The Bergamo conferences, 1973-1997: Reconceptualization and curriculum theory conferences. In William F. Pinar (Ed.), *Contemporary curriculum discourses: Twenty Years of JCT* (pp. 509-558). New York: Peter Lang.

Kridel, Craig (Ed.) (1999-2000). *Books of the century catalog.* Columbia, SC: University of South Carolina Museum of Education.

Kridel, Craig (2002). And gladly would she learn: Margaret Willis and The Ohio State University School. In Alan R. Sadovnik and Susan F. Semel (Eds.) *Founding mothers and others: Women educational leaders during the progressive era* (pp. 217-235). New York: Palgrave Macmillan.

Kridel, Craig (2006). Theodore Brameld: Reconstruction for our emerging age. In Karen L. Riley (Ed.) *Social reconstruction: People, politics, perspectives* (pp. 69-87). Greenwich, CT: Information Age Publishing.

Kridel, Craig and Newman, Vicky (2003). A random harvest: A multiplicity of studies in American curriculum history research. In William F. Pinar (Ed.), *International handbook of curriculum research.* Mahwah, NJ: Lawrence Erlbaum.

Kridel, Craig and Bullough, Jr., Robert V. (2007). *Stories of the Eight-Year Study: Reexamining secondary education in America.* Albany: State University of New York Press.

Kumashiro, Kevin (2001). *Troubling intersections of race and sexuality: Queer students of color and anti-oppressive education.* Lanham, MD: Rowman & Littlefield.

Kumashiro, Kevin (2004). *Against common sense: Teaching and learning toward social justice.* New York: RoutledgeFalmer.

Kumashiro, Kevin (2007). *Six lenses for anti-oppressive education: Partial stories, improbable conversations.* New York: Peter Lang.

Ladson-Billings, Gloria (2001). *Crossing over to Canaan: The journey of new teachers in diverse classrooms.* San Francisco: Jossey-Bass

Ladson-Billings, Gloria and Tate IV, William F. (1995). Toward a critical race theory of education. *Teachers College Record 97*(1), 47-68.

Langeveld, Martin (1983a). The stillness of the secret place. *Phenomenology + Pedagogy, 1*(1), 11-17.

Langeveld, Martin (1983b). The secret place in the life of the child. *Phenomenology + Pedagogy, 1*(2), 181-191.

Langness, L. L. and Frank, Gelya (1981). *Lives: An anthropological approach to biography.* Novato, CA: Chandler & Sharp Publishers.

Lasch, Christopher (1978). *The culture of narcissism: American life in an age of diminishing expectations.* New York: Norton.

Lasch, Christopher (1984). *The minimal self: Psychic survival in troubled times.* New York: Norton.

Lasch, Christopher (1995). *The revolt of the elites and the betrayal of democracy.* New York: Norton.

Lather, Patti (1991). Deconstructing/deconstructive inquiry: The politics of knowing and being known. *Educational Theory, 41*(2), 153-173.

Lazarus, Neil (1999). Disavowing decolonization: Fanon, nationalism, and the question of representation in postcolonial theory. In Anthony C. Alessandrini (Ed.), *Frantz Fanon: Critical perspectives* (pp. 161-194). London: Routledge.

Leck, Glorianne M. (2000). School uniforms, baggy pants, Barbie dolls, and business suit cultures on school boards: A feminqueering. In Susan Talburt and Shirley Steinberg (Eds.) *Thinking queer* (pp. 177-199). New York: Peter Lang.

Leonard, Timothy and Willis, Peter (in press). *Pedagogies of the imagination: Mythopoetic curriculum in education practice.* New York: Springer.

Lesko, Nancy (1998). Feeling the teacher: A phenomenological reflection on Maxine Greene's pedagogy. In William F. Pinar (Ed.) *The passionate mind of Maxine Greene* (pp. 238-246). London: Falmer.

Leitch, Vincent B. (1992). *Cultural criticism, literary theory, poststructuralism.* New York: Columbia University Press.

Lesko, Nancy (2000). Terms of identity: Ellen's intertextual coming out. In Susan Talburt and Shirley Steinberg (Eds.) *Thinking queer* (pp. 161-173). New York: Peter Lang.

Letts, Will and Sears, James (Eds.) (1999). *Queering elementary education.* Landham, MD: Rowman & Littlefield.

REFERENCES

Linne, Rob (2000). Choosing alternatives to the well of loneliness. In Susan Talburt and Shirley Steinberg (Eds.) *Thinking queer* (pp. 201-213). New York: Peter Lang.

Lipset, Seymour M. and Raab, Earl (1970). *The politics of unreason: Right-wing extremism in America, 1790-1970*. New York: Harper & Row.

Low, Marylin (2003). Radical contingencies in the words of a student: (Dis)placing, (re)marking, languaging. In Erika Hasebe-Ludt and Warren Hurren (Eds.) *Curriculum intertext: Place/language/pedagogy* (pp. 57-69). New York: Peter Lang.

Luce-Kapler, Rebecca (1998). The slow fuse of aesthetic practice. In William F. Pinar (Ed.), *The passionate mind of Maxine Greene* (pp. 148-159). London: Falmer.

Lukacher, Ned (1986). *Primal scenes: Literature, philosophy, psychoanalysis*. Ithaca, NY: Cornell University Press.

Lymburger, Julie (2004). Interwoven threads: Theory, practice, and research coming together. In Rita L. Irwin and Alex de Cosson (Eds.) *A/R/Tography: Rendering self through arts-based living inquiry* (pp. 75-88). Vancouver, Canada: Pacific Educational Press.

MacArthur, Jeannette Scott (2003). In the space between the threads: Reweaving the yarns of ethical research. In Erika Hasebe-Ludt and Warren Hurren (Eds.) *Curriculum intertext: Place/language/pedagogy* (pp. 51-55). New York: Peter Lang.

Macdonald, James B. (1964). An image of man: The learner himself. In R. Doll (Ed.), *Individualizing instruction* (29-49). Washington, DC: ASCD.

Macdonald, James B. (1967). An example of disciplined curriculum thinking. *Theory into Practice, 6*(4), 166-171.

Macdonald, James B. (1975a). Autobiographical statement. In William F. Pinar (Ed.), *Curriculum theorizing: The reconceptualists* (pp. 3-4). Berkeley, CA: McCutchan. [Reissued in 2000 by Educator's International Press as *Curriculum Theorizing: The Reconceptualization.*]

Macdonald, James B. (1975b). Curriculum theory. In William F. Pinar (Ed.), Curriculum theorizing: The reconceptualists (pp. 5-13). Berkley, CA: McCutchan. Reissued in 2000 by Educator's International Press as *Curriculum theorizing: The reconceptualization.*]

Macdonald, James B. (1975c). Curriculum and human interests. In William F. Pinar (Ed.), Curriculum theorizing: The reconceptualists (283-294). Berkley, CA: McCutchan. Reissued in 2000 by Educator's International Press as *Curriculum theorizing: The reconceptualization.*]

Macdonald, James B. (1986). The domain of curriculum. [Foreword by D. Huenchke.] *Journal of Curriculum & Supervision 1*(3), 205-214.

Macdonald, James B. (1988). Curriculum, consciousness, and social change. In William F. Pinar (Ed.), *Contemporary curriculum discourse* (pp. 156-174). Scottsdale, AZ: Gorsuch Scarisbrick.

Macdonald, James B. (1995). *Theory as a prayerful act: The collected essays of James B. Macdonald.* [Edited by Bradley J. Macdonald.] New York: Peter Lang.

Macdonald, James B. (1974). A transcendental developmental ideology of education. In William F. Pinar (Ed.), *Heightened consciousness, cultural revolution, and curriculum theory: The proceedings of the rochester conference* (pp. 85-116). Berkeley, CA: McCutchan.

Macdonald, James B., Anderson, D. and May, F (Eds.). (1965). *Strategies for curriculum development: The works of Virgil Herrick.* Columbus, OH: Charles E. Merrill.

Macdonald, James B. and Leeper, R. (Eds.) (1966). *Language and meaning.* Washington, DC: ASCD.

Macdonald, James B. and Leeper, R. (Eds.) (1968). *Theories of instruction.* Columbus, OH: Charles Merrill.

Macdonald, James B. and Macdonald, Susan Colberg (1988). Gender, values, and curriculum. In William F. Pinar (Ed.), *Contemporary curriculum discourse* (pp. 476-485). Scottsdale, AZ: Gorsuch Scarisbrick [First published in JCT, 1981].

Macdonald, James B. and Purpel, David (1987). Curriculum and planning: Visions and metaphors. *Journal of Curriculum & Supervision, 2*(2), 178-192.

Macdonald, James B. and Zaret, Esther (Eds.) (1975). *Schools in search of meaning.* [1975 yearbook]. Washington, DC: ASCD.

Macedo, Elizabeth (2007, January 24). Personal communication.

198

Malewski, Erik L. (in press). Curriculum studies: The next moment. New York: RoutledgeFalmer.

Marcuse, Herbert (1964). *One-dimensional man: Studies in the ideology of advanced industrial societies.* Boston, MA: Beacon Press.

Marshall, J. Dan, Sears, James T., Allen, Louise Anderson, Roberts, Patrick, Schubert, William H. (2006 [1999]). *Turning points in curriculum: A contemporary American memoir.* Englewood Cliffs, NJ: Prentice-Hall.

Matus, Claudia and McCarthy, Cameron (2003). The triumph of multiplicity and the carnival of difference: Curriculum dilemmas in the age of postcolonialism and globalization. In William F. Pinar (Ed.), *International handbook of curriculum research* (pp. 73-82). Mahwah, NJ: Lawrence Erlbaum.

McCarthy, Cameron, Crichlow, Warren, Dimitriadis, Greg, and Dolby, Nadine (Eds.) (2005) *Race, identity, and representation in education.* [Second edition] New York: Routledge.

McClintock, Robert (1971). Toward a place for study in a world of instruction. *Teachers College Record* 73(2), 161-205.

McCutcheon, Gail (1999). Deliberation to develop school curricula. In James G. Henderson and Kathleen R. Kesson (Eds.) *Understanding democratic curriculum leadership* (pp. 33-46). New York: Teachers College Press.

McNeil, Linda M. (2000). *Contradictions of school reform: Educational costs of standardized testing.* New York: Routledge.

Menzies, Heather and Newson, Janice (2006). No time to think? *The Journal of Higher Education*, 13-15.

Meyer, Karen (2003). (In)different spaces: Re-imagining pedagogy in the academy. In Erika Hasebe-Ludt and Warren Hurren (Eds.) *Curriculum intertext: Place/language/pedagogy* (pp. 11-22). New York: Peter Lang.

Miller, Janet L. (1977). *Curriculum theory of Maxine Greene: A reconceptualization of foundations in English education.* Columbus, OH: Ohio State University, College of Education, unpublished Ph.D. dissertation.

Miller, Janet L. (1990). *Creating spaces and finding voices: Teachers collaborating for empowerment.* Albany: State University of New York Press.

Miller, Janet L. (1998). Autobiography as a queer curriculum practice. In William F. Pinar (Ed.), *Queer theory in education* (pp. 349-364). Mahwah, NJ: Lawrence Erlbaum Associates, Publishers.

Miller, Janet L. (2005). *The sound of silence breaking and other essays: Working the tension in curriculum theory.* New York: Peter Lang.

Mirochnik, Elijah and Sherman, Debora C. (Eds) (2002). *Passion and pedagogy: Relation, creation, and transformation in teaching.* Lesley College Series in Arts and Education, v. 1. New York: Peter Lang.

Mirzoeff, Nicholas (Ed.) (1998). *The visual culture reader.* London: Routledge.

Miyoshi, Masao (2002). Ivory tower in escrow. In Masao Miyoshi and D. H. Harootunian (Eds.) *Learning Places: The afterlives of area studies* (pp. 19-60). Durham, NC: Duke University Press.

Miyoshi, Masao and Harootunian, D. H. (Eds.) (2002). *Learning places: The afterlives of area studies.* Durham, NC: Duke University Press.

Molnar, Alex (1985). Tomorrow the shadow on the wall will be that of another. *JCT*, 6(3). 35-42.

Moriarty, Michael (1991). *Roland Barthes.* Stanford: Stanford University Press.

Morris, Marla (1998). Existential and phenomenological influences on Maxine Greene. In William F. Pinar (Ed.), *The passionate mind of Maxine Greene* (pp. 124-136). London: Falmer.

Morris, Marla (2000). Dante's left foot kicks queer theory into gear. In Susan Talburt and Shirley Steinberg (Eds.) *Thinking queer* (pp. 15-32). New York: Peter Lang.

Morris, Marla (2001). *Curriculum and the Holocaust: Competing sites of memory and representation.* Mahweh, NJ: Lawrence Erlbaum and Associates.

Morris, Marla (2002a). A difficult road: Talk in (post) Holocaust voices. In Marla Morris and John A. Weaver (Eds.) *Difficult memories* (pp. 1-11). New York: Peter Lang.

REFERENCES

Morris, Marla (2002b). Curriculum theory as academic responsibility: The call for reading Heidegger contextually. In Marla Morris and John A. Weaver (Eds.) *Difficult memories* (pp. 227-247). New York: Peter Lang.

Morris, Marla (2006). *Jewish intellectuals in the university.* New York: Palgrave Macmillan.

Morris, Marla and Weaver, John (Eds.) (2002). *Difficult memories: Talk in a (post) Holocaust Era.* New York: Peter Lang.

Morrison, Toni (1992). *Playing in the dark: Whiteness and the literary imagination.* Cambridge, MA: Harvard University Press.

Munro, Petra (1998a). *Subject to fiction.* Philadelphia: Open University Press.

Munro, Petra (1998). Engendering curriculum history. In William F. Pinar (Ed.) *Curriculum: Toward new identities* (pp. 263-294). New York: Garland.

Naths, Anami (2004). Of mango trees and woven tales. In Rita L. Irwin and Alex de Cosson (Eds.) *A/R/Tography: Rendering self through arts-based living inquiry* (pp. 116-126). Vancouver, Canada: Pacific Educational Press.

Ng-A-Fook, Nicholas A. (2006). *Understanding an indigenous curriculum in Louisiana through listening to Houma oral histories.* Baton Rouge: Louisiana State University, unpublished Ph.D. dissertation.

Noddings, Nel (1984). *Caring.* Berkeley, CA: University of California Press.

Noddings, Nel (1999). Foreword. In Margaret Smith Crocco, Petra Munro, and Kathleen Weiler, *Pedagogies of resistance: Women educator activists, 1880-1960* (pp. ix-x). New York: Teachers College Press.

Nolan, Kathy (2003). conSCIENCEness land(e)scapes. In Erika Hasebe-Ludt and Warren Hurren (Eds.) *Curriculum intertext: Place/language/pedagogy* (pp. 71-72). New York: Peter Lang.

Oberg, Antoinette (2003). Paying attention and not knowing. In Erika Hasebe-Ludt and Warren Hurren (Eds.) *Curriculum intertext: Place/language/pedagogy* (pp. 123-129). New York: Peter Lang.

O'Gorman, Kathleen (1998). Maxine Greene: A religious educator's religious educator. In William F. Pinar (Ed.) *The passionate mind of Maxine Greene* (pp. 230-237). London: Falmer.

Opfer, V. Darleen (2000). Paranoid politics, extremism, and the religious right: A case of mistaken identity? In Susan Talburt and Shirley Steinberg (Eds.) *Thinking queer* (pp. 85-103). New York: Peter Lang.

Pagano, JoAnne (1990). *Exiles and communities: Teaching in the patriarchal wilderness.* Albany: State University of New York Press.

Pandey, Sid N. and Moorad, Fazlur R. (2003). The decolonization of curriculum in Botswana. In William F. Pinar (Ed.), *International handbook of curriculum research* (pp. 143-170). Mahwah, NJ: Lawrence Erlbaum.

Paraskeva, João Menelau (2005) Dwayne Huebner. A Curricologus avant la lettre. In "Dwayne Huebner: *Mitografias da Abordagem Curricular. Reconhecimento e Desafios*". Porto: *Didáctica Editora*, 6-21.

Pautz, Anne E. (1998). Views across the expanse: Maxine Greene's Landscapes of Learning. In William F. Pinar (Ed.) *The passionate mind of Maxine Greene* (pp. 30-38). London: Falmer.

Pearse, Harold (2004). Praxis in perspective. In Rita L. Irwin and Alex de Cosson (Eds.) *A/R/Tography: Rendering self through arts-based living inquiry* (pp. 184-197). Vancouver, Canada: Pacific Educational Press.

Pente, Patti (2004). Reflections on artist/researcher/teacher identities: A game of cards. In Rita L. Irwin and Alex de Cosson (Eds.) *A/R/Tography: Rendering self through arts based living inquiry* (91-102). Vancouver, Canada: Pacific Educational Press.

Pilder, William (1974). In the stillness is the dancing. In W. Pinar (Ed.), *Heightened consciousness, cultural revolution, and curriculum theory: The proceedings of the Rochester conference* (pp. 117-129). Berkeley, CA: McCutchan.

Pinar, William F. (1979). What is the reconceptualization? *JCT, 1*((1), 93-104.

Pinar, William F. (1985). A prayerful act: The work of James B. Macdonald. *JCT, 6*(3), 43-55.

200

Pinar, William F. (1994). *Autobiography, politics, and sexuality: Essays in curriculum theory 1972-1992*. New York: Peter Lang.

Pinar, William F. (Ed.) (1998a). *The passionate mind of Maxine Greene*. London: Falmer.

Pinar, William F. (1998b). Notes on the Intellectual: In Praise of Maxine Greene. In William Ayers and Janet L. Miller (Eds.), *A Light in dark times: Maxine Greene and the unfinished conversation*. New York: Teachers College Press.

Pinar, William F. (Ed.) (1998c). *Queer theory in education*. Mahwah, NJ: Lawrence Erlbaum.

Pinar, William F. (1998 [1983]). Curriculum as gender text: Notes on reproduction, resistance, and male-male relations. In William F. Pinar (Ed.) *Queer theory in education* (pp. 221-243). Mahwah, NJ: Lawrence Erlbaum. [First published in *JCT* 5 (1), 26-52.]

Pinar, William F. (Ed.). (2000 [1975]). *Curriculum theorizing: The reconceptualization*. Troy, NY: Educator's International Press.

Pinar, William F. (2001). *The gender of racial politics and violence in America: Lynching, prison rape, and the crisis of masculinity*. New York: Peter Lang.

Pinar, William F. (Ed.) (2003). *International handbook of curriculum research*. Mahwah, N.J.: Lawrence Erlbaum.

Pinar, William F. (2004a). *What is curriculum theory?* Mahwah, NJ: Lawrence Erlbaum.

Pinar, William F. (2004b). The problem of the public. In Rubén Gaztambide-Fernandez and James T. Sears (Eds.), *Curriculum work as a public moral enterprise* (pp. 119-126). Landham, MD: Rowman & Littlefield.

Pinar, William F. (2005). A lingering note. In William F. Pinar and Rita L. Irwin (Eds.), *Curriculum in a new key* (pp. 1-85). Mahwah, NJ: Lawrence Erlbaum.

Pinar, William F. (2006a). *Race, religion, and a curriculum of reparation*. New York: Palgrave Macmillan.

Pinar, William F. (2006b). *The synoptic text today: Curriculum development after the reconceptualization*. New York: Peter Lang.

Pinar, William F. (2006c). Independence. In J. Milam, S. Springgay, K. Sloan, and B. S. Carpenter (Eds.), *Curriculum for a progressive, provocative, poetic and public pedagogy* (pp. xi-xxiii). Troy, NY: Educator's International Press.

Pinar, William F. (2007a). Introduction: A queer conversation, toward sustainability. In Nelson Rodriguez and William F. Pinar (Eds.) *Queering straight teachers* (pp. 1-12). New York: Peter Lang.

Pinar, William F. (2007b). Punk'd. In Nelson Rodriguez and William F. Pinar (Eds.) *Queering straight teachers* (pp. 155-182). New York: Peter Lang.

Pinar, William F. (in press). On the agony and ecstasy of the particular. *JCT*.

Pinar, William F. and Grumet, Madeleine R. (2005 [1976]). *Toward a poor curriculum*. Troy, NY: Educator's International Press.

Pinar, William F. and Grumet, Madeleine R. (1988). Socratic Caesura and the theory-practice relationship. In William F. Pinar (Ed.), *Contemporary curriculum discourses* (pp. 92-100). Scottsdale, AZ: Gorsuch Scarisbrick.

Pinar, William F. and Irwin, Rita L. (Eds.) (2005). *Curriculum in a new key: The collected works of Ted T. Aoki*. Mahwah, NJ: Lawrence Erlbaum.

Pinar, William F. and Reynolds, William M. (Eds.) (1992). *Understanding curriculum as phenomenological and deconstructed text*. New York: Teachers College Press.

Pinar, William F. and Reynolds, William M. (Eds.) (1992). Appendix, section one: Genealogical notes on the history of phenomenology in curriculum studies. *Understanding curriculum as phenomenological and deconstructed text* (pp. 237-244). New York: Teachers College Press.

Pinar, William F., Reynolds, William M., Slattery, Patrick, and Taubman, Peter M. (1995). *Understanding curriculum*. New York: Peter Lang.

Pitt, Alice (2003). *The play of the personal: Psychoanalytic narratives of feminist education*. New York: Peter Lang.

REFERENCES

Ponder, Gerald (2006). Social Reconstructionist curriculum impulses: Pragmatism, collectivism and "The American Problem." In Karen L. Riley (Ed.) *Social reconstruction: People, politics, perspectives* (pp. 235-256). Greenwich, CT: Information Age Publishing.

Porter, Nichole (2004). Exploring the making of wonder: The A/r/tography model in a secondary art classroom. In Rita L. Irwin and Alex de Cosson (Eds.) *A/R/Tography: Rendering self through arts-based living inquiry* (pp. 103-115). Vancouver, Canada: Pacific Educational Press.

Price-Spratlen, Townsand (2000). Nurturing images, whispering walls: Identity intersections and empowerment in the academic workplace. In Susan Talburt and Shirley Steinberg (Eds.) *Thinking queer* (pp. 215-225). New York: Peter Lang.

Pryer, Alison (2004). Living with/in marginal spaces: Intellectual nomadism and artist/researcher/ teacher praxis. In Rita L. Irwin and Alex de Cosson (Eds.) *A/R/Tography: Rendering self through arts-based living inquiry* (pp. 198-213). Vancouver, Canada: Pacific Educational Press.

Ransom, John S. (1997). *Foucault's discipline: The politics of subjectivity*. Durham, NC: Duke University Press.

Ravitch, Diane (2000). *Left back: A century of battles over school reform*. New York: Simon and Schuster.

Reynolds, William M. (1989). *Reading curriculum theory: The development of a new hermeneutic*. New York: Peter Lang.

Reynolds, William M. (2000). Personal communication.

Reynolds, William M. (2003). *Curriculum: A river runs through it*. New York: Peter Lang.

Riley-Taylor, Elaine (2006). Grounding biological and cultural diversity in a postmodern world. *JCT* 22(1), 61-78.

Robison, Helen F. (Ed.). (1966). *Precedents and promise in the curriculum field*. Washington, DC: ASCD.

Rodriguez, Nelson M. and Pinar, William F. (Eds.) (2007). *Queering straight teachers: Discourse and identity in education*. New York: Peter Lang.

Rofes, Eric (2000). Transgression and the situated body: Gender, sex, and the gay male teacher. In Susan Talburt and Shirley Steinberg (Eds.) *Thinking queer* (pp. 131-150). New York: Peter Lang.

Rogan, J. (1991). Curriculum texts: The portrayal of the field. Part II. *Journal of Curriculum Studies* 23 (1), 55-70.

Rogan, J. and Luckowski, J. (1990). Curriculum texts: The portrayal of the field. Part I. *Journal of Curriculum Studies* 22(1), 17-39.

Rorty, Richard (1989). *Contingency, irony and solidarity*. Cambridge: Cambridge University Press.

Rorty, Richard (1991). *Essays on Heidegger and others. Philosophical papers. Volume 2*. Cambridge & New York: Cambridge University Press.

Rosenberg, Harold (1970). *The tradition of the new*. London: Paladin.

Ross, Andrew (1989). *No respect: Intellectuals and popular culture*. New York & London: Routledge.

Ruas, Charles (1984). *Conversations with American writers*. London: Quartet.

Russell, Bruce David (2003). Reaching haiku's pedagogical nature. In Erika Hasebe-Ludt and Warren Hurren (Eds.) *Curriculum intertext: Place/language/pedagogy* (pp. 93-102). New York: Peter Lang.

Sadovnik, Alan R. and Semel, Susan F. (2002). *Founding mothers and others: Women educational leaders during the progressive era*. New York: Palgrave Macmillan.

Said, Edward W. (1996, 1994). *Representations of the intellectual: The 1993 Reith lectures*. New York: Vintage.

Salvio, Paula M. (1998). Maxine Greene and the project of "making the strange liberty of creation possible." In William F. Pinar (Ed.), *The passionate mind of Maxine Greene* (pp. 99-121). London: Falmer.

Salvio, Paula M. (2007). *Anne Sexton: Teacher of weird abundance*. Albany: State University of New York Press.

Savran, David (1998). *Taking it a like a man: White masculinity, masochism, and contemporary American culture*. Princeton, NJ: Princeton University Press.

Schubert, William H. (1986). *Curriculum: Perspective, paradigm, and possibility.* New York: Macmillan.

Schubert, William H., Lopez-Schubert, Ann, Herzog, L., Posner, George and Kridel, Craig (1988). A genealogy of curriculum researchers. *JCT, 8*(1), 137-184.

Schwab, Joseph (1964). Structure of the disciplines: Meanings and significances. In G. Ford and L. Pugno (Eds.), *The structure of knowledge and the curriculum* (pp.1-30). Chicago, IL: Rand McNally.

Schwab, Joseph (1978). *Science, curriculum and liberal education: Selected essays, Joseph J. Schwab.* [Edited by Ian Westbury & Neil Wilkof.] Chicago, IL: University of Chicago Press.

Schwab, Joseph (1983, Fall). The practical 4: Something for curriculum professors to do. *Curriculum Inquiry, 13*, 239-266.

Searles, W. (1982). A substantiation of Macdonald's models in science curriculum development. *JCT, 4*(1), 127-155.

Sears, James T. (1998a). *Lonely hunters: An oral history of lesbian and gay southern life, 1948-1968.* Boulder, CO: Westview.

Sears, James (1998b). A generational and theoretical analysis of culture and male (homo)sexuality. In William F. Pinar (Ed.), *Queer theory in education* (pp. 73-105). Mahwah, NJ: Lawrence Erlbaum.

Sears, James T. (2001). *Rebels, rubyfruit, and rhinestones: Queering space in the Stonewall South.* New Brunswick, NJ: Rutgers University Press.

Sears, James T. (2005). *Gay, lesbian, and transgender issues in education: Programs, policies, and practices.* Binghamton, New York: Hawthorn Press.

Sears, James T. (2006). *Behind the mask of the Mattachine: The Hal Call chronicles and the early movement for homosexual emancipation.* New York: Harrington Park Press.

Seixas, Peter (2004). Introduction. To Peter Seixas (Ed.), *Theorizing historical consciousness* (pp. 3-20). Toronto: University of Toronto Press.

Sekyi-Otu, Ato (1996). *Fanon's dialectic of experience.* Cambridge, MA: Harvard University Press.

Serres, Michel (1983). *Hermes: Literature, science, philosophy.* Baltimore, MD: Johns Hopkins University Press.

Silberman, Bernard S. (2002). The disappearance of modern Japan: Japan and social science. In Masao Miyoshi and D. H. Harootunian (Eds.) *Learning places: The afterlives of area studies* (pp. 303-320). Durham, NC: Duke University Press.

Silverman, Kaja (1992). *Male subjectivity at the margins.* New York & London: Routledge.

Simmons, Ron (1991). Tongues untied: An interview with Marlon Riggs. In Essex Hemphill (Ed.), *Brother to brother: Collected writings by black gay men* (pp. 189-199). [Conceived by Joseph Beam. Project managed by Dorothy Beam.] Los Angeles: Alyson Books.

Sizer, Theodore R. (2004). *The red pencil: Convictions from experience in education.* New Haven, CT: Yale University Press.

Slattery, Patrick (2001). The educational researcher as artist working within. *Qualitative Inquiry 7*(3), 370-398.

Slattery, Patrick (2006 [1995]). *Curriculum development in the postmodern era.* [Second edition.] New York: Routledge.

Slattery, Patrick and Dees, David (1998). Releasing the Imagination and the 1990s. In William F. Pinar (Ed.) *The passionate mind of Maxine Greene* (pp. 46-57). London: Falmer.

Slattery, Patrick and Rapp, Dana (2002). *Ethics and the foundations of education: Teaching convictions in a postmodern world.* Boston: Allyn and Bacon.

Smith, David G. (2006). *Trying to teach in a season of great untruth: Globalization, empire, and the crises of pedagogy.* Rotterdam, The Netherlands: Sense Publishers.

Smith, Lillian (1963 [1949]). *Killers of the dream.* [Revised and enlarged edition. First published in 1949 by Norton & Co.] Garden City, NY: Anchor Books.

Smith, Lillian (1972 [1944]). *Strange fruit.* San Diego, CA: Harvest.

Sontag, Susan (1966a). *Against interpretation.* New York: Farrar, Struas & Giroux.

Sontag, Susan (1966b). *Preface to Roland Barthes, Writing degree zero.* New York: Hill & Wang.

REFERENCES

Sontag, Susan (1979). *On photography*. New York: Penguin.
Sontag, Susan (1983, 1980). *Under the sign of Saturn*. London: Writers and Readers.
Sontag, Susan (1987, 1969). *Styles of radical will*. New York: Farrar, Straus & Giroux.
Spivak, Gayatri Chakravorty (2003). *Death of a discipline*. New York: Columbia University Press.
Spodek, Bernard (1985). Reflections in early childhood education. *JCT, 6*(3), 54-64.
Springgay, Stephanie (2004). Body as fragment: Art-making, researching, and teaching as a boundary shift. In Rita L. Irwin and Alex de Cosson (Eds.) *A/R/Tography: Rendering self through arts-based living inquiry* (pp. 60-74). Vancouver, Canada: Pacific Educational Press.
Steinberg, Shirley (1998). Appropriating queerness. In William F. Pinar (Ed.). *Queer theory in education* (pp. 187-195). Mahwah, NJ: Lawrence Erlbaum Associates, Publishers.
Steinberg, Shirley (2000). From the closet to the corral: Neo-stereotyping in *In & Out*. In Susan Talburt and Shirley Steinberg (Eds.) *Thinking queer* (pp. 153-159). New York: Peter Lang.
Stephenson, Wendy (2004). Digging for "historical combines": Representing art education history research through art-making. In Rita L. Irwin and Alex de Cosson (Eds.) *A/R/Tography: Rendering self through arts-based living inquiry* (pp. 155-172). Vancouver, Canada: Pacific Educational Press.
Stinson, Susan W. (1998). Maxine Greene and arts education. In William F. Pinar (Ed.) *The passionate mind of Maxine Greene* (pp. 222-229). London: Falmer.
Stoler, Ann Laura (1995). *Race and the education of desire: Foucault's history of sexuality and the colonial order of things*. Durham, NC: Duke University Press.
Sumara, Dennis J. and Davis, Brent (1998). Unskinning curriculum. In William F. Pinar (Ed.) *Curriculum: Toward new identities* (pp. 75-92). New York: Garland.
Talburt, Susan (2000). Identity politics, institutional response, and cultural negotiation: Meanings of a gay and lesbian office on campus. In Susan Talburt and Shirley Steinberg (Eds.) *Thinking queer* (pp. 61-84). New York: Peter Lang.
Talburt, Susan and Steinberg, Shirley R. (Eds.) (2000). *Thinking queer*. New York: Peter Lang.
Taliaferro, Denise (1998). Signifying self: Re-presentations of the Double-consciousness. In William F. Pinar (Ed.), *The passionate mind of Maxine Greene* (pp. 89-98). London: Falmer.
Tanaka, Stefan (2002). Objectivism and the eradication of critique in Japanese history. In Masao Miyoshi and D. H. Harootunian (Eds.) *Learning places: The afterlives of area studies* (pp. 80-102). Durham, NC: Duke University Press.
Tang, Sannie Yuet-San (2003). Generative interplay of/in language(s) and culture(s) midst curriculum spaces. In Erika Hasebe-Ludt and Warren Hurren (Eds.) *Curriculum intertext: Place/language/pedagogy* (23-32). New York: Peter Lang.
Taubman, Peter (1979). *Gender and curriculum: Discourse and the politics of sexuality*. Rochester, NY: University of Rochester, Graduate School of Education and Human Development, unpublished doctoral dissertation.
Taubman, Peter (1992 [1990]). Achieving the right distance. In William F. Pinar and William F. Reynolds (Eds.), *Understanding curriculum as phenomenological and deconstructed text* (pp. 216-233). New York: Teachers College Press [First printed in *Educational Theory, 40*(1), 121-133.]
Thomas, P. and Schubert, William H. (1997). Recent curriculum theory: Proposals for understanding, critical praxis, inquiry, and expansion of conversation. *Educational Theory 47*(2), 261-285
Thomson, Rosemarie Garland (1997). *Extraordinary bodies: Figuring physical disability in American culture and literature*. New York: Columbia University Press.
Toback, James (1968, July). Whatever you'd like Susan Sontag to think, she doesn't. *Esquire*, 58-61.
Todd, Sharon (2003). *Learning from the other: Levinas, psychoanalysis, and ethical possibilities in education*. Albana, NY: State University of New York Press.
Tröhler, Daniel (2006). The "Kingdom of God on Earth" and early Chicago pragmatism. *Educational Theory 56*(1), 89-105.
Trueit, Donna (2005). Watercourses: From poetic to poietic. In William E. Doll, Jr., M. Jayne Fleener, Donna Trueit, and John St. Julien (Eds.) *Chaos, complexity, curriculum, and culture* (77-99). New York: Peter Lang.

Tyack, David and Cuban, Larry (1995). *Tinkering toward utopia: A century of school reform.* Cambridge, MA: Harvard University Press.

Tyler, Ralph (1949). *Basic principles of curriculum and instruction.* Chicago: University of Chicago Press.

van Manen, M. (1991). *The tact of teaching.* Albany: State University of New York Press.

Verriour, Patrick (2003). Stories of an itinerant wayfarer: Narrative in the space of healing. In Erika Hasebe-Ludt and Warren Hurren (Eds.) *Curriculum intertext: Place/language/pedagogy* (pp. 73-92). New York: Peter Lang.

von Humbolt, Wilhelm (2000 [1793-1794]). Theory of Bildung. In Ian Westbury, Stefan Hopmann, and Kurt Riquarts (Eds.) *Teaching as a reflective practice: The German didaktik tradition* (pp. 57-61). [Trans. By Gillian Horton-Krüger.] Mahwah, NJ: Lawrence Erlbaum.

Wang, Hongyu (2004). *The call from the stranger on a journey home: Curriculum in a third space.* New York: Peter Lang.

Watkins, William H. (2001). *The white architects of black education: Ideology and power in America, 1865-1954.* New York: Teachers College Press.

Webber, Julie A. (2003). *Failure to hold: The politics of school violence.* Lanham, MD: Rowman & Littlefield.

Whitlock, Reta Ugena (2007). *This corner of Canaan: Curriculum studies of place and the reconstruction of the South.* New York: Peter Lang.

Williamson, Joel (1984). *The crucible of race: Black-white relations in the American South since emancipation.* New York: Oxford University Press.

Williams, Patricia (1991). *The alchemy of race and rights.* Cambridge, MA: Harvard University Press.

Willinsky, John (1992). *Learning to divide the world: Education at empire's end.* Minneapolis: University of Minnesota Press.

Willinsky, John (1999). *Technologies of knowing: A proposal for the human sciences.* Boston: Beacon Press.

Willinsky, John (2005). *The access principle: The case for open access to research and scholarship.* Cambrige, MA: MIT Press.

Willinsky, John (2000). *Technologies of knowing: A proposal for the human sciences.* Boston: Beacon Press.

Wilson, Sylvia (2004). Fragments: Life writing in image and in text. In Rita L. Irwin and Alex de Cosson (Eds.) *A/R/Tography: Rendering self through arts-based living inquiry* (pp. 41-59). Vancouver, Canada: Pacific Educational Press.

Winfield, Ann Gibson (2007). *Eugenics and education in America: Institutionalized racism and the implications of history, ideology, and memory.* New York: Peter Lang.

Winnicott, D. W. (1965). *The maturational processes and the facilitating environment: Studies in the theory of emotional development.* Madison, CT: International Universities Press.

Wolfson, Bernice (1985a). Preface: Special issue in commemoration of James B. Macdonald, 1925-1983. *JCT,* 6(3), 5-7.

Wolfson, Bernice (1985b). Closing remarks. *JCT,* 6(3), 65.

Woolf, Virginia (1955 [1927]). *To the lighthouse.* New York: Harcourt, Brace & Company.

Wraga, William G. (1999, January-February). Extracting sun-beams out of cucumbers": The retreat from practice in reconceptualized curriculum studies. *Educational Researcher 28*(1), 4-13.

Wright, Handel Kashope (2004). *A prescience of African cultural studies: The future of literature in Africa is not what it was.* New York: Peter Lang.

Ziarek, Ewa Plonowska (2001). *An ethics of dissensus: Postmodernity, feminism, and the politics of radical democracy.* Stanford, CA: Stanford University Press.

Zimmerman, Jonathan (2002). *Whose America? Culture wars in the public schools.* Cambridge, MA: Harvard University Press.

Zizek, Slavoj (1993). *Tarrying with the negative.* Durham, NC: Duke University Press.

NAME INDEX

Addams, Jane, xv, xviii, xxvii
Adler, Mortimer, 138, 164
Allen, Elizabeth Amira, xxvii
Allen, Louise Anderson, xxvii
Althusser, Louis, 110
Anijar, Karen, 107, 125, 126
Aoki, Doug, xxviii, 87, 100
Aoki, Ted, xxvi, xxx, xxxii, 18, 28, 39-50, 53, 57, 61, 89, 90, 92-94, 95, 97, 99-101, 106, 177, 181
Appel, Stephen, xxviii, 87
Appelbaum, Peter, 105
Apple, Michael, 164
Arendt, Hannah, 143
Aronowitz, Stanley, 152
Asher, Nina, xxvii
Aswell, Duncan (see Bill Cutler)
Aswell, Edward, 169
Aswell, Mary Louise, 169
Atwell-Vasey, Wendy, xxviii, 87
Bagley, William, xviii
Baker, Bernadette, xxv, 20
Baldwin, James, 131
Banks, James, xxvii
Barone, Thomas, xxix, xxxiii, 115-123, 155
Barrington, Judith, 32
Barthes, Roland, 152
Baszile, Denise Taliaferro, 155, 182
Bateman, Donald R., 16, 184
Beckett, Samuel, 168
Bell, Daniel, 153
Bell, Quentin, 89
Bellack, Arno, 142
Bender, Thomas, 155
Benjamin, Walter, 152
Berdyaev, Nicholas, 143
Berger, Peter, 164
Berrill, Veronica, 113
Bersani, Leo, 84
Bestor, Arthur, 138
Bhabha, Homi, xxvii, 89
Black, Earl, 177
Black, Merle, 177
Blades, David, 91, 105
Blake, William, 164

Block, Alan, xxvii, xxviii, xxix, 87, 103, 156
Blomgren, Constance, 101
Bloom, Allan, 138
Bloom, Benjamin, 164
Bloom, Harold, 117
Blumenfeld-Jones, Donald, xxix, 155
Bobbitt, Franklin, xi, xiv, xvii, xviii, 141, 182
Bode, Boyd Henry, 133
Boler, Megan, xxxii, 113
Bourdieu, Pierre, 130
Bowers, C.A., xxvi, xxviii, xxix, 7
Bragg, Laura, xxvii
Brameld, Theodore, xxix
Britzman, Deborah P., xxviii, xxx, xxxii, 20, 81, 87, 113, 128
Bruner, Jerome, 164
Buber, Marin, 143, 164
Bullough, Jr., Robert, xxv, 181
Burke, Melva, 163
Butler, Judith, 76, 110, 113, 133
Cable, George Washington, 176
Camus, Albert, 60
Canella, Gaile, xxvii
Capote, Truman, 116, 169
Caputo, John, 46, 92
Carey, Lisa, xxiv
Carpenter, William B., 8
Casemore, Brian, 175
Castaneda, Carlos, 164
Chalmers, F. Graeme, 57
Chambers, Cynthia, 93, 97
Chandler, James, xix
Charters, W. W., xi
Clandinin, M. Jean, xxviii
Cleaver, Eldridge, 184
Clifford, Patricia, xxix, 1-8, 10-13, 92, 183
Coleman, James, 164
Connelly, F. Michael, xxviii
Counts, George, xxix, 181
Crary, Jonathan, 8, 9
Crocco, Margaret Smith
Cuban, Larry, xxvi, xxix
Cutler, Bill, 170

207

SUBJECT INDEX

ABOUT THE AUTHOR

Before moving to the University of British Columbia in 2005, where he holds a Canada Research Chair and directs the Centre for the Study of the Internationalization of Curriculum Studies, William F. Pinar taught curriculum theory at Louisiana State University, where he served as the St. Bernard Parish Alumni Endowed Professor. He has also served as the Frank Talbott Professor at the University of Virginia and the A. Lindsay O'Connor Professor of American Institutions at Colgate University. He has lectured widely, including Harvard University, McGill University, the University of Wisconsin-Madison as well as the Universities of Chicago, Oslo, and Tokyo.

Pinar took his B.S. in Education at Ohio State University, graduating in 1969. He taught English at Paul D. Schreiber High School in Port Washington, Long Island, New York from 1969-1971, returning to Ohio State to finish his M.A. in 1970 and the Ph.D. in 1972. Pinar is the founding editor of the scholarly journal *JCT*, and with Janet Miller, the founder of the Bergamo Conference on Curriculum Theory and Classroom Practice, as well as the founder and past-President of the International Association for the Advancement of Curriculum Studies and the founder of its U.S. affiliate, the American Association for the Advancement of Curriculum Studies.

The author, most recently, of *Race, Religion and a Curriculum of Reparation* (Palgrave Macmillan, 2006), Pinar received in 2000 a Lifetime Achievement Award from the American Educational Research Association; in 2004 he received an American Educational Association Outstanding Book Award for *What is Curriculum Theory?* (Lawrence Erlbaum, 2004).

TRANSGRESSIONS: CULTURAL STUDIES AND EDUCATION

Volume 17
Expanding Waistlines
An Educator's Guide to Childhood Obesity
David Campos
Paperback ISBN 978-90-8790-206-3 Hardback ISBN 978-90-8790-207-0

Volume 18
Harry Potter: *Feminist Friend or Foe?*
Ruthann Mayes-Elma
Paperback ISBN 978-90-8790-081-6 Hardback ISBN 978-90-8790-082-3

Volume 19
Intellectual Advancement through Disciplinarity: Verticality and Horizontality in
Curriculum Studies
William F. Pinar
Paperback ISBN 978-90-8790-236-0 Hardback ISBN 978-90-8790-237-7

Volume 20
Symbolic Movement: *Critique and Spirituality in Sociology of Education*
Philip Wexler
Paperback ISBN 978-90-8790-273-5 Hardback ISBN 978-90-8790-274-2